LOST WORLDS

Jonathan Dewald

L⊕ST WORLDS

THE EMERGENCE OF FRENCH SOCIAL HISTORY, 1815–1970

THE PENNSYLVANIA STATE UNIVERSITY PRESS
UNIVERSITY PARK, PENNSYLVANIA

Library of Congress
Cataloging-in-Publication Data

Dewald, Jonathan.
The emergence of French social history, 1815–1970 / Jonathan Dewald.
p.   cm.
Includes bibliographical references and index.
ISBN 978-0-271-05866-5 (pbk : alk. paper)
1. France—Historiography—19th century.
2. France—Historiography—20th century.
3. Historiography—France—History—19th century.
4. Historiography—France—History—20th century.
5. France—History—Study and teaching.
6. Social history—19th century.
7. Social history—20th century.
I. Title.

DC36.9.D49 2006
944.0072—dc22
2006007771

FOR Patricia

La science historique est une forme de la conscience qu'une communauté prend d'elle-même,
un élément de la vie collective, comme la connais-
sance de soi un aspect de la conscience personelle,
un des facteurs de la destinée individuelle.

—RAYMOND ARON, 1938

But no symbol can long exist merely as the indication of one thing; it begins to take on meanings for
itself and begins to have powers beyond the
power of the thing it represents.

—LIONEL TRILLING, 1929

CONTENTS

PREFACE

The chapters assembled here were first presented as separate essays, and each can be read on its own. But they were written as elements of a single investigation, addressing a set of core questions and developing a cumulative argument. The questions concern the genesis of modern historical thought, which I define as characterized by two fundamental ideas: that all domains of human life have histories and deserve study; and that a society's multiple parts affect one another and need to be understood as in some sense a whole. In this book I ask how these ideas came into being and how they came to be widely accepted. My answers center on the contributions of freelance intellectuals in nineteenth-century Paris, most of them little known to contemporary students of historiography. I seek to show that well before 1900 these intellectuals had developed a broad program for social history, a term that they had already begun to use. Historians today, I argue, share more with these nineteenth-century predecessors than is usually understood.

Hence this book is primarily a history of ideas, an effort to trace the responses of successive generations of intellectuals to basic problems about the relationship between past and present. At the same time, any discussion of historical writing in the recent past inevitably touches on what historians write in the present. Such reverberations remain mostly implicit in what follows, and I offer no prescriptions for contemporary historical practice. But one of my intentions here is to deepen historians' understanding of the conceptual apparatus that we regularly use, by drawing attention to what we have inherited from our predecessors. Like us, they wrestled with ideas about the agency of historical actors, the professionalism of the historian, the otherness of the past, and the barriers between classes and cultures; and like us they were preoccupied with the problem of defining modernity itself, with understanding what differentiated their own society from its antecedents. Our use of these concepts often differs substantially from theirs, but (like other heirs to powerful intellectual traditions) we cannot altogether disentagle our usages from the histories behind them. When we deploy concepts that others developed, we also call back to life overtones and allusions, some obvious, many hidden. We need a better understanding than we have of the concepts that we use, and a history of them is a first step in that understanding.

It is relevant to these intentions that this is an American book, written by an American student of French society and culture. As such, it participates in the work of translation that attends all efforts to understand societies to which one does not belong. The outsider's perspective produces both blind spots and magnifications. Some differences that seem important to participants seem less so at a distance, while other similarities, differences, connections, and resemblances acquire greater importance. Like the historians whom I examine here, then, I write from a particular viewpoint, with particular concerns and interpretive expectations, without claiming universality for them. This book is offered as illustrating the view of historical knowledge that I apply to its subject matter, that is, a discipline that addresses universal questions with intellectual tools that are irreducibly personal.

I began this project in 1995, near the end of a year's fellowship at the Institute for Advanced Study. The project was not part of my plans when I showed up there, but it could only have developed as it did in the institute's lively atmosphere and with the help of its extraordinary facilities. Since then, support from other institutions has allowed me to study these questions in greater detail and forced me to sharpen my understanding of them. It is a great pleasure to thank the Deutsche Akademische Austauschdienst, the Max Planck Institut für Geschichte at Göttingen, the École des Hautes Études en Sciences Sociales, and Stanford University. I have also benefited enormously from presenting versions of these ideas to a range of academic audiences: at Georgetown University; York University (U.K.); the University at Buffalo; the University of Waterloo; Catholic University; the University of California, Irvine; Rutgers University; the joint Seminar in French History of the University of Toronto and York University; the École des Hautes Études en Sciences Sociales; the American Society for French Historical Studies; the British Society for the Study of French History; the University of Pennsylvania; the Western Society for French History; the National Humanities Center; and the Baltimore-Washington Old Regime Group. Participants in those discussions will perhaps note here my belated answers to some of their probing questions, and their encouragement has been immensely important over the course of what has become a long project. I will not try to list all those who have helped me in these ways, but I owe special debts to Donald Kelley, Bonnie Smith, Robert Descimon, André Burguière, Orest Ranum, Roger Chartier, Patricia Marino, and Patricia Mazòn. A generous subvention from the College of Arts and Sciences of the University at Buffalo helped cover costs of publication.

A version of Chapter 1 first appeared in the *American Historical Review*; a version of Chapter 4, in *French History*; and a version of Chapter 6, in *The French Nobility and the Eighteenth Century: Reassessments and New Approaches*, edited by Jay Smith. I am grateful to the editors of each for permission to reprint them here.

INTRODUCTION:

HISTORIANS AND MODERNITY

This book examines French historical thought from the early nineteenth through the mid-twentieth century. Its focus is on a central fact about modern historical consciousness. Whereas Western historical writing long concerned itself mainly with political doings and the great men who performed them, contemporary writers and readers want to know how people in the past lived, related to one another, and understood the basic conditions of their lives; in short, we want to know about the collection of topics that receives the conventional (and imperfect) label social history. This interest has applied to all categories of people, women as well as men, the disreputable as well as the esteemed, the weak and the powerful. Our historical thought is thus democratic, in that it resists assigning hierarchical value to different categories of actors and life-domains, and particularistic, in assuming that each human society organizes itself in its own ways, according to specific values and logics. So defined, contemporary historical practice seems to express a larger cultural modernity, both manifesting and contributing to our broader commitments to pluralism and egalitarianism. In this book, I ask how such ideas about the historian's task came into being and what they imply for a broader view of European culture. Understanding modern historical practice, I argue, is central to understanding modernity itself.

This is so partly because European culture during the nineteenth and twentieth centuries accorded an immense place to historical knowledge. This commitment to history was itself a historical phenomenon, and already in 1961 Hannah Arendt believed that it was receding; a loss of interest in history, she wrote, was "inevitable in all completely modernized societies."[1] But things were otherwise through the mid-twentieth century. From the aftermath of the French Revolution through World War II, intellectuals of diverse ideological commitments and personal circumstances shared the belief that historical study could reveal the essentials of the human condition. "We know only one science, the science of history," wrote Karl Marx, in 1845; in 1874 Friedrich Nietzsche wrote of the "mighty historical orientation of the age" (an orientation that he himself disliked); on the eve of World War II Raymond Aron added that "for man history is not an exterior fact, but the essence of his being. . . . I [as an individual] merge with my life-story, as humanity merges with its history."[2] Professional historians spoke more forcefully still. The development of historical thought during the nineteenth century, wrote the German historian Friedrich Meinecke in 1936, "was one of the greatest intellectual revolutions that has ever taken place in Western thought."[3]

So important a component of European thought has of course attracted a great deal of historical research and reflection. A central argument in the chapters that follow, however, is that scholars have misunderstood important aspects of the process by which contemporary historical ideas developed. Thus I offer at the outset an extended overview of recent discussions of the topic, against which my arguments are directed. Conventional accounts stress nineteenth-century intellectuals' interest in political

1. Arendt, *Between Past and Future*, 58. See also Modris Eksteins's remark that "our century has . . . been an antihistorical age, . . . [primarily] because this century has been one of disintegration rather than integration." Eksteins, *Rites of Spring*, 291.

2. Marx, *Selected Writings*, 107 (*The German Ideology*); Nietzsche, *On the Advantage and Disadvantage of History for Life*, 7; Aron, *Introduction à la philosophie de l'histoire*, 12.

3. Meinecke, *Historism*, liv.

history. History (so run these accounts) first became an academic discipline in nineteenth-century Germany, and it manifested the intellectual preoccupations of its era. It sought to address the cultural needs of developing nation-states, most of them still marked by an aristocratic past.[4] Wanting to give chronological depth to the politics of their own time, the great nineteenth-century historians viewed the state's development as their principal subject matter, and they focused on the leaders who had made the state the organizing matrix of national life.[5] Such a history was inevitably progressive, centering on the movement from inferior to superior modes of social organization, tracing a "grand narrative" that ultimately had religious foundations. In 1828, the French historical philosopher Victor Cousin summarized for his Sorbonne audience the Hegelian philosophy that he had learned during an exile in Germany: "It is because Providence is in history that humanity has its necessary laws and history its necessary course. History is the demonstration of God's providential design for humanity; history's judgments are God's own judgments." Across Europe, most nineteenth-century historians agreed. The great Prussian historian Leopold von Ranke spoke of "the religious foundation on which our efforts rest."[6]

Already in the late nineteenth century, so continues the standard account, some dissent from these views could be heard, in the works of historians such as the Frenchman Jules Michelet, the Swiss Jacob Burckhardt, and the German Karl Lamprecht. But the real challenges came after 1900, and they came from France. In fin de siècle Paris a variety of philosophies contested the worldviews on which historical thought had long rested. Psychology and sociology were emerging as distinct social sciences, posing interpretive challenges to any understanding of the past; and new developments in the hard sciences disrupted ideas about knowledge itself. World War I added existential crisis to the mix. Intellectuals who had experienced trench warfare and the collapse of centuries-old states could accept neither a providentialist view of history's unfolding nor a history centered on political leadership. Hence a new kind of history

4. Berlin, *Power of Ideas*, 205 ff.

5. See, for instance, Carbonell, *Histoire et historiens*, 586–87: French historical writing of the period "se moque de 'l'histoire sociale,' qu'elle confond, les rares fois qu'elle s'y intéresse, avec une histoire polissonne des moeurs de jadis ou avec l'étude de quelques familles distinguées d'autrefois."

6. Quoted in Gossman, *Basel in the Age of Burckhardt*, 219–20; Ranke, "On the Character of Historical Science," 38.

began to emerge before 1914, a history as much concerned with social groups and cultures as with politics. New problems became legitimate subjects of inquiry, and new kinds of documents demanded attention. Narrative became less central as a mode of historical representation, because historians now attended to questions that had little to do with the established stories of national development. A history focused on problems in turn required new methods: quantification, comparison across national boundaries, insights derived from geography, sociology, psychology, and anthropology.

After the war, this kind of history began a steady march to prominence, first within French academia, eventually elsewhere. Its most prominent advocates were the French historians Lucien Febvre and Marc Bloch, both of them war veterans. As colleagues at the postwar University of Strasbourg, they began planning their journal *Annales d'histoire économique et sociale* almost immediately after demobilization; it began publication in 1929, providing a forum both for new kinds of research and for theoretical reflections on where historical studies ought to be going. Such insistence that historians give more attention to the real life of past societies (so runs the conventional account) aroused suspicion among the political historians who dominated European universities, and Febvre and Bloch faced a difficult struggle in establishing the legitimacy of their enterprise. Peter Burke has recently described them as leading a "small, radical and subversive" band, "fighting a guerrilla action against traditional history, political history, and the history of events."[7] Georg Iggers describes Febvre and Bloch as occupying "a somewhat marginal position in the 1930s," as "they pursued their conflict with [historian Charles] Seignobos and the traditional political historians at the Sorbonne."[8]

But after World War II the situation changed dramatically. Historians associated with the *Annales* acquired increasingly absolute preeminence within the French historical profession, and their example resonated

---

7. P. Burke, *French Historical Revolution*, 2. Burke offers some nuances to this position (7–10), but also argues that the *Annales* represented first "the substitution of a problem-oriented analytical history for a traditional narrative of events. In the second place, the history of the whole range of human activities in the place of a mainly political history. In the third place . . . a collaboration with other disciplines" (2).

8. Iggers, *Historiography in the Twentieth Century*, 54. Cf. Revel, "Histoire et sciences sociales," 1347–59, and Burguière, "Histoire d'une histoire," 1360–75, each noting Febvre and Bloch's closeness to the center of contemporary academic influence. For nuances to conventional descriptions of Seignobos's "positivism," see also Noiriel, *Sur la "crise" des histoires,* 220–29.

abroad, among North American, British, and German historians. Bloch was executed in 1944 for his role in resisting the German occupation, but Febvre survived until 1956, to the end working to strengthen the framework that underlay the *Annales*. His lobbying bore abundant results. "The *Annales* school" ceased being a mere intellectual orientation, and became instead an institution: first a section of the already existing École Pratique des Hautes Études, then in the 1970s the fully autonomous, degree-granting École des Hautes Études en Sciences Sociales, with its buildings, research centers, publication series, and programs for international outreach. In 1972, the American historian J. H. Hexter humorously noted the success of these efforts: he spoke of his "eerie feeling that . . . the *Annalistes* are on a march that by friendly persuasion is about to conquer the historical world."[9] Fifteen years later, in an essay mainly concerned with Anglo-Saxon historical writing, Gertrude Himmelfarb suggested that "even some of the *Annalistes* are beginning to suspect that they have unleashed a force that they cannot control. The very disciplines they have used to subvert the conventions of the old history threaten to subvert history itself."[10] Whether as subversion or inspiration, observers have repeatedly stressed the impact of French writers on historical consciousness throughout the twentieth-century West.

Conventional views of social history's development thus offer an appealing narrative of intellectual progress. On this account the vigorous creativity of a few individuals combined with larger currents in the world around them to enlarge history's subject matter, methods, and sympathies; at the same time these historians brought the discipline back into creative dialogue with society, allowing it to address pressing concerns of the age. The narrative includes elements of drama, notably the tragedy of Bloch's death, and a happy ending: Febvre and Bloch confronted the incomprehension of their traditionalist colleagues, and they had to fight to bring their ideas from the margins of academic life to its center, but in the end they triumphed. Finally, this is a narrative authorized by an important historical source, the abundant writings of Lucien Febvre himself.[11] Febvre wrote often and emphatically about the movement that he led. He emphasized the deficiencies in the traditions of historical knowledge on which he and Bloch had been raised, and he stressed the impact on his generation

---

9. Hexter, *On Historians*, 83.
10. Himmelfarb, *New History and the Old*, 8.
11. For overviews, see Müller, *Bibliographie des travaux de Lucien Febvre* and *Marc Bloch, Lucien Febvre*.

of the cultural shocks of the early twentieth century. As he explained in a 1933 lecture, the experience of World War I, "the repeated shock of new ideas, . . . the bankruptcy of old ideas, old doctrines thrust into the void by the new" had produced a "crisis of everything that surrounded and framed historical thought."[12] It is reasonable that historians have taken seriously his claims that the *Annales* represented "a new kind of history."

In the chapters that follow, however, I argue that these narratives are oversimple. They distort both our understanding of our own historical enterprise and our view of our predecessors. Valuable though it has been, I argue, the research underlying conventional interpretations has been marked by two closely related failings. First, it has tended to focus on a limited number of historians, and especially on those who fitted within the professional discipline of history, historians attached to university faculties and a few others who produced eventually canonical works. Second, research has given more weight to programmatic statements about how history should be practiced than to practices themselves. Here I emphasize instead practices, and I emphasize the breadth of interest in historical study in nineteenth- and twentieth-century France. The very importance of historical knowledge within the culture of these years ensured that professional historians were only one among many groups to think seriously about the past and to apply high levels of scholarship to its study.

A different picture of historical thought emerges if one considers this full range of intellectuals who studied the past—essayists, philosophers, amateur historians, antiquarians, and novelists, as well as university professors. Examining their work shows that interest in the history of society and of private experience was not the invention of twentieth-century professional historians. From the 1820s on, numerous writers argued that history consisted of much more than politics, and they produced numerous examples of what we today term social history. Including such figures in our genealogy of modern historical thought is not a matter of historical accuracy alone, although it is partly that: these writers deserve attention simply because of the quality of their research and thought. More important, neglecting them has obscured the intellectual contexts from which the canonical works emerged, the books that figure so prominently in most discussions of historiography. I will suggest that these histories acquired some of their meaning and force from the implicit dialogues that

12. Febvre, "De 1892 à 1933," 99–100.

they carried on with other works around them. Explicating their broader intellectual contexts, in other words, is a necessary step in understanding the intellectual choices that more recent historians have made and in decoding the messages in their work. In some ways, I argue here, reverberations from these implicit debates continue in the historical writing of our own time.

Such an approach is especially appropriate in the case of France, for throughout the modern period the French university has remained open to influences from outside its walls. Until the 1860s, courses given by prominent professors attracted crowds of auditors from polite society, often leaving serious degree candidates a small minority in the lecture hall, and lecturers sought to speak to the interests of this dilettante audience.[13] In their published works as well, historians sought to reach this broad middle-class public, and many succeeded in dramatic fashion. In the 1850s and 1860s the historian Jules Michelet was able to earn twenty thousand francs annually from his book sales, according to the envious report of Hippolyte Taine, a sum about three times the income of a university professor.[14] Publication for a broad market has remained characteristic of French academics, in history as in other disciplines; even today the gap between the university and the middle-class public is easily and often crossed. At the same time, French academics have taken participation in public life to be an appropriate extension of their intellectual activities. A number of them have played prominent roles in French political life, among them Victor Cousin, François Guizot, Jean Jaurès, and Jérôme Carcopino, and others have figured prominently in French journalism.[15]

Conversely, French academics have understood that they constituted only one force among the many that shaped educated opinion. They both allied and competed with writers who lacked academic degrees and relied on the literary marketplace to supply their livelihoods. French society has always accorded such writers a great deal of respect. "France being without universities according to the German pattern," observed Stendhal in 1825, with good-humored exaggeration, "conversation used to constitute the entire education of a Frenchman. Today, it is conversation and the

13. Keylor, *Academy and Community*, 21–22.

14. Goncourt and Goncourt, *Journal*, 1:1029; Charle, *Les intellectuels en Europe*, 210.

15. Recent examples include Philippe Ariès (see Chapter 5, below), and François Furet (see Christofferson, "François Furet Between History and Journalism," 421–47, and the selection of Furet's journalism in Furet, *Un itinéraire intellectuel*).

newspapers."[16] Complaints that academics were pedantic and narrow-minded remained vigorous through the 1950s, and academics themselves often joined in the criticism.[17] A history of historical thought limited to professors and canonical works risks obscuring the main tendencies in French intellectual life, tendencies to which even the professors were highly sensitive.

So also does a history that fails to balance attention to historians' statements of their intentions (such as Febvre's 1933 lecture) with a close reading of what they said about specific historical problems and situations. It is in the nature of historical research that labels and programmatic statements repeatedly prove inadequate to the realities that they claim to describe. Important works that are commonly termed social history include extensive discussions of politics, ideas, and personalities; and practitioners of the genre have used a variety of approaches to the past, shifting easily among them, in some instances within a single historical work. Even definitions of what a social history ought to be have differed widely, in some instances producing heated public debates.[18] New historical approaches inevitably incorporate ideas and techniques from previous generations of scholarship. Focusing on what historians hoped to achieve risks missing these elements of continuity and recombination, while at the same time producing exaggerated images of generational differences and disagreements. The study of historical thought needs to look closely at what historians have actually done.

Historians have noted the variety of forces that contributed to giving history its centrality in nineteenth- and twentieth-century Europe. The experience of the French Revolution forced both intellectuals and the public to think about differences between historical eras, and suggested as well the difficulty of understanding the directions in which history was moving. Industrialization likewise heightened concerns about defining historical change and identifying its sources; even in a relatively slowly developing country such as France, intellectuals had an overwhelming sense that modes of life were changing around them and that all aspects of society would eventually be affected. History served more immediate political needs as well. Acquiring a clear vision of their past served both nations

16. Stendahl, *Racine and Shakespeare*, 56.
17. See Chapter 1, below.
18. For a very helpful summary of one such debate, see Lepetit, "Un regard sur l'historiographie allemande," 466–86.

and social groups as a mechanism for asserting autonomy and identity; in the nineteenth century, new states sponsored historical research in order to bolster their positions, while in the twentieth emerging social groups have insisted on their own histories as an element in their identities. Ideas about the direction and pace of historical change have likewise cemented religious and political convictions, on both the Left and the Right.[19]

Underlying this multiplicity of functions, though, has been a fundamental idea. As a science of what actually happened, a depiction of true events and real people, history, more forcibly than other humanistic disciplines, has claimed to represent the real. Hannah Arendt suggested many years ago that "'reconciliation with reality' . . . has been the secret motor of all historiography that transcends mere learnedness"; more recently, Hayden White has pursued this idea, suggesting that history confers "a kind of transcendental authority upon a given system of social praxis," both by defining specific events in the past and by delineating the larger field of plausible human motives and behaviors.[20] The case studies presented here take these observations as a starting point. I argue that thinking about the past has been a way for European intellectuals to define for themselves the dividing line between realism and fancy, and that nineteenth- and twentieth-century historians used the techniques of scholarship as means of thinking about the character of their own world.

Well into the twentieth century, I argue here, a crucial task in this project of defining the real was that of exploring the nature of modernity itself. As even the most sheltered scholars came to terms with the French and Industrial Revolutions, they found themselves having to define the specificities of their society; they also needed to think about social groups that directly posed the problems of modernity. The working class, political radicals, and urbanites raised questions from one direction, as visible representatives of societal transformation. On the other side stood peasants and aristocrats, who seemed to have survived from an earlier world. But as the nineteenth century advanced there were also increasing contacts with colonized peoples, and they too posed the problem of how modern and premodern differed. The encounter retained its full force through the 1960s, as a wide range of intellectuals concerned themselves with the problems of decolonization and with the economic development of former colonial territories. No Western scholar could altogether avoid these

19. For a clear and eloquent summary of these causes, see Berlin, "The Bent Twig," 238.
20. Arendt, *Between Past and Future*, 262; White, *Content of the Form*, 102.

questions, and French scholars found them especially urgent, given their nation's experiences of both revolution and colonial empire. I argue here that these issues lurk in even the purest scholarship of the period; surprisingly often, French historians addressed them directly, using the contemporary underdeveloped world as a metaphor for understanding early Europe.

Hence another theme running throughout this book is the problem of historical time. Writers on French history (I suggest here) returned repeatedly to the problem of periodization, asking when their nation had undergone the transition from premodern to modern and what the main causes of the change had been. Industrialization and political revolution might have provided easy answers to such questions, allowing French intellectuals to use 1789 as the divide between premodern and modern, but most found that solution unsatisfactory. The Revolution was too violent and too disconnected from much that intellectuals valued to define the nation's modernity; and in France industrialization advanced more slowly than elsewhere. Rather, French intellectuals tended to see the decisive moment in their nation's modernization as coming in the seventeenth century, with its great cultural achievements, newly effective bureaucratic government, and military triumphs. These considerations help explain a distinctive aspect of French historical writing in these years, its preoccupation with what historians today term the early modern period, the period from about 1550 to 1789. Studying their nation's own preindustrial, predemocratic past, as I claim here, was a means for French historians to reflect on the nature of modernity and on the processes that led to it. As a result, apparently narrow scholarly debates about historical chronology had large implications. Discussing differences between the sixteenth and seventeenth centuries was implicitly to discuss the character of modern life.

Because the problem of modernization presented itself so forcefully to historians in these years, the politics of writing the history of society were complex, more complex than most students of the subject have recognized. Scholars have tended to see a sharp division between conservative and radical schools of history, and they have tended see interest in social history as attaching to political radicalism. Georg Iggers, for instance, has linked the triumph of the French *Annales* school in the 1950s to a "critical reconsideration" of "the attitudes that [historian Marc] Bloch, in *Strange Defeat*, charged had helped to pave the way for the catastrophe of 1940"; and he has similarly viewed the German social history of Hans Ulrich

Wehler as reflecting a "political message" affirming social-democratic values.[21] A German student of the working class has described the genesis of his own work in similar terms: "[T]he anti-authoritarian protest movement at the end of the 1960s, the period of socialist-liberal coalition," and other movements from the period "stimulated a turn to themes that for decades only a handful of embittered outsiders had concerned themselves with."[22] From an explicitly conservative viewpoint, Norman Cantor has spoken of the "leftist political views" underlying Bloch's *French Rural History;* conversely, from the Left E. P. Thompson described his own studies of English working-class history as designed to reinforce a radical understanding of the contemporary world.[23]

Such descriptions (so runs another of this book's main arguments) conceal the wide array of political positions from which historians actually considered the European past. Many influential historians of European society have held conservative political views. Others have oscillated in their positions or refrained from taking any. Enlarging our genealogies of modern historical practices makes it clear that much study of European society in fact derived from fears about the political future and eagerness to defend existing social arrangements, both of these stimuli to careful study of how society had functioned in the past. As important, I argue here, historical writing had (and continues to have) political effects that go well beyond its authors' intentions, and that sometimes contradict those intentions. Lucien Febvre, for instance, was solidly on the republican Left, but his great work on religious values in sixteenth-century France shared many ideas with the essays of the nationalist anti-Semite Charles Maurras, founder of the Action Française; in particular, both drew a sharp line between modern rationality and the savage thought of premodern groups.[24] Conversely, the nineteenth-century historian Hippolyte Taine was frightened of democracy and advocated racist ideas of social differences. But his efforts to establish a history that made no reference to divine providence deeply unsettled his contemporaries; and he saw the Old Regime's monarchy as the direct cause of many of the ills from which modern France suffered.

In both the questions that it asks and the answers that it proposes, this book treats historical writing as a form of literature, and it thus inevitably

21. Iggers, *Historiography in the Twentieth Century,* 54, 69.
22. Gruettner, *Arbeitswelt an der Wasserkant,* 11.
23. Cantor, *Inventing the Middle Ages,* 40; Thompson, *Making of the English Working Class.*
24. Chapters 2, 4, and 5, below.

engages to some degree with long-standing debates about the relationship between history and other forms of writing.[25] A brief summary of how I view that engagement may be helpful at this point. This study takes for granted that history, like other writing, requires its authors to choose both the facts and the explanatory schemes that they deploy. Like novelists, historians must select among the immense array of episodes that their accounts might include, and like novelists they try to offer descriptions and explanations that their own contemporaries will find persuasive. I have also assumed that even the most scientific historical work repays literary analysis, attention to its language, imagery, and allusions. These formal elements helped constitute the meanings that it conveyed to its original readers, the more so in that historians (again like novelists) are borrowers, whose work advances through recycling and referring to that of others. Finally, I have assumed that historical writing contributes to the functioning of the society to which it is addressed, engaging (if only implicitly) with the world in which it is written, and thus possessing ideological content. In some instances it does this directly, through comments on the historian's own world. More commonly, history's ideological content is indirect, expressed through the historian's ideas about causation, motives, and social structure. History thus contributes—alongside many other forms of cultural activity—to the store of ideas and judgments that people use as they deal with the world around them, but its contributions are the more influential insofar as history attempts to present the truth about the past. I thus see no contradiction between affirming history's ideological functions and recognizing its scientific claims, its claims to provide accurate descriptions of the past based on hard evidence. On the contrary: historians' very commitment to scholarship implies an engagement in their society's efforts to define its vision of what the world is like and what constitute sensible approaches to it. Historians' commitment to the factual makes their discipline more, not less, ideological.

These are not novel or radical claims, nor do they imply skepticism about historians' knowledge of the past. To note resemblances between novels and histories is not to argue for their identity. I take seriously the scholarly standards that characterize the historical works addressed here, and I have sought to distinguish between more and less serious scholarly work. In one respect, however, these ideas do lead to what may seem a

---

25. For an overview of these debates, see Smith, Dewald, Sewell, and Chartier, "Forum," 213–64.

radical conclusion: this study argues for looking critically at the distinction between academic historians and other students of the past, and it emphasizes interactions between and commonalities among these groups.[26] Such emphasis is especially appropriate in a consideration of nineteenth-century historical thought, for nineteenth-century writers themselves stressed the relatedness of different literary genres, and several of the writers considered here moved among them, producing in turn history, literary criticism, philosophy, and fiction. In a 1912 overview of French literary criticism, an American observer claimed that such a blending of genres was characteristic of the age.[27] In an 1887 letter, Taine made a similar point in somewhat different terms. "Five writers and thinkers . . . ," he wrote, "in my opinion are the men who, since Montesquieu, have added the most to the knowledge of human nature and human society": despite his own well-known emphasis on science as the basis for historical thought, his list included two novelists (Honoré Balzac and Stendhal), a literary critic (Charles-Augustin Sainte-Beuve), and two historians (François Guizot and Ernest Renan).[28] Such nineteenth-century readiness to see connections among history, fiction, and other genres makes the disciplinary anxieties of twentieth-century historians especially striking. I suggest here that we need to examine the twentieth-century rhetoric of intellectual professionalism as a distinctive intellectual choice, one move in a long-term discussion about the intellectual's functions and social position.

These problems and themes have shaped the methods that I have followed here. They have led me to organize these studies around a series of moments in intellectual history, rather than attempting an overview of them, and to emphasize close readings of specific historical works and close attention to their contexts, as means of understanding how historians responded to one another and to their times. Texts and contexts of course overlap, especially in the ways that I use the terms here. I have given limited attention to the personal lives of the scholars that I have studied, and especially little attention to their social backgrounds. Whether academics or not, French intellectuals during this period lived in a coherent cultural world, marked by commonality of education and accomplishment, and by the overwhelming magnetic attraction of Paris; intellectuals of any

26. In addressing this issue, I have been especially influenced by the work of Bonnie G. Smith; see, for instance, Smith, *Gender of History*.

27. Irving Babbitt, discussed in Chapter 1, below.

28. Taine, *Sa vie et sa correspondance*, 4:232.

ambition had to make their careers there, and in doing so they encountered the same books, people, and ideas as did their friends and competitors. In this world, differences of background and experience quickly faded, as writers found their places and made contact with one another.

Each chapter in this volume thus includes both close readings of individual texts and exploration of how different intellectuals engaged with one another. But in some chapters I am especially concerned with contexts, describing specific groups of writers and the flow of influences among them. In Chapter 1, I describe the Parisian writers who clustered around Charles-Augustin Sainte-Beuve and Hippolyte Taine in the mid-nineteenth century. The chapter shows their preoccupation with historical questions and their vision of history as concerned with social life and personal experience; and it argues for the distinctively modern quality of their understanding of the intellectual's role. Chapter 4 deals with a second important group of intellectuals, those around the historians Lucien Febvre and Marc Bloch, founders of the journal *Annales d'histoire économique et sociale,* between about 1920 and the 1960s. Here the focus is on university history-writing, and I seek to show the ideological concerns that underlay the group's scholarly activity, with particular attention to their ideas about the dividing line between modernity and the premodern past. In Chapter 5 I look closely at two amateur historians, both of them fascinated by the history of private life, and both of them committed to establishing it as an important subject of research: from the late nineteenth century, the antiquarian Alfred Franklin; from the later twentieth century, the conservative intellectual Philippe Ariès and some of his associates. The example again shows important continuities between nineteenth- and twentieth-century scholarship, and it suggests the artificiality of conventional divisions between professional scholarship and antiquarianism. Chapter 7 compares French historians with Germans, as each group dealt with the specific problems of constructing a history of the peasantry, the group within European society that most vividly exemplified the issues of backwardness and modernization. Comparison of these two national traditions of writing history demonstrates the force of each; French and German scholars found different issues important, and they turned to different explanatory schemes for historical understanding.

The remaining chapters are concerned more strictly with ideas. There I examine a series of historical problems and the solutions that different historians proposed to them. In Chapter 2, I ask how historians have defined the chronology of French history, where they have seen its most important turning points; and I seek to account for French historians' fascination with the seventeenth century and its culture. Chapter 3 pursues this question, by examining an especially important case study: I consider intellectuals' interest in seventeenth-century Catholicism and explore linkages between that interest and their understanding of their own functions and intellectual underpinnings. In Chapter 6, I examine historians' treatments of the nobility, another group closely associated with premodern forms of social organization, showing how the group was repeatedly redefined so as to preserve interpretations of French history that centered on the bourgeoisie and on certain forms of modernization. The old nobles, it was commonly agreed, could not fully cope with the modern world; examining approaches to them thus offers yet another point of access to historians' understanding of the divide between their own world and its antecedents.

Taken together, these specific inquiries are meant to answer broad questions about modern historical thought. They point to a basic fact: interest in the history of society has been central to French historical consciousness since the early nineteenth century. It could scarcely have been otherwise, given the importance that contemporaries attached to historical knowledge during these years and the societal dramas that they witnessed. This interest centered on a specific problem, that of understanding the nature of the premodern world and defining the qualities that divided it from modernity. In turn, these interests helped shape these writers' understanding of the historian himself (and more rarely, herself),[29] producing for the first time an image of historians as disengaged scientists, indifferent to the societal developments that they traced, without allegiance to any particular ethical system, unmoved even by hopes for social progress. Finally, all this entails a rereading of some of the great twentieth-century contributors to historical thought. In writing their own social histories, I argue here, Lucien Febvre and his colleagues entered an already existing field of inquiry, rather than creating something altogether new. But in doing so they gave this form of history a particular orientation, as ultimately a defense of modernity and of the French path to it. Their historical writing, like the other histories examined here, served the present in which they lived—as all good history ultimately must.

---

29. A problem briefly taken up in Chapter 1, below.

1

"À LA TABLE DE MAGNY":
MEN OF LETTERS AND HISTORICAL WRITING
IN NINETEENTH-CENTURY PARIS

In 1938, the philosopher Raymond Aron sought to define the essential qualities of historical thought. "The biographer interests himself in the private man," he wrote, "the historian primarily in the public man. An individual enters history only by his impact on collective development, by his contribution to the moral future."[1] Aron's definition of history as the study of public realms derived from ancient traditions, which gave primacy to the history of political life. Although his own views allowed for some forms of social history, and indeed highlighted the importance of economic development and social class, they excluded both private experience and the many social groups that failed to have an impact on humanity's development. Despite Aron's magisterial assurance, however, these topics

1. Aron, *Introduction à la philosophie de l'histoire*, 97.

already interested some historians in 1938, and they have become central to historical thought since World War II. Contemporary historians insist that as much attention be given to private persons and intimate doings as to those of public significance, and that apparently marginal groups matter within the larger historical record. Emerging from these commitments, their studies of sexuality, childhood, deviance, women, and a long list of other topics have changed interpretations of most periods. Despite occasional protests, this vision of the historian's task has today become a norm guiding both professionals and members of the broader public in their understanding of the past.[2] In this book I seek to explain how this redefinition of knowledge about the past came about and how it fitted within larger patterns of European intellectual history.

At the center of that process, I argue, was a group of nineteenth-century Parisian men of letters, all of them deeply engaged by historical studies but none of them a university historian in the modern sense. Well before 1900, they developed the idea that history included the study of social structures and psychologies; some of them went further, claiming that these topics deserved far more of the historian's attention than politics, wars, and great men. In the present chapter I examine these writers and their ideas. I ask a series of questions about the place of historical thought and the role of the intellectual in nineteenth-century culture. How did history relate to other intellectual projects, and how did contemporaries define the proper scope of historical inquiry? What position did intellectuals occupy, and how specialized were their interests? How did engagements with the contemporary world affect thinking about the past? Asking such questions allows us to situate the origins of contemporary historical thought in the literary culture of the nineteenth century.

An 1887 letter from Friedrich Nietzsche conveniently lists the intellectuals on whom this chapter focuses—and suggests how important they seemed to contemporary observers. "The second volume of the *Journal des Goncourts* has appeared—a most interesting new publication. It concerns the years 1862–65; in it, the famous *dîners chez* Magny [a Parisian restaurant] are described in an extremely vivid way, the dinners at which

---

2. Among numerous examples, see the articles and reflections collected in Revel and Hunt, *Histories*; Dosse, *New History in France*; Carrard, *Poetics of the New History*. For a critical view that nonetheless stresses the prevalence of these ideas, see Himmelfarb, *New History and the Old*, esp. 4–5, 18, 25–26; for related ideas from a more sympathetic perspective, see Appleby, Hunt, and Jacob, *Telling the Truth About History*.

the most intelligent and skeptical troupe of Parisian minds at that time met together (Sainte-Beuve, Flaubert, Théophile Gautier, Taine, Renan, the Goncourt brothers, Schérer [*sic*] Gavarni, sometimes Turgenev, and so on). Exasperated pessimism, cynicism, nihilism, alternating with a lot of joviality and good humor; I would have been quite at home there myself—I know these gentlemen by heart, so well that I have actually had enough of them. One should be more radical; at root they all lack the principal thing—'*la force.*'"[3] Nietzsche's reservations about these men of letters matter less for now than his conviction that they in some sense anticipated his own vision of the world, and that they had an important and unsettling effect on contemporaries.

Nietzsche's cast of characters began meeting in 1862, at a restaurant favored by the literary critic Charles-Augustin Sainte-Beuve, one of the group's organizers. The biweekly meetings quickly acquired some fame for their mixture of personal confession, scabrous, atheistic talk, and literary seriousness. The Goncourts' *Journal* described the group discussing classical literature, recent works, and recent historical writing. But it also quoted Sainte-Beuve confessing "a secret despair, buried but still alive; he wished he were handsome, having, as he put it, a physique" that would instantly attract women. In the following year, they described an intoxicated Hippolyte Taine vomiting out the window, then turning back in to continue an argument about religious belief. Two weeks later, there were debates about the psychological effects of visiting whorehouses, with Taine arguing (against Gustave Flaubert, who insisted on the necessity of personal engagement) that real benefits came from venal sex. New members regularly joined, usually after having already attained literary prominence; others eventually left as a consequence of evolving personal enmities. Sainte-Beuve's death in 1869 and the fall of the empire the following year accelerated this turnover among the diners, and in 1874 Edmond de Goncourt (another of the original organizers) noted sadly that the dinners had lost much of their interest, having become mainly the preserve of political figures.[4] While the empire lasted, however, ties among the diners were reinforced by their encounters in other settings, and these balanced the dinners' bohemian tone. Most important, Sainte-Beuve, the Goncourts, Taine, Ernest Renan, Flaubert, and others met one

3. Middleton, *Selected Letters of Friedrich Nietzsche,* 275.
4. Goncourt and Goncourt, *Journal,* 1:886 (on first meeting), 1:897 (on Sainte-Beuve), 1:1039 (on Taine), 1:1047 (on sex), 1:1082 (on notoriety), 2:614 (on decline), 2:668 (30 November 1875; on the dinners as "tout politique").

another frequently in the salon of the princess Mathilde, Napoleon III's cousin, who provided a haven for liberal artists and writers and used her influence on their behalf when they ran into political difficulties.

The group included five writers whose careers included significant works of history and who will be the focus in what follows. The oldest of these (born in 1804), Sainte-Beuve exemplified much about Parisian intellectual life during the first two-thirds of the nineteenth century. He was born into the straitened middle class, the posthumous son of a provincial tax official. As such he could rely on a small network of familial connections and some financial support, but any larger ambitions would have to be met on his own—and they would have to be met in Paris, whose absolute domination of French cultural and social life had been cemented by the Napoleonic regime. Hence, as a teenager, Sainte-Beuve himself insisted on completing his education in Paris, following the rigorous course of classical literature supplied by the city's lycées; eventually his mother and aunt joined him there, keeping house as he began medical studies then turned to a career of writing. He published poems and a novel, but his real success came as a literary journalist. Starting in 1824 he began publishing commentaries and reviews in leading newspapers, and these eventually became his "Lundis," weekly articles that significantly shaped French literary tastes over the following forty years. There were also books on French literary history, the most important of which was his massive history of Port-Royal, to which he devoted two decades of scholarly research.

Sainte-Beuve's personal life was disorderly, to some extent as a matter of choice. Until his late thirties he lived for long stretches in rented rooms, and he fought at least one duel, a common experience for mid-nineteenth-century journalists. (It rained that morning, and he held an umbrella throughout, explaining that he was willing to die but not to be soaked to the skin.) While still a struggling journalist, he turned down the possibility of a respectable teaching position, which would have secured him both an income and social rank.[5] He also carried on a brief affair with the wife of Victor Hugo, at the time his closest friend. But this bohemianism did not prevent a relentless pursuit of the social connections needed for literary success. Early on he became a regular at the literary salon of the aging René de Chateaubriand, about whom he eventually wrote a book, and he soon established warm relations with Victor Cousin, the philosopher and literary historian who dominated French university life during

5. Sainte-Beuve, *Portraits littéraires*, cii. However, he did seek a position that would allow him to stay in Paris. Molho, *L'ordre et les ténèbres*, 280–81.

the Restoration and July Monarchy. Such connections began to pay off in the 1840s. At the start of the decade, Cousin's influence secured him the directorship of the Mazarin library, a position that included a substantial salary and a spacious, rent-free apartment. The appearance of *Port-Royal*'s first volume brought election to the Académie française in 1844, and in 1854 he was named to the Collège de France, a short-lived experiment, since radical students hooted him off the podium; in 1865, with Mathilde's support, he became a member of the imperial Senate, a mainly honorific position that brought the considerable salary of thirty thousand francs.[6] By his late thirties, Sainte-Beuve had thus become a prosperous member of the French literary establishment, but the bohemian aura remained with him throughout his life. He never married, continuing to the end a series of clandestine affairs with working-class women, and his views of society became more radical with age. After their first meeting, in 1861, Taine noted privately that for Sainte-Beuve "youth is arriving at age fifty-five"; Mathilde commented that "he's turning to socialism. He's against both literary and territorial property."[7]

The others on Nietzsche's list were a full generation younger. They had come of age in the years around 1848, and they embodied new career paths and sensibilities. Sainte-Beuve himself described them as more serious and less sociable than his own coevals, and less susceptible to romantic follies: "a generation shaped by solitude, books, sciences." Having to absorb modern science and scholarly methods, "they had at the outset a heavy weight to lift; they devoted themselves entirely to the task, and succeeded at it."[8] In keeping with this more scholarly orientation, Hippolyte Taine and Ernest Renan both sought conventional academic careers; after intensive preparations—Taine at the École Normale Supérieure, Renan at the seminary of Saint-Sulpice—both took the *agrégation* in philosophy, and both wrote dissertations. But despite academic ambitions and prudent calculations, in the end Sainte-Beuve's younger friends had careers that paralleled his to a remarkable degree.[9] Like Sainte-Beuve, Taine and Renan were provincials raised by widowed mothers, and both knew from

6. Casanova, *Sainte-Beuve*, esp. 418. For an important recent effort to assess Sainte-Beuve's importance within modern culture, see Lepenies, *Sainte-Beuve*.

7. Taine, *Sa vie et sa correspondance*, 2:241.

8. Sainte-Beuve, *Nouveaux lundis*, 8:79, 8:81.

9. For appreciative overviews of their careers, see Monod, *Les maîtres de l'histoire*. For an important recent effort to situate Taine especially within contemporary intellectual life, see Charle, *Paris fin de siècle*, 97–123. For a description of Taine's sensible, hardworking life, see also Goncourt and Goncourt, *Journal*, 2:1.

the outset that they had to succeed on their own, with limited familial support: Taine's father had been an unsuccessful small-town lawyer, who left him a small fixed income, and Renan relied mainly on the support of his devoted older sister, a governess and teacher. Support became especially necessary when, in the midst of his seminary studies, Renan lost his faith and had to remake himself as a university philosopher and historian. He succeeded dramatically, passing his examinations and publishing a well-received thesis on the medieval philosopher Averoes, then securing government funding for extended researches in Palestine. The 1863 publication of his *Life of Jesus* transformed his situation yet again. The book outraged Christians for its treatment of Jesus as a human figure, and under pressure the government suspended Renan from his teaching position at the Collège de France. But *The Life of Jesus* was also one of the nineteenth century's great best sellers, establishing Renan as a wealthy man, now married to the daughter of a society painter and with a growing family. With the fall of the Second Empire, he returned triumphantly to the Collège de France, and in 1878 he was elected to the Académie française.

Taine's career followed a similar path, with additional complications. He too was a brilliant provincial, whose family counted on his success. With that in mind, he was sent to the same Parisian lycée as Sainte-Beuve had attended and lived in one of the several *institutions* that served to prepare bright students for competitive examinations; in 1848, fulfilling his family's hopes, he moved on to the École Normale Supérieure, which then as now brought together the country's most brilliant and ambitious students. Taine did well there, but his school years concluded with an academic disaster: he failed the *agrégation*, the competitive examination that would have guaranteed him a teaching career. The failure reflected both the tense political mood of the times and Taine's unwillingness to conform to it. Taine's answers, the jury found, reflected a skeptical, irreverent outlook that the educational establishment could not accept, least of all during a time of political revolution. Taine nonetheless spent a year teaching provincial high school students, on a temporary appointment, but he refused the offer of a second year, deciding instead on a freelance career like Sainte-Beuve's; he tutored privately, gave courses at the cramming school that he himself had attended, and wrote—at an astonishing pace. By 1854 he had completed a doctoral dissertation on Jean de La Fontaine, a secondary thesis on Plato, and a book on the Roman historian Livy, the last written in ninety-eight days in response to a prize competition held

by the Académie française. In the following year he began writing articles for the middlebrow press, partly for the money and partly to establish his literary reputation, and these led to other literary commissions.

At the cost of such efforts, Taine was making a substantial income in
the mid-1850s, and he had come to be viewed as a significant literary
figure. Sainte-Beuve praised him in a long article in 1857 and a few years
later helped secure him positions at the École des Beaux-Arts and the
military academy of Saint-Cyr, near-sinecures that supplied a substantial
income. Like Renan, Taine reached his full glory after 1871. His books
criticizing the French Revolution shielded him from accusations of dangerous radicalism, and he too was elected in 1878 to the Académie française. In his youth Taine had resisted marriage, in this respect imitating
Sainte-Beuve's self-conscious refusal of societal convention. "If I were
married," he wrote to his best friend in 1855, "I would no longer have
the right to consider life as it is, that is, a bad joke concocted by necessity and chance. I would be condemned to consider society just, destiny
good, denying my reasoning and my experience."[10] But in the end he, like
Renan, remade his life in more conventional terms, with a family and a
country house in Savoy. His correspondence from that phase of his life
includes lengthy discussions about what grapes would grow best on the
property and worries that his daughters might fall into unsound reading
habits; "all this," he wrote of a series of modern authors, "is decidedly
unhealthy."[11]

Alone among the group, the Goncourt brothers were born wealthy.
They enjoyed a fixed income that allowed them a comfortable Paris apartment, and (as Taine described them) "they go off every summer to their
relatives, where they regain their strength, save some money, do some
boating, eat, fence."[12] So comfortably situated, they had no interest in the
advanced degrees and academic positions that Renan and Taine sought.
But they had received much the same education as the others, at leading
Parisian lycées, and they shared the others' intense ambition. Writing
together, between 1851 and Jules's death, of syphilis, in 1870, they produced
more than forty works of history, art history, and fiction; they also produced near-daily entries in their journal on contemporary literary life,
which Edmond eventually published. Like Sainte-Beuve, Renan, and Taine,
they pursued the connections that would help bring attention to their

10. Quoted in Leger, *La jeunesse d'Hippolyte Taine*, 305.
11. Taine, *Sa vie et sa correspondance*, 4:327.
12. Taine, *Sa vie et sa correspondance*, 2:239.

literary productions, and they fumed privately when their books failed to achieve the renown they thought appropriate. Neither married, and their personal relations were unconventional; for a time they shared a mistress. But they too mixed more conventional behavior with bohemianism. Edmond was named to the very official Legion of Honor in 1868, and late in life, established in an elegant suburban villa, he enjoyed considerable public eminence.[13]

Magny was thus characterized by its blurring of the lines that divided intellectual life elsewhere in nineteenth-century Europe. It brought together men who were in some ways cultural outsiders, men who—willingly or not—had made their way outside the institutional structures of French academic life and the norms of settled family life. The aura of scandalous opinions attached to all of them, bringing both denunciations from religious conservatives and more practical dangers: the imperial government prosecuted both Flaubert and the Goncourts for obscenity, dismissed Renan from his academic position, and blocked Taine's career.[14] Yet in other ways these were insiders, intellectually, socially, and even economically. By 1862, when the dinners began, Sainte-Beuve's opinions dominated contemporary French literature, making the careers of those whose works he praised, and the other diners were all well-known literary figures. They enjoyed a significant social position as well, especially as the imperial regime sought to improve its relations with liberal intellectuals. These same figures occasionally encountered the emperor himself at Mathilde's salon and regularly socialized there with some of the regime's leading administrators, including Alfred de Nieuwerkerke, who was both Mathilde's lover and the director of the regime's massive art purchases.

Taine's only novel, *Notes sur Paris: Vie et opinions de M. Frédéric Thomas Graindorge,* illustrates how these two outlooks, that of the outsider and that of the insider, might fit together. It appeared in 1868, and like all of Taine's work it was popular, partly because of its comic elements.[15] The fictional Graindorge, whose ideas and observations it recounts, is a Frenchman who has traveled, in the process acquiring a German doctorate of philosophy and an American fortune, won by producing salt pork on a Louisiana slave plantation and oil in Pennsylvania; he spends his days

13. Their careers are summarized in Billy, *Goncourt Brothers.*
14. For the views of religious conservatives and contemporary responses to them, see Chapter 3, below.
15. It reached an eighteenth edition in 1913.

with his mistress, a Spanish dancer; and he punctuates his narrative with reminiscences of the outlandish behavior he witnessed during his American sojourn. But alongside the comedy the book offers serious reflections about aesthetic issues and about upper-class life in Second Empire Paris, presented in enough detail to suggest that Taine knew what he was talking about. We last hear directly from Graindorge as he discusses, with insight and depth of feeling, the emotional impact of Beethoven's late piano sonatas. Before that, he has described for the reader embassy balls, the opera, expensive dinner parties, girls' educations, marital relations, all with a sharp interest in contemporary material life: we learn from him the cost of women's dresses, their fabrics and colors, how marriage proposals were made and what went through the minds of the parties to them, how much income the different levels of Paris society required.

By his midthirties, the novel shows, Taine himself had become enough of a man-about-town to know, close up, how high society worked, what it felt like to live in it, and how much it cost to do so. Hedonistic appreciation for all this material comfort runs through the book, but Graindorge's opinions also display a radical detachment from conventional moralities and a readiness to acknowledge the harsh realities of modern life. "To have a proper idea of man and of life, " he comments, "one must have oneself gone to the brink of suicide or madness, at least once."[16] *Notes sur Paris* can thus be read as exemplifying the mode of intellectual life that the Magny group represented, one that combined engagement with contemporary social life, philosophical materialism, and freedom from institutional constraints and pious moralizing.

Taine reinforced the point in the novel's conclusion, which consists of Graindorge's obituary. It is the work of a university professor who, having resisted the government's demand for absolute, abject conformity (the ministry had demanded that all professors shave their beards), has become the hero's servant and pedicurist. The university professor is ready for any indignity, it appears, but he is also angry and envious, stealing his master's wine, peeping through the keyhole at his trysts, and claiming to have contributed to his writing style. Despite these efforts, the servant-professor is appalled to discover, Graindorge had simply ignored his literary opinions: "What gratitude did M. Graindorge display? Where does he cite my name? Is there a single sentence in which he alludes to my services? . . . Let him keep for himself his incorrect sentence structure,

16. Taine, *Notes sur Paris*, 308.

his vulgar phrases, his abrupt and bizarre style."[17] *Notes sur Paris* thus forcibly juxtaposes the narrow absurdity of university culture with the subtlety, cultivation, aesthetic responsiveness, and ethical freedom of the merchant Graindorge.[18] Fifteen years later, even Taine himself found the book's radicalism somewhat shocking. To an admirer of the novel, he wrote, "[T]he Graindorge whom you have the kindness to remember died long ago; fifteen years are such a long time in a man's life! When I reread the books I wrote then, I no longer recognize myself."[19]

Self-consciously placing themselves in a borderland between the university and high society, the Magny diners also claimed a liminal position within contemporary literature. They represented widely differing literary genres, including history, literary criticism, philosophy, and fiction, and they readily mixed these genres over the course of their own careers. Sainte-Beuve wrote poetry and novels, and he only reluctantly decided that his primary vocation was as a literary historian; the Goncourts first became known for their historical writing, then shifted to fiction; Taine and Renan both wrote works of fiction, though this was never their primary focus, and Taine wrote studies of psychology and philosophy, as well as history; privately Taine worried that Renan had brought novel-writing techniques into his historical writing.[20] But Taine himself took fiction very seriously, and his literary taste was excellent; he was the first literary critic to give serious attention to Stendhal, for instance. One boundary remained largely intact. George Sand appears to have been the only woman to attend the Magny dinners. But in other settings, members of the group had intense intellectual contacts with women—yet another way in which their intellectual lives visibly diverged from the ideals of contemporary university culture. From the 1840s, Sainte-Beuve corresponded regularly with his former lover Hortense Allart, who spent most of her time in the countryside near Paris. She commented on his recent work, urged that he take up particular topics, and described her other reading, abruptly mixing these literary discussions with stories from her own love life and inquiries about his, much in the spirit of the Magny

17. Taine, *Notes sur Paris*, 343. Taine's professor appears to be a literary ancestor of Vladimir Nabokov's Charles Kinbote in *Pale Fire*.

18. Along with Graindorge's meditations on Beethoven, music to which Taine himself was especially drawn, the book includes numerous other aesthetic reflections.

19. Taine, *Sa vie et sa correspondance*, 4:135. I will argue below that this wildly understates the continuities in Taine's thinking over the course of his career.

20. Taine, *Sa vie et sa correspondance*, 3:242 ff.

discussions.[21] Renan's researches in Palestine were carried out in close partnership with his sister, and they corresponded about both personal and intellectual matters until her death, in 1861.

In these encounters, as among themselves, the Magny writers repeatedly stressed the relatedness of their scholarly writing to their personal lives. "Cold, lifeless, unphilosophical, all that *littérature universitaire*," Renan confided to his journal, in 1846; "have these men no other purpose in their literary exercises than to produce good professors?"[22] In an 1853 letter to his mother, Taine drew a similar contrast. Having completed his thesis and his work on Livy, he explained, he was about to set off in directions of his own choosing. "For the first time, I'm going to speak freely, in the form that suits me, without the restrictions of the Sorbonne or the Académie. There lies my future. If the work is good and is read, all will be well."[23] This was a rhetoric of intellectual activity that differed sharply from that of the historical seminars that had already developed in contemporary Germany and that would emerge in France and the United States during the 1880s and 1890s. But at the same time, the Magny writers stressed the seriousness and fruitfulness of their discussions. The Goncourts quoted Sainte-Beuve's claim that his weekly articles emerged from discussions at the dinners, and added their own comment: "[I]t is true, Magny will be seen to have been . . . one of the last centers of real liberty of thought and speech."[24]

Given their prominence, these men of letters offer an obvious test case for an argument about the nineteenth-century's contribution to the twentieth century's historical outlook, but they also illustrate the difficulties with such an argument. None of the group trained as a professional historian or taught history in the university, and even their nonfiction was often written with a mass audience in mind; all of them needed to make money through literary journalism, writing for such middlebrow periodicals as the *Revue des Deux Mondes*. These literary orientations were at the core of the historian Alphonse Aulard's critique of Taine, first presented in 1905–6 as a course at the Sorbonne, where Aulard held France's first chair in French Revolution studies. Taine failed to meet the standards of

21. See Allart de Méritens, *Lettres inédites à Sainte-Beuve*. At the end of her life, Allart apparently destroyed Sainte-Beuve's side of this correspondence.

22. E. Renan, *Histoire et parole*, 210.

23. Taine, *Sa vie et sa correspondance*, 2:19.

24. Goncourt and Goncourt, *Journal*, 2:107.

professional historical study, argued Aulard; his citations were sloppy and partial, and he failed to confront questions that mattered to professionals. "At the Sorbonne," Aulard proclaimed, asserting the importance of professional boundaries, "a candidate for a diploma in historical studies or a doctorate would disqualify himself if he cited Taine as an authority on a historical question."[25] Insofar as contemporary historical thought rests on clearly defined standards of professional expertise, its origins would seem to lie elsewhere.

A more serious problem with connecting the Magny group to contemporary historical practice lies in its ideas about human nature: most of the group believed in racialist explanations of social phenomena. The Goncourts publicly voiced their anti-Semitism, and made it the subject of one of their novels (*Manette Salomon*); they dedicated it "à la table de Magny," implying that the group as a whole had some sympathy for their views.[26] Privately, their language was even stronger, and Edmond responded enthusiastically to Édouard Drumont's *La France juive* when it appeared in 1885; its claims about Jewish power over Parisian newspapers, he thought, might explain unsympathetic reviews of his own work since *Manette Salomon*.[27] Taine and Renan adopted the rhetoric of scientific racism, and both applied Darwinian ideas to social phenomena very soon after the *Origin of Species* first appeared. "A race like the Aryan people," wrote Taine, "scattered from the Ganges to the Hebrides, established under all climates, ranged along every degree of civilization, transformed by thirty centuries of revolutions, shows nevertheless in its languages, in its religions, in its literatures, and in its philosophies, the community of blood and of intellect which still today binds together all its offshoots. However much they may differ, their parentage is not lost." Such racism led Taine to hierarchical judgments about different cultures' possibilities, contrasting the limited aptitudes of "the Semitic races" and the Chinese with those of

25. Aulard, *Taine historien de la Révolution française*, viii; for stress on Taine's literary, rather than historical, interests, see also 50. A generation later, March Bloch described Taine as an "ill-instructed philosopher." Bloch, *French Rural History*, 169.

26. As an example of the specifically racial nature of their anti-Semitism: "Des entrailles de la [future] mère, la juive avait jailli. Et la persévérance froide, l'entêtement résolu, la rapacité originelle de sa race, s'étaient levés des semences de son sang. . . . Comme toutes ses pareilles, elle avait ce restant de croyances, la foi insolente dans sa chance, la certitude religieuse de son bonheur, de l'arrivée de tout ce qu'elle désirait." Goncourt and Goncourt, *Manette Salomon*, 351–52. On Renan's complicated attitude toward Jews, see Sorel, *Le système historique de Renan*, 69–70.

27. Goncourt and Goncourt, *Journal*, 2:1242: "[L]e livre de Drumont m'a causé une certaine épouvante par la statistique et le dénombrement de leurs forces occultes."

"the Aryan races."[28] Renan drew out the practical consequences of these views. In response to the crisis of 1870–71, among other recommendations, he urged colonialism as "a political necessity of the absolutely first order. . . . [T]he regeneration of inferior or corrupted races by superior races is a part of the providential order of humanity." China and Africa offered the logical targets for this activity, he believed, since their inhabitants were naturally suited to manual labor. In contrast, even working-class Europeans descended from "a race of masters and soldiers." With its factories and offices, modern society restricted these masterly men "to labors contrary to [their] race," and socialist agitation inevitably ensued. Far better, Renan thought, to send them off on colonizing missions, where their innate heroism could serve the larger good.[29]

Racism of this kind allied closely with mistrust of democracy, which they saw advancing all around them and whose impact seemed especially frightening after the crisis of 1870–71. Sainte-Beuve followed a complicated political evolution and late in life became a left-wing hero for urging liberal reforms on the empire. But his works included enough criticism of democracy that Charles Maurras could claim them as sources of his own views. In 1898 he argued that in Sainte-Beuve "one would find the first indications of that resistance to the ideas of 1789 that, later, would bring honor to such figures as Taine and Renan." The literary group around Sainte-Beuve, he added, "brings together everything . . . solid and healthy in our nature. It includes nearly all those writers of our century who do not go on all fours"; and thus the Action Française sought to establish a national holiday in his honor.[30]

Having witnessed the Paris Commune, Taine and Renan were more explicit in their anxieties. Taine's *Les origines de la France contemporaine* famously argues that the revolution of 1789 was made by men who had found themselves unable to succeed in the Old Regime; the Revolution resulted from bitterness and envy, rather than reason and philosophy. Individual revolutionary leaders such as Jean-Paul Marat showed as well the destabilizing effects of their mixed racial backgrounds, but such leadership was not surprising in democratic situations; "universal suffrage," he wrote of his own times, "has had the effect of pushing aside the true notables, . . . the men who by their education, their preponderant role in taxation, their still-greater influence on production, work, and business,

28. Taine, *History of English Literature*, 2:12, 10.
29. E. Renan, *Histoire et parole*, 628, 629.
30. Maurras, *Trois idées politiques*, 259.

are the social authorities and ought to be the legal authorities."[31] Renan
spoke still more bluntly. "Democracy," he wrote in response to the calami-
ties of 1870–71, "causes our military and political weakness, our ignorance,
our silly vanity; together with our backward Catholicism, it causes the
inadequacy of our educational system."[32] The Goncourts, whose family
claimed eighteenth-century ennoblement and who prided themselves on
never having voted, shared both this fear of democratic government and
a related fear that Europe was being Americanized. "It is the barbarians
. . . who will swallow up the Latin world, just as the horde of uncivilized
barbarians devoured it in a former age."[33] Renan envisioned the same
prospect, with greater resignation. "The world is headed toward a form
of Americanism that wounds our delicate ideas, but that, once the current crises have passed, may well be no worse than the Old Regime for
the only thing that matters, that is, the freedom and the progress of the
human soul."[34]

Their confident expression of such ideas suggests the distance separating the Magny writers from twentieth-century assumptions about historical explanation. But there are also reasons for looking more closely at
the group's influence. In the first place, history held a central place in its
thinking and writing. "History is the real philosophy of the nineteenth
century," wrote Renan at the start of his career, in 1849. "Our century is
not metaphysical. . . . Its great concern is history, and above all the history of the human mind. . . . In our times, one is defined by the way one
understands history."[35] Taine agreed. In 1858, he summarized the mood
of his contemporaries as so deeply historical as to crowd out the philosophical approaches of earlier eras. The eighteenth century's classics of
social theory, such as Jean-Jacques Rousseau's *Social Contract*, "are now
just decorations for the library," and any modern who attempted the genre
would join these classics in oblivion. Hence the writer with sociological
theories to advance "discovers an excellent method, the use of history."[36]
"Everyone knows," he added a few years later, "that this science is the
greatest concern and the greatest achievement of the century. It is our

31. Taine, *Les origines de la France contemporaine*, 2:97–100, 598–99.
32. E. Renan, *Histoire et parole*, 618.
33. Quoted in Billy, *Goncourt Brothers*, 189.
34. E. Renan, *Souvenirs d'enfance et de jeunesse*, 42; see also 45.
35. E. Renan, *L'avenir de la science*, 261.
36. Taine, *Essais de critique et d'histoire*, 258.

contemporary; in Voltaire's day, it was barely imagined; in Bossuet's, it didn't exist."[37]

In establishing this outlook, Taine argued, Sainte-Beuve had played a central role.[38] Although he practiced as a literary critic, in his writings Sainte-Beuve gave more attention to historical and social questions than to literature. A survey of the 640 essays that he produced for his weekly newspaper column between 1849 and 1869 finds only 150 literary topics, and even fewer instances of pure literary criticism; and his greatest work remains his history of Port-Royal.[39] To the American critic and Harvard professor Irving Babbitt, writing in 1912, Sainte-Beuve illustrated the larger confusion of nineteenth-century thought, its refusal of disciplinary conventions: "Criticism in Sainte-Beuve is plainly moving away from its own centre towards something else; it is ceasing to be literary and becoming historical and biographical and scientific. It illustrates strikingly in its own fashion the drift of the nineteenth century away from the pure type . . . towards a general mingling and confusion of the *genres*. We are scarcely conscious of any change when Sainte-Beuve passes . . . from writers to generals or statesmen."[40] If we are to understand the historical culture of the late nineteenth century, we need to understand these writers.

This is the more important in that they had an immense influence on their contemporaries. Taine wrote of Sainte-Beuve that "we are all his pupils," and Anatole France called him the Thomas Aquinas of the nineteenth century.[41] Despite Aulard's criticisms, leading academic figures also read Taine's work carefully. Gabriel Monod, among the architects of French academic history, founder of the *Revue Historique,* and supervisor of Lucien Febvre's doctoral dissertation, had an altogether different political outlook from Renan and Taine's, but he nonetheless counted them as two of the three most important French historians (the other was Jules Michelet). "To Taine goes the glory of having understood, better than any other, the state of his generation's soul and mind; philosopher, aesthetician,

37. Taine, *Les philosophes classiques,* 303.

38. Taine, *History of English Literature,* 1:7.

39. Wellek, *History of Modern Criticism,* 56.

40. Babbitt, *Masters of Modern French Criticism,* 161. Cf. the similar assessment offered by René Wellek: Saint-Beuve "should be described as the greatest representative of the historical spirit in France in the sense in which this spirit is understood by modern Germany theoreticians such as Meinecke." Wellek, *History of Modern Criticism,* 36–37.

41. Taine, *History of English Literature,* 1:7; Anatole France quoted in Maurras, *Trois idées politiques,* 257.

literary critic, historian, he displayed all of his generation's tendencies, with rigor, brilliance, and force; he had a profound influence on it."[42] From another wing of the Sorbonne, the philosophy professor Lucien Lévy-Bruhl added his assessment of Renan and Taine's intellectual impact— and Lévy-Bruhl was also an important influence on Febvre, who cited him often and with respect. (Some years later Lévy-Bruhl invented the term "mentalité," which was to have such an impact on Febvre's thinking). Taine's "influence upon minds has perhaps been equal to that of Renan, and still makes itself strongly felt even in his very adversaries."[43]

These writers' effect on the larger reading public was comparable, appropriately, given their efforts to reach that public. Renan's *Life of Jesus* was one of the great best sellers of the nineteenth century, allowing its author to respond with perfect indifference when the imperial government stripped him of his academic position. Taine was almost as popular. By 1923, his *Les origines de la France contemporaine* had reached a twenty-eighth edition, and his literary criticism was almost as widely read. This popularity only added to Alphonse Aulard's vexation as he looked critically at Taine's work: though university historians had begun questioning it, "neither in France nor abroad has the larger public yet been alerted."[44] Even the Goncourts, whose historical works sold badly, had considerable impact on their literary contemporaries. Their study of eighteenth-century society, wrote the often-critical Edmond Scherer, was "one of the works that best allows us to understand the century, . . . which at least best helps us enter into its intimate life."[45] Their influence was especially strong on Émile Zola, who acknowledged that he had adapted their concept of the novel as an exploration of societal patterns. In 1896, only two years before he intervened in the Dreyfus affair, Zola presented the principal eulogy at Edmond de Goncourt's funeral; despite Goncourt's anti-Semitism and Zola's own concerns about anti-Semitic injustice, Zola described Goncourt as having had a "noble gallantry of mind"; his "errors, if he were guilty of any, were errors arising only from his burning passion for literature."[46] For better and worse, ideas from the Magny group loomed large in the

42. Monod, *Les maîtres de l'histoire*, 140.

43. Lévy-Bruhl, *History of Modern Philosophy in France*, 435.

44. Aulard, *Taine historien de la Révolution française*, ix. Their closeness to the mood of their middlebrow contemporaries may help explain Nietzsche's sense that the group lacked his own critical seriousness.

45. Scherer, *Nouvelles études sur la litterature contemporaine*, 96; on the Goncourts' disappointment with their book sales, see Billy, *Goncourt Brothers*, 176–77.

46. Quoted in Billy, *Goncourt Brothers*, 334–35.

intellectual landscape of pre–World War I France, the era in which Febvre and Bloch began their studies.[47]

Nor was the group's impact limited to France. Already in 1866 the Goncourts noted the presence at a Magny dinner of "an American passing through, some kind of Yankee journalist"; he had been attracted by the group's widening renown and was especially voluble in his admiration for Taine, commenting even on Taine's forthcoming studies of psychology.[48] Nietzsche had reservations about the group as a whole and especially disliked Renan, but he had enormous admiration for Taine, whom he described as "the educator of all the more serious learned characters in France" and as one of the few contemporary intellectuals who formed the true audience for his own ideas.[49] In Vienna, the novelist and cultural critic Stefan Zweig wrote his 1904 doctoral dissertation on Taine's philosophy; the dissertation was hastily thrown together and remained unpublished, but (scholars have suggested) Taine had an important influence on Zweig's later thinking.[50] The American critic Babbitt devoted one of the ten chapters in his 1912 book *The Masters of Modern French Criticism* to Taine and another to Renan; as the leading critic of his age, Sainte-Beuve received two.[51] In England Matthew Arnold expressed his admiration, and the literary critic Edmund Gosse noted Sainte-Beuve's influence on his own work and that of other British critics, adding that "all the world has read him."[52] In Italy, Benedetto Croce criticized Taine's methods and argued that his influence had been destructive, partly because of the pessimism that Nietzsche so admired; but criticism was necessary, he explained, forty-four years after Taine's death, because of "the widespread celebrity of his work. . . . Taine's is an example that everyone remembers."[53] For Aulard as well, the "servile admiration" of

47. Febvre himself referred to this intellectual presence. He spoke of "that great and penetrating mind, Sainte-Beuve"; referred to Renan as "one of the most original thinkers of that magnificent nineteenth century, whose riches we still we have not exhausted"; and, with much less enthusiasm, noted Taine's place among the "great men" of the era. Febvre, "Une mise en place," and "Taine et son temps," 356; "Renan retrouvé," 201.

48. Goncourt and Goncourt, *Journal*, 2:60 (31 December 1866).

49. Nietzsche, *On the Genealogy of Morality*, Third Treatise, sec. 27, 114 (on Renan); *Selected Letters*, 276, 279 (on Taine).

50. Dumont, *Stefan Zweig et la France*, 28–29; Prater, *European of Yesterday*, 24–25.

51. Babbitt, *Masters of Modern French Criticism*.

52. Matthew Arnold, quoted in Casanova, *Sainte-Beuve*, 355; Gosse, *More Books on the Table*, "The Prince of Critics," 13–18.

53. Sprigge, *Philosophy, Poetry, History*, 597 (from the essay "History Prepares Action Without Determining It," 1938).

Italian and German scholars for Taine heightened the need for critical review.[54]

To understand this influence, it is helpful to start with the Magny group's conception of historical inquiry itself. Despite differences among them, these writers were alike in stressing the novelty of their approaches to the past, in terms that foreshadow Lucien Febvre's own idea of a new history. "The political history of the Revolution has been done and is being redone every day. The social history of the Revolution has been attempted for the first time in these studies," wrote the Goncourts in the preface to a new edition of their 1854 book. "For this new history, we have had to discover new sources of Truth."[55] "Through psychological analysis," they wrote in another work, "through observing individual and collective life, and assessing habits, passions, ideas, moral as well as material fashions, we intend to reconstitute a whole vanished world, from the base to the summit, from the body to the soul."[56] They thus claimed innovation in regard to subject matter, methods, and sources alike, and in each domain they contrasted themselves to the political historians around them. They did not dismiss political history as irrelevant, but they argued that it could give only a partial representation of the past and that its methods were unsuited to explicating other domains of life.

Taine used similar language: a new kind of history needed to be written, one that would deal with the real life of the past, rather than its politics or ideas. "We too often forget it these days: questions of finances, tactics, politics, administration, the details of beliefs, philosophy, arts, science—all these ought to enter the portrayal of human life, but only to serve the depiction of the human passions; the true subject of history is the soul."[57] Taine thus expressed himself as a vigorous advocate of social history, which he described as a history both of the ordinary facts of daily life and as a history of ordinary people. In the absence of such a history, he wrote, "in truth, the history of the Revolution seems still unwritten." Only the use of new documents could "show us living figures, the petty nobles, priests, monks and nuns of the provinces, lawyers, civic dignitaries,

54. Aulard, *Taine historien de la Révolution française*, ix n. 1.

55. Goncourt and Goncourt, *Histoire de la société française*, v.

56. Goncourt and Goncourt, *La femme au dix-huitième siècle*, 1:8.

57. Taine, *Essai sur Tite Live*, 359. Taine's argument is the more striking in that he had prepared his essay for a contest sponsored by the conservative Académie française, and in that the Académie awarded him its prize. It could be assumed by a very young and ambitious author that such sentiments would find positive responses.

and bourgeois of the cities, country lawyers and village leaders, farmers and artisans, officers and soldiers. Only they can show us in detail and close up the condition of men, . . . a worker's salary, how much a field produced, how much a peasant paid in taxes."[58]

Both admirers and critics understood that this represented a new and important approach to the past. In *The Genealogy of Morals* Nietzsche contrasted Leopold von Ranke's arid "prudence" with Taine's willingness to confront the frightening psychological realities of the past. Only "with a *Taine*-like dauntlessness, out of *strength of soul*" would history of real significance be written.[59] Less enthusiastic, Edmond Scherer saw Taine's study of English literature (first published in 1864) as "not just a history, but also and above all a manner of seeing history," which was now to focus on "everything that constitutes social life." Scherer believed that the method "changes the idea of history. . . . History . . . as it has always been understood, is above all a narrative. It proposes to make known men's actions. It does indeed seek the causes of those actions, . . . but it inquires only into causes that are witnessed and documented. . . . More-over, what will become of narrative in the midst of these researches?"[60]

As with the Goncourts, Taine's choice of subject matter had implica-tions for his approach to documents: this kind of history required a wider and more heterogeneous range of sources. In 1899 the novelist Paul Bour-get admiringly summarized this situation: "For M. Taine, everything in human history interests the psychologist and provides him with docu-mentation. From people's ways of furnishing a room and serving a meal, to their manners of praying to God and honoring their dead, there is nothing that does not merit examination, commentary, and interpretation, for there is nothing in which men do not engage some aspect of their intimate being . . . no evidence, no matter how small, is absolutely insignificant or negligible."[61] Aulard too noted Taine's readiness to use unconventional sources, but believed that they deformed his historical

58. Taine, *Les origines de la France contemporaine,* 1:6.
59. Nietzsche, *On the Genealogy of Morality,* 100 (Third Treatise, sec. 19); emphasis in the original.
60. Scherer, *Études sur la littérature contemporaine,* 6:112–14.
61. Bourget, *Oeuvres complètes,* 1:174–75. In 1864, Fustel de Coulanges's *La cité antique* provided yet another example of the nineteenth century's hospitality to such views. Fustel opened with a ringing statement of historical difference, "the radical and essential differ-ences that once and for all separate those ancient peoples from modern societies." See Fustel de Coulanges, *La cité antique,* 1.

understanding. Taine's vision of the early Revolution, resting as it did on extreme events recounted in popular pamphlets, had no more value than would a description of France in 1907 based on "a selection of horrify-ing *faits-divers* published by the *Petit Journal* or the *Petit Parisien*."[62] At the same time, Taine had given more thought than the Goncourts to the new methods that such different kinds of documentation required. Whether literary or archival, he wrote in 1864, a document resembles "a fossil shell[,] . . . one of those forms embedded in a stone by an animal which once lived and perished. Beneath the shell was an animal and behind the document there was a man. Why do you study the shell unless to form some idea of the animal? In the same way do you study the document in order to comprehend the man; both shell and document are dead frag-ments and of value only as indications of the complete living being. The aim is to reach this being; this is what you strive to reconstruct. . . . True history begins when the historian has discerned . . . the living active man, endowed with passions, furnished with habits."[63] History needed to con-cern itself with real life, rather than with institutional abstractions.

One result of these orientations was an interest in the history of women. The subject had surprising popularity among nineteenth-century writers, sufficiently so that in 1844 controversy erupted between two lit-erary eminences over priority in the field. In that year, both Sainte-Beuve and Victor Cousin published studies of women during the Old Regime. Sainte-Beuve was especially irritated by the overlap, and he asserted his own methodological originality in terms similar to those used by Taine and the Goncourts. "I have preserved these technical details," he wrote of an erudition-filled footnote that he included in the republished version of an essay on the duchesse de Longueville, because they "indicate my priority in this kind of research, which has since been so worked over."[64] In 1862 the Goncourts also contributed to the genre, with their *La femme au dix-huitième siècle,* and that work too attracted significant attention. The princess Mathilde, whom they had met only once before, used her read-ing of the book as the occasion for a dinner invitation; and Jules Michelet himself cited it with praise in a new volume of his history of France.[65]

62. Aulard, *Taine historien de la Révolution française*, 84.
63. Taine, *History of English Literature*, 1:1, 2.
64. Sainte-Beuve, *Portraits de femmes*, 2:1288.
65. Goncourt and Goncourt, *Journal*, 1:901, 1031. When the brothers paid Michelet a grate-ful visit, he offered further praise and urged on them additional research in the area: "[Y]ou sirs, who are observers, you should write a history of chambermaids. . . . It's a remarkable

Sainte-Beuve's review suggested the breadth of topics that seemed worth pursuing in this kind of history. The Goncourts, he wrote, had depicted women "of all ranks and all classes, . . . at every level of society, every hour, and every age. The book is a mine of information."[66]

Bonnie Smith has shown that during the first half of the nineteenth century numerous female scholars explored women's history, and it is likely that Sainte-Beuve and Cousin were influenced by these efforts.[67] But the question of Sainte-Beuve's originality matters less here than his approach to the topic. He insisted in his studies that women's history belonged in the mainstream of historical analysis, and he gave serious attention to women's place within the modern world. There was nothing inevitable about this approach. Cousin, for instance, idolized the aristocratic ladies of the seventeenth century and expressed horror at the public roles that women had come to exercise in his own times. "Woman is an *être domestique,* as man is a public personage," he wrote; "what are we to say of the *femme auteur?* What! a woman who, thanks to God, has no public cause to defend, throws herself into the public sphere, and her modesty is not revolted at revealing to all eyes, selling to the highest bidder . . . her most secret beauties, her most mysterious and touching charms, her soul, her sentiments, her sufferings, her inner struggles. Though we see this every day, and even among the most honest women, it will be eternally impossible for us to understand."[68]

At points Sainte-Beuve too used condescending language in discussing women's history, and his friend Hortense Allart complained that the studies were too delicate in tone, failing to convey the intellectual force of his best work.[69] But in contrast to Cousin, Sainte-Beuve consistently stressed the severe limitations under which even the most free-spirited women labored during the seventeenth century, and he contrasted these with the liberating effects of modernity. The seventeenth-century duchesse de Longueville, for instance, lacked "a will of her own," however dazzling

---

and important thing, the role of domestic servants in history." They ignored the advice, but took it seriously enough to note it verbatim in their journal.

66. Sainte-Beuve, *Nouveaux lundis,* 4:2.

67. Smith, *Gender of History,* 50–59. Consisting of essays written from 1829 on, it is worth noting, Sainte-Beuve's studies of women come early in the sequence of studies that Smith cites.

68. Cousin, *Jacqueline Pascal,* 28, 31. (In this quotation as throughout, I have eliminated paragraph breaks.) For Sainte-Beuve's critique of Cousin's approach as sentimental and superficial, see Sainte-Beuve, *Portraits de femmes,* 2:1293–95 n.

69. Allart de Méritens, *Lettres inédites à Sainte-Beuve,* 140–41.

her personality, and could scarcely distinguish among religion, flirtation, and politics.[70] Conversely, he treated the revolutionary leader Madame Roland as a heroic figure, "one of the most eloquent and honest representatives for studying that political generation that wanted 1789, and that 1789 neither wearied nor satisfied"; and he expressed no doubts about the legitimacy of her ambitions to participate in public affairs.[71] He praised Germaine de Staël in similar terms for her determination to enter the male public world. He spoke of her "male and serious outlook"; noted that she adopted "an openly, nobly ambitious state of mind and inspiration"; and placed her in a line of leading male writers.[72] Her fiction, centering on the situation of the creative woman trapped by romantic feeling, especially stimulated Sainte-Beuve's enthusiasm: her novel "*Corinne* is precisely the image of the sovereign independence of genius, even in a time of the most complete oppression."[73]

Politics lurked in this literary assessment, drawing attention as it did to the Napoleonic repression under which de Staël suffered, and Sainte-Beuve insisted on the fruitfulness of her engagement in the politics of her era. Her posthumous *Considérations sur la Révolution française* had an enormous influence on political debate in the early Restoration, he wrote; and her death in 1817 deprived liberals of an important influence.[74] At a less lofty level, he offered the example of Pauline de Meulan, who would become François Guizot's first wife. Because of her family's financial collapse, de Meulan supported herself for a decade as an unmarried "femme journaliste" (her own term). Having quoted at length her defense of that position against others' pity, Sainte-Beuve concluded by praising her commitment to "the ideas of duty and work, such as the new society increasingly demands"; de Meulan offered "a model of the strong, sensible, hardworking woman, in the front rank of the middle class." In precise opposition to Cousin, Sainte-Beuve's *Portraits de femmes* argued in favor of women's entry into the public sphere.[75]

70. Sainte-Beuve, *Portraits de femmes*, 2: 1280. Cf. Cousin, *Jacqueline Pascal*, 25–26.

71. Sainte-Beuve, *Portraits de femmes*, 2:1140, 1155.

72. Sainte-Beuve, *Portraits de femmes*, 2:1090, 1099, 1098.

73. Sainte-Beuve, *Portraits de femmes*, 2:1123.

74. Sainte-Beuve, *Portraits de femmes*, 2:1132. Only in recent years have feminist scholars such as Nancy Miller and Bonnie Smith restored assessments of de Staël to so positive a level; see Miller, *Subject to Change*, 162–203; Smith, "History and Genius," 1059–81.

75. Sainte-Beuve, *Portraits de femmes*, 2:1194, 1195. Cf. Smith, *Gender of History*, 59, for the claim that in this period "the insider/male history written by both men of letters and professionals was based on the activities of great men and set in political and military narrative about them."

Their literary orientations and mass audience did not prevent the Magny group from claiming scientific status for their approaches to the past or from criticizing the flimsy or fictional accounts produced by some of their literary friends. Renan's views were the most ambiguous. As a skilled linguist and diligent editor of ancient inscriptions, he in some ways exemplified the nineteenth century's ideas about scientific history. But the very fervor of his belief in the natural sciences led him to stress the gap between their methods and those of historical investigation. "The natural sciences remained for me the sole source of truth," he recalled in his memoirs; had he followed his interest in them, he would have studied physiology and perhaps arrived at "several of Darwin's results, that I had some inkling of." The natural sciences remained the model of real knowledge, which historical study could never fully attain.[76] The Goncourts wrote history in a more literary and impressionistic manner, but they too insisted on rigorous methods, demanding that "at each step the historian remove prejudices [and] return to the facts" concerning eighteenth-century women; "the novel has given a false idea of everything."[77]

Of the group, Taine expressed the greatest enthusiasm for applying science to historical study, arguing that these were overlapping rather than contradictory modes of investigation. His 1853 dissertation made the point bluntly: "We may view man as something of a superior animal, which produces philosophies and poems in about the same way as silkworms make their cocoons and bees their hives." Toward this idea-making animal, he proposed taking the stance of a naturalist, who would dissect the writer and make clear how his or her various parts functioned together.[78] He returned to the image in the preface to his literary essays of 1858, describing himself as an anatomist of human systems, probing beneath the surface beauties of works of art to get at their underlying structures. "History's aim is not to drown us in detail, as it is commonly thought today," but rather to understand the "main forces" that govern each era, uniting the diversity of its surface manifestations. Only when thus pursued "will history cease being a compilation and become a science; only then will we be able to perceive and measure the secret forces that move us; then perhaps will we be able to *predict*."[79]

76. E. Renan, *Souvenirs d'enfance et de jeunesse*, 158, 163, 164.
77. Goncourt and Goncourt, *La femme au XVIIIe siècle*, 1:25.
78. Taine, *La Fontaine et ses fables*, v.
79. Taine, *Essais de critique et d'histoire*, ix, x, xi, xvi, preface to the 1st ed.; emphasis in the original.

His history of English literature (1864) likewise opens with a vigorous invocation of scientific method. "Vice and virtue," his introduction declares, "are products like vitriol and sugar; every complex fact grows out of the simple facts with which it is affiliated and on which it depends. We must therefore try to ascertain what simple facts underlie moral qualities just as we can ascertain those that underlie physical qualities. . . . There is, then, a system in human ideas and sentiments."[80] Objections that scientific history produced ugly writing or unsettling moral implications, objections that "could be sustained in the Middle Ages, cannot today be applied to any science, no more to history than to physiology or chemistry, since the right to determine human beliefs has passed entirely to the side of empirical experience, and since precepts and doctrines, instead of founding observation, [now] derive from it their own plausibility."[81] This remained his position in old age, despite the political shocks of his later years. "It is certain," he wrote Bourget, "that everything—physiology, psychology, history—can and should be seen from a deterministic, mathematical, geometrical viewpoint," though this did not (he added) preclude ethical and aesthetic judgments.[82] "The more I study moral issues," he noted in the same year, "the more I find at base mathematical ideas. . . . [T]he essential notion in the moral sciences is that of quantity."[83]

Taine believed that race science supplied one such underpinning to historical analysis, but this was not the only resource he offered. Thus, his *Les origines de la France contemporaine* asked what linguistic possibilities France had available to it in the eighteenth century and what forms of thought this linguistic apparatus permitted. During the two centuries leading up to 1789, he argued, French writers had sought to purify their language of uncouth words and to give it clarity and balance. The culture that resulted allowed only certain worldviews and prohibited others; having cut away the linguistic richness inherited from the Middle Ages, classicism produced an intellectual impoverishment that eventually allowed "only a portion of the truth, a miserable portion." In turn, linguistic poverty helped explain the Enlightenment's fatal inability to ground its social theories in human realities. In this case, Taine turned to quantification to

---

80. Taine, *History of English Literature*, 1:7, 9.
81. Taine, *Essais de critique et d'histoire*, xxi, preface to the 2d ed..
82. Taine, *Sa vie et sa correspondance*, 4:171 (1 November 1883).
83. Taine, *Sa vie et sa correspondance*, 4:159–61 (22 April 1883); for another example, see also 4:109.

prove his point, comparing the limited number of acceptable words in French with the abundance of contemporary German and English.[84]

A note to the text indicates another approach to establishing the history of culture on scientific foundations. "For the past twenty years," Taine wrote with regard to the workings of religious belief, "thanks to the researches of psychologists and physiologists, we are beginning to understand the subterranean regions of the soul and the latent work [*travail latent*] that goes on there. The storage, residues, and unconscious combining of images . . . , the composition, disassociations, and sustained doubling of the self [*moi*—the term used in French psychoanalytic writing for our *ego*] . . . the physical effects of mental sensations . . . —all these recent discoveries add up to a new conception of the mind, and psychology thus renewed offers strong insights for history."[85] Scientific psychology was to illuminate the historian's practice, by allowing understanding of the irrational and mysterious in human behavior. In particular, the historian could come to understand "latent" ideas that guided social actors, without their knowledge. Elsewhere, he described as a firm result of recent studies of psychology "that the conscious feelings, memories, desires, and so on are composed of elements that we are unaware of, and that the visible self [*le moi visible*] is only the end point, the surface manifestation, of this hidden self [*ce moi obscur*], that thousands and tens of thousands of latent events combine to construct our visible actions [*nos événements manifestes*]."[86]

Hence Taine stressed the mutability of the self, its provisional status. By its nature, the soul was a historical phenomenon, heavily subject to outside influences. "What do we mean by a self [*moi*], in other words, by a person, a soul, a mind?"[87] That the question required asking, amid the supposed self-assurance of the late Victorian era, is itself significant, as is the equivalence that Taine saw among his terms; for him soul, person, self, and mind all pointed to the same reality. Rigorously materialistic, Taine answered his question by arguing that the self had no real existence. It was merely the space within which the impressions of life were registered, an interior that remained amidst the continual flux of exterior impressions. Such stability as it had derived from its placement, not its content. Its coherence rested on memory, the series of sensations built up over a

84. Taine, *Les origines de la France contemporaine*, 1:145.
85. Taine, *Les origines de la France contemporaine*, 2:670 n. 3.
86. Taine, *Derniers essais de critique et d'histoire*, "Études de psychologie, I. Th. Ribot," 186.
87. Taine, *De l'intelligence*, 2:203.

life. This vision led Taine to an interest in the circumstances that might disrupt the continuity of selfhood: false memories, delusions, insanity, and cerebral disturbances, concerning which he undertook researches with specialists at Parisian asylums.[88] He concluded from these that no firm boundary separated madness from sanity, because selfhood had no firm ontological status. "Our idea of our selfhood [*notre personne*] actually refers to a group of coordinated elements, whose mutual associations, constantly under attack, constantly triumphing, hold together so long as our reason watches over them. . . . But madness is always at the mind's door, just as sickness is always at the body's; for the normal combination is only an achievement [*réussite*]; it only results from, and renews itself by, the defeat of opposing forces."[89] Taine thus pioneered the later nineteenth century's critique of the bounded, freely reasoning, freely choosing individual of mid-Victorian ideology. But in this respect as in others, his scientific argument accorded with the larger outlook of the Magny group. In 1847, Sainte-Beuve had already written that "often, if I may say so, there is no deeper reality [*fond véritable*] in us, only an infinite array of surfaces."[90]

These orientations placed the Magny group in a complex relationship with other historians of their day. Although they believed that their contemporaries had dramatically improved the methods of historical study, they also expressed reservations about contemporary historical writing;[91] and these doubts applied even to Jules Michelet, whose interest in social history might seem akin to their own. Sainte-Beuve produced immediate and enthusiastic reviews of books by Taine, the Goncourts, and Renan, but he declined an informal invitation to review early volumes of Michelet's *History of France,* and only thirty years later did he comment on the work in one of his regular columns. Trivial causes help to explain this failure. Although the two enjoyed cordial relations, Sainte-Beuve was a notoriously unhelpful friend in literary matters, and he disliked Michelet's flamboyant prose style.[92] More important, however, he disagreed with Michelet's conception of historical change itself. In an 1850 review of a

88. Taine, *De l'intelligence,* "Note sur les éléments et la formation de l'idée du moi," 2:465–74.

89. Taine, *De l'intelligence,* 2:230–31.

90. Sainte-Beuve, *Portraits littéraires,* "M. de Rémusat," 929.

91. For Renan's statement of this view, see above; Goncourt and Goncourt, *Journal,* 1:880 (7 November 1862).

92. Proust, *Contre Sainte-Beuve,* esp. 161–69; Goncourt and Goncourt, *Journal,* 1:880 (7 November 1862).

work on François Rabelais, Sainte-Beuve made fun of Michelet for "pursuing, three centuries after the fact, that war against the Middle Ages, which he believes still threaten us." For Michelet, Rabelais was to be understood as a warrior for cultural progress. For Sainte-Beuve and his colleagues, there could be no such simple progress through history, indeed no clear identification of a successful end point to historical development. "Every century has its mania," Sainte-Beuve wrote; "ours . . . is the humanitarian mania, and we think we honor Rabelais in attributing it to him." Although he expresses admiration for Rabelais's educational ideas, he ends the essay by stressing Rabelais's mysterious qualities, the gap that separates contemporary readers from an author in the past.[93]

Five years later, Taine offered similar ideas in a series of three reviews of Michelet. He too complained about Michelet's style, which he found intoxicating but ill suited to scientific inquiry. Taine saw this style as closely linked to Michelet's capacity to see empathetically the inner currents of the periods he wrote about, and he admired many of Michelet's insights; "that ability to see into the souls of his characters makes the author a psychologist." But ultimately Michelet's history entailed a degree of simplification that Taine could not accept. "This book," he wrote of Michelet's treatment of the Reformation, "is a long defense of the modern spirit struggling to be born, and bringing with it art, science, liberty, and humanity. For the author, the enemies that this spirit encounters are so many personal enemies."[94] Taine's own understanding of historical evolution was almost precisely the opposite. Seventeenth-century style and sentiments, he wrote elsewhere, "are so distant from our own that we understand them with difficulty. . . . A transformed society has transformed the soul. . . . [E]ach century, with its own conditions, produces feelings and beauties particular to it."[95] Conversely, he praised Sainte-Beuve for the absolute love of truth that led him to "mistrust great names, fine words, enthusiasm; not to take our aspirations and the demands of our sensibilities for proofs and certitudes . . . ; to be on his guard against the illusions of the human word."[96]

The group's response to the historian and political theorist Alexis de

93. Sainte-Beuve, *Causeries du lundi*, 3:16 (7 October 1850). For similarities between Sainte-Beuve and Michelet, cf. Molho, *L'ordre et les ténèbres*, 398.

94. Taine, *Essais de critique et d'histoire*, "M. Michelet," 84–129, quotations at 103, 98–99. For a more nuanced reading of Michelet's idea of progress, which gives attention to the doubts and anxieties accompanying it, see Gossman, *Between History and Literature*, 201–24.

95. Quoted and discussed in more detail in Chapter 4, below.

96. Taine, *Derniers essais*, "Sainte-Beuve," 92.

Tocqueville was similar. "Only one man has touched on the history of prerevolutionary society with some impartiality, M. de Tocqueville," commented the Goncourts. "But he was too close to the passions of his day, engaged in its liberalism, prejudiced even in his good faith. We [are] free from everything, . . . independent even of the future. . . . A general idea: there is no progress, merely evolution in human life."[97] Moral relativists, doubting the reality of historical progress, and reluctant to see in past societies prefigurations of contemporary achievements, the Magny group could not accept Michelet's and Tocqueville's ideas about how past and present interacted. They shared their interest in the history of society, but not their confidence about what that history meant.

Sainte-Beuve, Taine, and their associates, I have argued, believed that history was a central method for understanding the human condition and that, as such, it needed to move beyond its fixation on politics, institutions, ideas, and narrative. Because it concerned itself with private persons and inner lives, this new history also demanded new sources and techniques of analysis, notably through the development of a scientific psychology. But this claim raises two further questions, both of them suggested in somewhat different terms by Alphonse Aulard in his 1905–6 critique of Taine. One concerns the apparent contradiction between the innovations that the Magny group called for in historical method and its difficulties with the modern world itself. In one way or another, all may be described as social conservatives; why then did they turn so readily to novel conceptions of the past, conceptions that (as they emphasized) differed sharply from traditional ways of relating past to present?

In answering this question, it is important to note that the group was not unambiguous in its conservatism. Sainte-Beuve was thought to be turning toward socialism in his last years; and Paul Bourget noted in 1883 that "until these past few years," Taine "was placed by the majority of his readers among what might be called the far Left of contemporary thought."[98] The Magny diners as a group were notorious for their atheism, and as such were treated as a social menace by conservatives during the Second Empire.[99] Their comments on the Old Regime also tended to be

97. Goncourt and Goncourt, *Journal*, 1:703.

98. Bourget, *Essais de psychologie contemporaine*, 125–26.

99. In 1863, the leading Catholic intellectual Monsignor Dupanloup publicly denounced Taine and Renan for atheism, leading Sainte-Beuve in turn to defend them (Casanova, in *Sainte-Beuve*, 414, summarizes the episode; it is discussed in more detail in Chapter 3, below).

negative, and they vigorously defended the culture of the nineteenth century. The aristocratic Goncourts, to be sure, viewed themselves as "deep within, immigrants from the eighteenth century . . . déclassé contemporaries of that refined, exquisite, supremely delicate society."[100] Yet even they, it has been seen, enjoyed cordial intellectual relations with Michelet and Zola, pillars of republican culture during the late nineteenth century. Sainte-Beuve questioned the value even for the seventeenth century of "a brilliant, ephemeral, artificial, superficial monarchy, without deep links to the past or future of France, or even to the manners of its own time."[101] He suggested that "our century's style . . . will be less correct and less learned, freer and more daring" than that of the seventeenth-century classics—but it would nonetheless produce its own masterpieces.[102]

Both before and after the crises of 1870–71, Taine was still more vigorous in his contempt for the old French aristocracy. During the Old Regime, he wrote in 1858, they had been ready traitors to the larger nation, "paid thugs" of foreign kings against their fellow countrymen and -women; "within the country, they had power only to ruin the people and pillage the state's finances. They were the enemies of civilization, of order, of public peace. Every wound they received was a blessing for the country."[103] "If you mean by [revolution]," he wrote a friendly critic in 1881, "the abolition of the Old Regime (arbitrary kingship, feudalism), nothing more reasonable; not only in France, but in Italy, in most of Germany and in Spain, the old machine was rotten and called only for overthrowing."[104] Even his studies of academic philosophy brought forth defense of bourgeois society. "When a society's law establishes unequal conditions, no one is exempt from insults; . . . human nature is humiliated at every level, and society is only an exchange of affronts." Insofar as the Revolution established legal equality and ended aristocratic power, Taine approved of it.[105] Renan also praised the Revolution—and even some aspects of the ongoing revolutions that he witnessed during the nineteenth century. They showed the emergence of new societal energies and the consequent need for new social arrangements.[106]

100. Goncourt and Goncourt, *Journal*, 1:905.
101. Sainte-Beuve, *Tableau historique et critique*, 281.
102. Sainte-Beuve, *Tableau historique et critique*, 284.
103. Taine, *Essais de critique et d'histoire*, 290, 291.
104. Taine, *Sa vie et sa correspondance*, 4:126.
105. Taine, *Les philosophes classiques*, 113.
106. Rétat, *Religion et imagination religieuse*, 144–56; Rétat speaks of Renan's "solidarité intérieure avec un parti avancé" (147), "sa sympathie spirituelle pour la révolution" (148).

Nor were these writers altogether critical of modernity. "I envy the future," wrote Renan in his memoirs. "It is to one's advantage to arrive on this planet as late as possible. . . . We must not, because of our personal tastes, stand in the way of what our era is achieving."[107] In an early work that he published only in 1890, two years before his death, he stressed his faith in material progress and its cultural benefits: "[T]he human spirit will not be altogether free until it is perfectly freed from the material needs that humiliate it and block its development. . . . Everything that serves the progress of humanity, however humble and profane it may seem, is by that fact deserving of respect and sacred."[108] Taine spoke more straight-forwardly. He believed the nineteenth century to have been far more inventive and productive than its predecessors, and he viewed inventiveness as a sign of a society's health. "It's invention that measures moral force," he wrote in 1858. "To search, to discover, to apply, one must want with passion. The decay of invention among the Romans demonstrated their failure of nerve; our fecundity of invention shows our internal energy. This century, which is not yet finished, has produced more than its predecessors"; and he offered a list of what the sciences had recently achieved and seemed on the verge of discovering. These changes affected the humblest in French society in that "the new science and industry have reached into the most distant villages, feeding, clothing, transporting, agitating men."

But (again following Sainte-Beuve) Taine also believed that the changes of the nineteenth century extended beyond the material realm, to include philosophy and culture as well. He argued that nineteenth-century literature was "as abundant in thought, as rich in masterpieces, as its predecessors, appropriate in both ideas and form to the class and civilization that have produced it." If it was cruder than that of previous centuries, it was also more alive: "hardier, less enslaved to the proprieties, more universal . . . more passionate."[109] Such appreciation for the vitality of modern life contrasted sharply with the pessimism of many contemporaries. Tocqueville, for instance, claimed that eighteenth-century France "had not yet become the land of dumb conformity it is now," and that "eighteenth-century man had little of that craving for material well-being which leads the way to servitude."[110] Sainte-Beuve, Taine, and Renan viewed the modernity around them as in fact representing a distinctive civilization, with a

107. E. Renan, *Souvenirs d'enfance et de jeunesse*, 42.
108. E. Renan, *L'avenir de la science*, 249–50.
109. Taine, *Essais de critique et d'histoire*, 277, 278.
110. Tocqueville, *Old Regime and the French Revolution*, 115, 118.

particular mix of virtues and vices. They showed no interest in the idea that material abundance might lead to moral weakness, and worried instead about the brutalizing effects of poverty.

Among the group's writings, Taine's *Les origines de la France contemporaine* (written with explicit reference to the crises of 1870–71) raised the deepest questions about both democracy and the processes by which it had been established. The book pleased conservatives, and they responded by electing both Taine and Renan to the bastion of French conservative culture, the Académie française. Yet even this passionate critique of democracy neither defended the Old Regime's social order nor criticized the modern world. Rather, Taine's primary concern lay in the problem of revolutionary violence. He sought first to depict violence, and then to explain it; and in both efforts he focused on its irrational qualities, the fact that so much of it was ill connected to the real problems and dangers that the Revolution faced and that it so often involved dramatic cruelties. These interests led him to pay close attention to the gruesome details of revolutionary violence, such as the symbolic indignities to which crowds subjected victims before and after their deaths: he described the seventy-four-year-old Joseph Foullon, for instance, being marched to Paris with "a bundle of hay on his head, a necklace of thistles around his neck, his mouth stuffed with hay."[111] For Aulard, Taine's deployment of such lurid detail conformed to the other weaknesses in his work. Seeking after literary effect and lacking professional training, Aulard argued, Taine heaped up examples of violence without considering their larger contexts. Like the tabloid journalists from whom he drew so many examples, he retold horrific particulars with excessive relish, dwelling on the victims' sufferings while ignoring the real dangers under which the revolutionary leadership worked. Taine failed as a historian because he focused on details and neglected the larger circumstances from which they emerged.[112]

Reviewing the debate in 1909, the conservative historian Augustin Cochin drew attention to the importance within it of the concept of otherness. Aulard, he suggested, explained the revolutionaries' choices as utilitarian political responses to extraordinary threats, to the principles of 1789 and to the nation itself, whereas for Taine the Revolution could not be understood as an extension of ordinary life or as following its rules. Understanding the Revolution therefore demanded a new kind of science, the

111. Taine, *Les origines des ls France contemporaine*, 1:347.
112. For instance, Aulard, *Taine historien de la Révolution française*, 178–81.

application of psychological theory and comparison, rather than the commonsense reasoning that ordinarily characterized political history; and contemporaries recognized the book as a "work of historical psychology."[113] Cochin was not altogether happy with this psychological approach and argued that Taine had posed an intellectual problem without having the analytical framework needed to resolve it. From a desire to understand the revolutionaries' behavior, Taine's methods led him to focus on their failings as individuals and obscured from his view the systems that determined behavior. He could only understand the revolutionary leaders as criminals, their actions to be explained by particular facts in their backgrounds and personality.[114] The criticism applies even more strongly to Taine's friends. Sainte-Beuve's work was primarily biographical, a compilation of individual stories and a summary of individual works. Renan himself noted the irony that his plan to write a large-scale history of Mediterranean religion had culminated in a *Life of Jesus*, though he also defended the choice.[115] Historical psychology of the sort that he and his friends practiced seemed to have collapsed into mere biography.

Cochin suggested an alternative source of interdisciplinary inspiration in the newly founded sociology of Émile Durkheim. As François Furet noted, Cochin appears to have been the first French historian to propose that academic sociology might supply useful guidance to research, but in the decade before his death Taine himself had already begun reading the English sociologist Herbert Spencer.[116] In any case, despite his questions about method, Cochin applauded Taine's definition of the problem and adopted it as his own: the phenomenon of revolution confronted the historian with extraordinary behavior, which could not be explained in terms of utilitarian calculations of means and ends. Understanding it required new sources and methods, which would draw historians' attention to irrationality and allow them to make sense of it. Cochin, Taine, and the other conservative historians considered here thus turned to social history partly because of their very fears about modernization. These posed for them the problem of the irrational in history, forcing them to ask about the nature of social differences and about the force of unconscious motivations. Like other aspects of modern culture to which scholars have recently

113. Cochin, *La crise de l'histoire révolutionnaire*, 55.

114. Cochin, *La crise de l'histoire révolutionnaire*, 55–66.

115. E. Renan, *Life of Jesus*, 62.

116. Cochin, *La crise de l'histoire révolutionnaire*, 55–66, passim; François Furet drew attention to Cochin's insight in this regard in *Interpreting the French Revolution*, 172 ff.; Taine, *Sa vie et sa correspondance*, 4:30.

drawn attention, these historians' modernism had complex linkages with conservative, even reactionary politics.[117]

The second question that Aulard raised in 1905–6 concerned professional standards and the relationship between literature and scientific history. To what extent, he asked, could literary figures like the Magny diners be compared with the highly professionalized historians of the twentieth century?[118] For Aulard and his colleagues, the answer was clear. An enormous gap separated university historians, who devoted themselves to scientific method and the verification of facts, from the amateurs, who (in the words of two other Sorbonne historians) "consider history an art rather than a science, an exercise within the competence of any dilettante, and who, instead of confining themselves to the critical and exact determination of the facts, lose themselves in vain political or religious declamations." Rather than follow scientific procedures, the amateurs left everything "to individual caprice, passions, and above all, the interests of the writers."[119]

But during these years the boundaries between amateur and professional approaches were less clearly marked than such comments suggest. For one thing, Taine and his fellows enjoyed close relations with some of the early advocates of professional, university-based history. Ernest Lavisse regularly attended Taine's Monday-afternoon salon in the mid-1880s, and Gabriel Monod had been a friend since the 1860s; as noted above, Monod thought highly of both Taine and Renan.[120] Equally important, like the university historians, Taine and the others proclaimed their own allegiance to scientific methods, and in fact their efforts appear roughly to have met professional standards. Cochin verified a large sample of Taine's citations and found them as accurate as Aulard's own; some of Taine's free transcriptions of them merely reflected literary conventions of his age. As for Aulard's complaint about Taine's readiness to use local histories and memoirs, rather than the documents produced by governmental authorities,

117. See, for instance, Carroll, *French Literary Fascism*; compare Lionel Trilling's remark that "it is one of the cultural curiosities of the first three decades of the twentieth century that, while the educated people . . . tended to become ever more liberal and radical in their thought, there is no literary figure of the very first rank (though many of the next rank) who, in his work, makes use of or gives credence to liberal or radical ideas." Trilling, *Moral Obligation to Be Intelligent*, "The Leavis-Snow Controversy," 417–18.
118. My understanding of the issues implicit in discussions of professionalization owes much to Smith, *Gender of History*.
119. Pierre Caron and Philippe Sagnac, quoted in Keylor, *Academy and Community*, 175.
120. Taine, *Sa vie et sa correspondance*, 4:194, 3:20; see above.

it was precisely this that made Taine's work original and fruitful.[121] Nor were the standards of university history always very high during the years before World War I. Following a thorough and sensitive overview of the university historians between 1870 and the war, William R. Keylor concludes by noting how "exaggerated and premature" were their assertions of scientific method, given "the egregious absence of it in much of their written work."[122] Aulard himself had trained in literature, with a dissertation on Italian poetry. Lavisse's early career was based on his personal connections with the Bonaparte family and with leading figures in the imperial administration, rather than on scientific attainments, and one of his students described him as "not a scholar," though "a great historian."[123] Similar disparities between the rhetoric and the realities of scholarly training have been noted for Germany and the United States in these years.[124] Through World War I, the professors' vision of a scientific history was more a statement of aims than an than accurate description.

As important for an evaluation of Aulard's critique is an assessment of the relative places of academics and intellectuals within French intellectual life at the end of the nineteenth century. Christophe Charle and others have drawn attention to the lofty standing that Parisian professors enjoyed during the nineteenth century and to their close connections with other elites; claims to professional expertise, like Aulard's, helped to sustain this position.[125] But the professors' position was hardly so secure as they would have liked, and a countervailing tradition mocked the narrowness of their outlook and their lack of creativity. In 1863 the Goncourts recorded their salon encounter with a philosopher, "typical of that horrible race, the jolly university professor. . . . [H]e makes professorial jokes and defends labored paradoxes. . . . There is in his whole person a certain low and disgusting smell of the provincial schemer."[126] In 1868 Taine made the same point in his novel *Notes sur Paris: Vie et opinions de M. Frédéric-Thomas Graindorge*, presenting the professor as poor, envious,

121. Cochin, *La crise de l'histoire révolutionnaire*, 9–32; compare a recent suggestion that "Aulard was able to marginalize conservative interpretations of the Revolution, ridiculing the amateurism of Hippolyte Taine's frightened account." Baker and Kaplan, editors' introduction, xii.

122. Keylor, *Academy and Community*, 209.

123. Keylor, *Academy and Community*, 68–69, 94–95, 107; see also den Boer, *History as a Profession*, 309–22.

124. Novick, *That Noble Dream*, 48.

125. Charle, "Academics or Intellectuals?" 94–116, esp. 100–101.

126. Goncourt and Goncourt, *Journal*, 1:999 (19 August 1863).

angry, and deluded.[127] In the following generation, Marcel Proust likewise offered a fictionalized version of the professor. His Professor Brichot is yet another pathetically subservient character, fawning on a salon hostess and so poor that he considers marrying his servant. He nonetheless draws from his salon attendance "a glamour that set him apart from all his Sorbonne colleagues. They were dazzled by his descriptions of dinners to which they would never be invited."[128] Such images survived intact through World War II, and in 1954 Philippe Ariès offered a sweeping overview of what the Goncourts, Taine, and Proust claimed to have observed in particular cases. "We must think of the social origins of those who taught or wrote [history]," Ariès explained. "During the second half of the nineteenth century, the bourgeoisie turned away from university careers. . . . Even today, recruitment is loftier in the law schools and at Saint-Cyr than in the humanities." Intellectually able young men from the lower-middle class "had few chances to shine in the literary salons. . . . The Académie française snubbed them, as did the cultivated public. In contrast, the upper university offered a field open to their ambitions. So, rather quickly, the professors' audience became one of future professors"—and the professors' writing (as Ariès saw it) became correspondingly narrow and dull.[129]

Early in the twentieth century, then, historical writing was less a defined field of expertise than a focal point for competing visions of intellectual life; and even leading advocates of professionalization had difficulty with the alternatives that these visions placed before them. Lavisse, Charles Seignobos, and Charles-Victor Langlois all complained in these years about the narrowness of much historical research and urged historians to address larger questions.[130] Lucien Febvre himself returned frequently to this theme, and from 1929 on he and Marc Bloch made it an important component of their journal *Annales d'histoire économique et sociale*. The journal's prospectus insisted on its engagement with the contemporary world and on the need for exchanges between historians and those dealing with contemporary problems. It proclaimed that even the distant past could not be understood without "study of today's living reality." At the same time, politicians and managers needed the perspectives that

127. Taine, *Notes sur Paris*, 334 ff.
128. Proust, *Sodome et Gomorrhe*, 262.
129. Ariès, *Le temps de l'histoire*, 274–75. Carbonell, in *Histoire et historiens*, 444–50, offers a somewhat different view of the professors' marginality, in stressing the Protestant views of the group surrounding the *Revue Historique*.
130. Keylor, *Academy and Community*, 105–8.

history could supply: "here we will assist men of action only by offering them the means to a better understanding of their own times; it is permitted to think that this is in itself a great deal."[131] In keeping with its manifesto, the *Annales* devoted far more space to contemporary history than did its competitors: between 1929 and 1939 more than one-third of its articles dealt with the period since 1871, as opposed to 8 percent in the *Revue Historique,* and Febvre and Bloch both wrote articles on contemporary subjects.[132] In 1933, in his inaugural lecture at the Collège de France, Febvre pursued the theme, arguing that historical education neglected the contemporary world and suffered as a result.[133] Febvre and Bloch stressed the technical competence that they expected even in discussions of modern society, and they too had harsh criticisms of literary approaches to historical study. But the widening influence of their journal ensured a measure of institutional permanence for the tradition of criticizing university history-writing. Alphonse Aulard's vision of an entirely professional historical practice had failed to persuade even French academics themselves.

By the mid-nineteenth century, I argue in this chapter, French intellectuals had developed a robust conception of social history. They believed that history should concern itself with the real life of past societies, rather than limiting itself to politics and great men, and they insisted that new sources and methods would be needed for getting at these realities. They were especially concerned to understand the psychological patterns of life in the past, which they believed differed widely from one society to another, and which they saw as involving a complex mixture of conscious and unconscious motivations. Addressing such questions, they understood, required attention to groups that had scarcely figured in earlier historical accounts—women, peasants, small-town elites. All these expectations implied a new kind of history, one that conflicted with the traditions of the genre, and nineteenth-century intellectuals regularly used language that revealed their awareness of having broken with older visions of historical study.

These ideas emerged in a specific milieu, the group of freelance intellectuals who in the 1850s and 1860s associated with the literary critic

---

131. Müller, *Marc Bloch, Lucien Febvre,* 1:42, 43.

132. Dosse, *New History in France,* 48. This orientation would change dramatically after 1945.

133. This episode and the larger issues surrounding it are discussed in detail in Chapter 4, below.

Sainte-Beuve. These writers depended for their livelihoods on reaching a broad public, and, often under acute financial pressure, they worked quickly, sometimes overconfidently. But their best writing meets high scholarly standards, a result both of the ferocity with which they worked and the excellent literary educations that they had received. Their writing was also extraordinarily influential. In the years around 1900, these were among the most widely read of all French writers. In a variety of ways, I argue here, their circumstances help account for the kind of history that these intellectuals advocated and wrote. All were attentive to literary culture, and all wrote works of fiction at some point in their careers. As in their novels, in their historical writings they sought to explicate how people lived in the world and how their personalities functioned. Equally important, these intellectuals were only loosely connected to the official institutions and programs around them. Willingly or not, they had made their way through journalism and the world of the salons, rather than through the university. This irregular pathway to success seems to have produced a detached skepticism toward many of their society's official values, including its belief in progress and its Christian ethics. The nineteenth-century French university was committed to both, and so could not tolerate doubters like Taine and Renan among its faculty.

Their detachment from conventional career paths left these writers unusually ready to explore the psychological workings of their own society, and unusually willing to see valid ethical and cognitive systems in societies that were not their own. This hardly resulted in a full cultural pluralism. Like many of their contemporaries, they believed that racial characteristics permanently shaped how different societies developed; and the events of 1870–71 brought to the fore their nationalism and their fears of the lower classes. But their relativism remained sufficiently strong to give a distinctive orientation to their historical thought, enlarging their ideas about human psychologies and allowing them to see history as something other than a march to the present. A generation after the Magny dinners, Nietzsche was correct in underlining the group's "exasperated pessimism, cynicism, nihilism, alternating with a lot of joviality and good humor." That outlook was unacceptable within the French university, but it was a necessary element in the development of a new mode of historical thought.

2

ORDERING TIME:

THE PROBLEM OF FRENCH CHRONOLOGY

"Modern France does not date from 1789," in-
toned Jules Michelet in a lecture of 1841; "it is
eternal [*de tous les temps*]."[1] His comment reflected a concern
shared by many intellectuals in nineteenth- and twentieth-
century France. What was the shape of French history? When
had France become modern, and what were the respective
contributions of the Old Regime and the Revolution to its
modernity? In this chapter I examine a series of efforts to
answer such questions. I ask how French writers understood
their nation's chronology, where they saw its turning points
and its lines of continuity, how they defined the relationship
between the historical past and the present within which
they themselves lived.

These were in part technical questions of historical interpretation, and their answers depended on how different

1. Michelet, *Cours au Collège de France*, 1:442.

historians read specific documents. But (I argue in this chapter) much more basic issues were also at stake. For these debates touched on the nature of historical time itself, expressing the participants' ideas about how history advanced and about its possible destinations. As writers sought to understand when their country had become "modern," they necessarily deployed their assumptions about what constituted modernity and identified the specific qualities in the present whose antecedents they thought it necessary to trace. Their views of French chronology also expressed their ideas about the element of progress in historical change. The best-known nineteenth-century historians saw historical processes as fundamentally progressive. For Victor Cousin, Leopold von Ranke, and even Jules Michelet, progress had theistic underpinnings; God's existence guaranteed that history had a meaningful direction.[2] The university historians of later nineteenth-century France toned down these providentialist assumptions, but they continued to see a direction in the movement of history. As respected officials within a newly established republican polity, they saw the nation's history as a long progress toward their own form of government, with its limited democracy, national unity, prosperity, educational advances, and humanitarian ideals. In contrast, Sainte-Beuve, Taine, Renan, and the other writers on whom this study focuses contested all progressive visions of historical development. They did so from an explicitly atheistic position, which disturbed their contemporaries, but they were equally critical of secular visions of progress. Their doubts derived in part from their ambivalence about the modern world itself. Reluctant to accord moral superiority to the world they inhabited, these writers could not see previous history as simply the story of how that world unfolded.

Because such large issues lay behind discussions of historical chronology, these discussions persisted through the nineteenth and twentieth centuries, and the terms of debate changed remarkably little. Although they disagreed in their specific views, French historians and other intellectuals defined the relevant questions in similar ways, and their answers clustered around a few fundamental themes. None could avoid seeing the Revolution of 1789 as an important moment in the nation's history, yet most shared Michelet's sense that the Revolution had emerged from deeper tendencies in the nation's past; in any case, as a brief moment, marked by bewildering violence, the Revolution could not suffice to mark the division between premodern and modern France. Instead, writers

2. These ideas are briefly discussed in the Introduction, above.

focused their attention on the seventeenth century, the age of Richelieu and Louis XIV, Molière and Racine, and it became the focal point for debate on how French modernity had developed and what it meant. This chapter thus focuses on a very specific problem, how French writers understood the seventeenth century, as a means of access to much larger issues: how did these writers define modernity, how did they understand the nature of historical change, and ultimately how did they define Frenchness itself?

I want to take as a starting point the simple fact of the nineteenth century's interest in the seventeenth: from 1815 on, readers and authors alike found the subject fascinating. At the popular level, there were of course the tales of Alexandre Dumas, which sold in legendary quantities, and which one observer described as the history lessons of ordinary people.[3] Higher up the cultural ladder, the literary critic Charles-Augustin Sainte-Beuve described a wave of enthusiasm for the seventeenth century that had arisen among the educated around 1810: "In that time, when everything was coming back to life, in some circles there was a reflowering, as it were, a second growth, of the pure Louis XIV outlook." The great seventeenth-century authors were reprinted, but also many minor ones; and "it was claimed that there were circles where ladies wore mourning on the anniversary of Madame de Sévigné's death."[4] Seventeenth-century subjects, Sainte-Beuve suggested, attracted men and women, the irreverent and the pious, culture professionals and the broad public. Sainte-Beuve himself profited from this interest. He had begun writing his history of Port-Royal in isolation, he claimed, but by the time he completed the work's second volume the subject had become fashionable.[5]

Why so much interest, in a nineteenth century that already saw itself as decisively set on the road to modernization? Some of it, of course, reflected the anguished response of conservatives to the discomforts of life after 1789, and there were milder forms of nostalgia as well, for a world that was slower and quieter.[6] Ernest Renan fondly recalled the Breton scenes of his childhood, where "one thinks oneself completely in the seventeenth century"; and he claimed that he was "at ease only at the Institut and the

3. Goncourt and Goncourt, *Journal* 1:995.
4. Sainte-Beuve, *Portraits de femmes*, 2:1406 (Madame de Rémusat).
5. *Port-Royal* is the subject of the following chapter.
6. For excellent analysis of the political stakes of this interest in the seventeenth century, see Molho, *L'ordre et les ténèbres*, 29–38.

Collège de France," where forms of politeness survived that had long since disappeared elsewhere.[7] The antiquarian Alfred Franklin used similar language to describe the Bibliothèque Mazarine, officially the library of the Institut and professional home to several important nineteenth-century intellectuals, and his own professional home for the forty years of his career. That institution "had resisted the invasion of modern ideas; it kept the cult of the past, and, confined within its traditions, remained unchanging in the midst of a world in transformation"; surrounded by its books, most of its personnel shared a "cult of the seventeenth century."[8]

But the readership to which Sainte-Beuve drew attention extended well beyond the reactionary and the sentimental. It touched also some of the movers and shakers of nineteenth-century academic life, and notably the philosopher and historian Victor Cousin. Cousin dominated the French university during the Restoration and July Monarchy, having become professor of philosophy at the Sorbonne in 1815, at the age of twenty-three. Political disputes with the Bourbons interrupted his tenure between 1820 and 1827, but he then returned in triumph and served as director of the École Normale Supérieure and minister of education under the July Monarchy. During these years, with only brief interruptions, he reigned as France's semiofficial philosopher, setting examination questions, controlling academic appointments, and lecturing to enthusiastic crowds of students. Cousin made full and arbitrary use of his power. In an 1848 letter to his sister, Renan himself regretted that he would sit for the *agrégation* during a year when Cousin happened to be absent from the jury, even though he ordinarily dominated the proceedings with "ses boutades et ses caprices": "At least he's a lofty thinker, and perhaps after all I might have found my way into his good graces."[9] Cousin's doctrine of "eclecticism" stressed reconciliation between religious belief and the moderate achievements of the French Revolution, a tricky melding of progress and tradition that appealed enormously to political leaders after 1815, helping to account for Cousin's stranglehold over the era's academic life.[10] But Cousin also touched feelings in the educated public at large, where there were similar yearnings for synthesis. While beginning his studies at the pious seminary of Saint-Sulpice, Renan and his fellows were not allowed

7. E. Renan, *Souvenirs d'enfance et de jeunesse*, 165, 207.

8. Franklin, *Histoire de la Bibliothèque Mazarine*, xi, xvii. Franklin and his setting are discussed in Chapter 5, below.

9. Rétat, *Histoire et parole*, 170.

10. On Cousin, see Kelley, *Descent of Ideas* 14–23.

to attend Cousin's lectures—but they nonetheless ardently followed and debated Cousin's ideas.[11]

For Cousin, the significance of the seventeenth century could be easily summarized: it represented the opening phase of modernity itself. "We know," he told his student audience in 1828, "the day and the year when modern philosophy was born, . . . the philosophical spirit that today animates Europe"; Cousin referred to 1637 and the publication of René Descartes's *Discourse on Method*.[12] This was not a matter of intellectual history alone. Cousin believed that philosophy constituted the essence of the historical process, at once reflecting and forming its other dimensions: philosophy "simply reflects in a more precise and clear manner the character of the industry, the art, the state, the religion of each era." Descartes's work thus marked the founding of modernity in the broadest sense. Accordingly, "this new Socrates" appeared in France, "the nation farthest advanced in the ways of European civilization."[13] In place of nostalgia or reaction, Cousin offered genealogy: the dynamic and enlightened present had its origins in the seventeenth century, leaving the French Revolution only a brief deviation of the deep currents of national life. In this respect, at least, Cousin showed the continuing influence of Voltaire in the postrevolutionary world, for Voltaire too had celebrated the achievements of Louis XIV's great century—indeed, had counted the era among the handful of crucial moments in humankind's evolution.[14]

As the ultimate insider-intellectual, pillar of a regime that seemed to have combined monarchical stability with modernity, Cousin was unusually eager to see the origins of the present in the seventeenth century. But more radical thinkers took more or less the same position. Thus Auguste Comte, writing in 1820: Descartes along with other seventeenth-century scientists "irrevocably destroyed the mental yoke of authority in scientific matters. It was then that natural philosophy came into being and that scientific capacity assumed its true character, that of the spiritual element of a new social system." To a significant degree, he believed, these achievements reflected the efforts of the French monarchy. Since the thirteenth century, according to Comte, "royal power in France and feudalism in England have constantly and increasingly encouraged the sciences and raised the political standing of scientists." Kings came to recognize "the

11. Renan, *Souvenirs d'enfance et de jeunesse*, 157.
12. Cousin, *Cours de philosophie*, 59, 60.
13. Cousin, *Cours de philosophie*, 184, 59.
14. Discussed by Pocock in *Barbarism and Religion*, 2:86.

obligation to encourage the sciences and to submit to the decisions of scientists. The establishment of the Academy of Sciences, instituted under
Louis XIV by his minister Colbert, is a solemn declaration of this principle."[15] Likewise Michelet, lecturing in 1844 at the Collège de France:
in the early seventeenth century, following the devastation wrought by
France's religious wars, "an idea surged to the fore, *that man is sacred,
man, the life of man, the blood of man* . . . [the idea that] amidst so many
uncertain things, man is the one certainty, the living truth, not to be
sacrificed to any merely verbal truth. This humanist [*humaine*] thought,
unknown to Antiquity and the Middle Ages . . . constitutes the legitimacy
of the modern world, its holiness."[16] For Michelet, this focus on the human
constituted the foundation for France's intellectual maturity—with bene-
ficial consequences for all of Europe. "When the century of combat . . .
gave way to the century of work, to the seventeenth century, more than
one great mind set itself on the task of understanding, and succeeded. . . .
Observe, after that violent sixteenth century, the honest seventeenth, [age
of] *la vie moderne*. . . . The regular, solitary, hardworking life of modern
times is strikingly present in the first efforts of the Grand Siècle."[17]

Intellectuals of widely divergent political temperaments might thus see
in the seventeenth century an important dividing line in French chronology, the line between modern and medieval—and the modernity that then
emerged included new social relations as well as new ideas. In Michelet's
account, the seventeenth century came in fact to have attributes of a bourgeois society: hardworking, calculating, this-worldly, committed to human
progress rather than to vain quarreling over abstractions. Monarchs and
philosophers alike contributed to this modernity, enshrining science and
establishing the political peace needed for social progress.

But this was not the only possible view of the matter, and in the same
years other intellectuals offered an almost precisely opposite reading of
the seventeenth century. In a series of articles, the novelist Stendhal
argued that the nineteenth century needed to give up its preoccupation
with French classical culture altogether, and turn instead to stronger,

15. Comte, *Early Political Writings*, 32–33.
16. Michelet, *Cours*, 1:660. Cf. the widely held view that Michelet saw modern thought
beginning only with the revolution, as expressed by, for instance, François Furet: "C'est
comme dans Michelet: l'Histoire de France est exemplaire, parce qu'elle incarne par excellence
des idées et des valeurs. . . . pour Michelet cette histoire commence, avec les philosophes des
Lumières et 1789." Furet, *Un itinéraire intellectuel*, 526.
17. Michelet, *Cours*, 1:669.

more direct forms of expression. Poetry from the seventeenth century could not meet his contemporaries' "growing thirst for strong emotions," he wrote in 1817, for in the seventeenth century "any expression of deep emotions seemed crude. A cumbersome *politesse*, followed a few years later by manners that were more lively and free of any feeling, repressed and in the end seem to have done away with any enthusiasm and any energy."[18]

Here was a fundamentally different understanding of French historical development from that offered by Cousin, Comte, and Michelet. Where they saw linear development from seventeenth-century past to the present, Stendhal saw the world of Louis XIV as essentially separate from his own; and differences of experiences in turn created new aesthetic standards. "In every century, beauty is simply *the expression of useful qualities*," and what had been useful in Louis XIV's world could have little use in his own. "Even in 1670, in the best days of Louis XIV, the court was merely an assemblage of enemies and rivals. How could true gaiety have shown itself there? . . . In the eyes of Louis XIV, Henri IV, or Louis XIII there were never more than two classes of people in France: the nobles . . . and the *canaille*, to whom one threw sausages and hams on great occasions, but whom it was necessary to hang or massacre without pity the moment they took it into their heads to express their opinions. . . . It was people like this whom, in the intervals between their amusements, Molière undertook to entertain. He succeeded like the great man he was; that is, almost perfectly. The comedies that he produced for the courtiers of the *sun-king* were probably the best and the most amusing that one could write for such people. But, in 1825, we are no longer this kind of people."[19] "Nothing resembles us less than those *marquis* in embroidered coats and big black periwigs costing a thousand *écus* who, around 1670, judged the plays of Racine and Molière. . . . It is my contention that henceforth tragedies should be written for us, the young people of the year of Our Lord 1823, who are argumentative, serious, and a bit envious."[20]

Like Cousin, Stendhal had followers. In the following generation, Charles Baudelaire argued in similar terms for the specificity of modern aesthetic conditions and the irrelevance to them of models from the past. Ancient art, he argued was "the idealization . . . of ancient life," a life of warfare and grandeur. Modern life had its own "heroism," and representing it formed a necessary part of modern beauty. "Since every century and

18. Stendhal, *Stendhal*, 109, 107; emphasis in the original.
19. Stendhal, *Racine and Shakespeare*, 47–49. I have slightly modified this translation.
20. Stendhal, *Racine and Shakespeare*, 15.

every people have their beauty, we of course have our own. . . . Absolute
and eternal beauty does not exist." Baudelaire acknowledged that his fellow moderns lacked confidence in the specific aesthetic of modern life,
and he attributed to this uncertainty their taste for "eclecticism," the mixing of inherited philosophies into a new synthesis. Baudelaire's language
betrayed his reflections as (among other things) a thinly veiled attack on
Victor Cousin himself. Cousin proudly described his own intellectual project as "eclectic" and claimed precisely that moderns of good sense could
combine the best ideas from different eras in the past, producing an intellectual climate that allowed for moderate progress. The idea attracted Baudelaire's particular sarcasm. "Eclecticism in every era has always thought
itself greater than older doctrines . . . but this impartiality demonstrates
the eclectics' impotence. . . . However artful the eclectic, he's a weak
man. . . . An eclectic is not a man."[21] In other words, historicity could not
be evaded. Real boundaries separated one thought-world from another
and severely restricted cross-border transactions.

Early nineteenth-century intellectuals thus presented their successors with
an apparently straightforward antithesis. For Cousin, Comte, and Michelet,
the seventeenth century was the origin and defining point of French
modernity; for Stendhal and Baudelaire, a pointless museum piece, irrelevant to the conditions of contemporary life, illustrating only the absolute
differences that separated one historical era from another. Lurking behind
these viewpoints, of course, was the reality of 1789. As a glaring rupture
in the nation's development, the Revolution required all French intellectuals to address the problem of periodization, if only implicitly. Cousin
and Michelet stressed the deep continuities of French culture across that
gap, Stendhal and Baudelaire its impassibility. Intellectuals of the following generations might situate themselves at many points along the spectrum that stretched from Cousin to Stendhal, but they could not avoid the
problem itself. Reflection on the seventeenth century stood at the center
of any effort to understand the larger shape of French history. But as the
nineteenth century advanced, few intellectuals were willing to accept the
choice in its extreme form. However critically they viewed seventeenth-
century culture, it remained an obvious presence in national life. Conversely, no one could deny the novelty of the conditions that the Revolution
had created, or the implications of the new technologies and industrial
organizations that already were becoming visible in the 1820s.

21. Baudelaire, *Écrits esthétiques*, 183, 184, 162.

Sainte-Beuve played a crucial role in these debates, one that testifies to the nineteenth-century's conflicted views of seventeenth-century culture. Over the forty-five years of his career, he returned again and again to the problem of fitting the seventeenth century into a larger understanding of French culture.[22] The problem stands at the center of his greatest single work, *Port-Royal*, which occupied him from the 1830s until 1859, just ten years before his death—the subject of the chapter that follows. But the problem is also important to his first work of literary criticism, the *Tableau historique et critique de la poésie française et du théâtre française au XVIe siècle*, completed in 1828, just as Cousin and Stendhal were debating classicism's place in the nation's life. In his opening statement as a critic, Sainte-Beuve presented sixteenth-century literary history in terms of a tension between popular traditions, still vigorous early in the sixteenth century, and the efforts of the mid-sixteenth-century Pléiade poets, who sought to imitate ancient models. However vulgar, Sainte-Beuve argued, François Villon and other medieval poets had expressed genuine feeling in vigorous language, thereby voicing both universal emotions and specific qualities of French national character. In their classicizing zeal, the Pléiade poets turned away from this authentic tradition, and sought to build a "langue savante" atop the "langue populaire" that they inherited; inevitably, so artificial an edifice could not stand for long. "Popular language shifted slightly," wrote Sainte-Beuve, "and the whole scaffolding of learned language collapsed."[23] Thus, despite some real qualities, sixteenth-century poetry constituted "a true literary disaster," whose unhealthy influence continued down to his own times. The Pléiade poets cut France off from its "national traditions," in sharp contrast to what happened elsewhere in sixteenth-century Europe. Shakespeare, Lope de Vega and Cervantes, Dante, and Tasso—all worked within national traditions, rather than rejecting them wholesale, and all managed to speak to popular as well as aristocratic audiences.[24]

In contrast, France's seventeenth-century writers inherited an essentially

22. Literary history conventionally presents him as evolving over the course of his career from Romantic to neoclassical views, but in fact he returned to these questions repeatedly without ever coming to a straightforward assessment of what the seventeenth century had meant. Cf. Babbitt, *Masters of Modern French Criticism* 137 ff.; René Wellek, in *History of Modern Criticism*, 50–60, sees classicism as the guiding thread of Sainte-Beuve's career. Raphaël Molho, in *L'ordre et les ténèbres*, passim, also stresses Sainte-Beuve's deep love of seventeenth-century literature and the extent of his retreat from the Romanticism of his young adulthood, but he also points to the ambiguity in Sainte-Beuve's view of the seventeenth century.

23. Sainte-Beuve, *Tableau historique et critique*, 54.

24. Sainte-Beuve, *Tableau historique et critique*, 165.

hollow literary tradition. French poetry had lost the "naive inspirations," "those simple and profound beliefs, melancholy or humorous," that characterized "the childhood of the modern nations." Writers such as François de Malherbe, Racine, and Molière restored sound language and sensible exposition, after the sixteenth century's baroque excesses, but they could not restore to French culture its lost authenticity and depth of feeling. French literary greatness would always be colder, less emotional, than that of neighboring nations. For Sainte-Beuve, there were gains as well as losses in this specifically French pattern of cultural development. France had no Dante or Shakespeare, but other countries had no Racine, no writers who united ancient and modern cultural forms to produce "an enchanting and pure ideal" of beauty; and some medieval vitality survived in the work of Molière, allowing French national traditions to continue flowing, though in new and constricted channels. But even these seventeenth-century successes, Sainte-Beuve argued, had little connection to the deeper realities of French life. They mattered only within the settings where they were performed, the preciously decorated apartments of Versailles, with spectators and actors alike dressed in the rigid fashions of the age, or in the icy atmosphere of Saint-Cyr, Madame de Maintenon's convent school. "That false atmosphere," he concluded, with its "uniformity of etiquette . . . applied without exception to every subject," meant that the seventeenth century too could only be a blind alley.[25]

Sainte-Beuve's troubled uncertainty about the place of the seventeenth century in French cultural development was directly related to his uncertainties about his own era. He found great beauty in classicism and even admired aspects of the society from which it emerged; in the same spirit, he worried as well about the spread of "industrial literature" in his own times, "the invasion of literary democracy," along with "the arrival of all the other democracies."[26] But in the end his position was fundamentally historicizing, in the terms that Stendhal and Baudelaire had proposed: his own world, he suggested, differed fundamentally from that of the seventeenth century. Adaptation to this new world would be difficult, but in the end new beauties would emerge, specific to it. "Modern society," he wrote in 1834 in an article on women's literature, "once it is somewhat more settled . . . will also have its calm, its corners of cool mystery, its retreats suited to perfect sentiments." "At times of change [*marche*] . . . like the

25. Sainte-Beuve, *Tableau historique et critique*, 165, 166–67, 256.
26. Sainte-Beuve, *Pour la critique*, "De la littérature industrielle" (1839), 197–222, 206.

present, it's natural that one go straight for the most important, that one concern oneself with the main tasks, and that everywhere—even in literature—there be the habit of striking hard, aiming high, with trumpets and megaphones blaring. The discreet graces will return eventually, perhaps." However difficult this period of transition, Sainte-Beuve stressed the benefits that modern society already offered its citizens: "Nonetheless, we've already acquired indisputable results, of well-being if not of glory."[27]

A more extreme statement of adherence to the Revolution's ideals came in 1846, when Sainte-Beuve published an "unpublished description of the last illness of Louis XV," which he had come upon in a Parisian library. His introduction made clear his view that the anger of 1789 was justified, indeed inevitable. In this as in other cases, he wrote, the king's misdoings explained "the ease with which, on the day that divine and popular angers suddenly erupted, the storm uprooted them, and neither the belated advice of the wise nor the innocence of the victims could in any way forestall disaster." Indeed, without the combined efforts of the duc de Choiseul and Madame de Pompadour, "the revolution, or rather the societal dissolution, would have arrived thirty years earlier." Louis XV was, he wrote, "the most worthless, the most vile, the most cowardly" of all kings, but his successor was only slightly better.[28] For Sainte-Beuve the men and women of 1789 were in fact the agents of national regeneration. Thirty years later, he had become more confident about nineteenth-century society. He praised the social theorist Frédéric Le Play, for instance, as "a man of modern society par excellence, nourished by its life, raised in its progress, its sciences, and their applications," and ready to work with "all the living forces of contemporary civilization, without trying to strangle or repress their development."[29] Raw, intense, often excessive, incompletely formed—the aesthetics of modernity bore a noticeable resemblance to the crude but authentic literature of the fifteenth and early sixteenth centuries. Sainte-Beuve loved seventeenth-century literature, but his comments suggested that authentic Frenchness was rather to be found in these rougher times.

For Sainte-Beuve as for Stendhal and Baudelaire, then, discussion of the seventeenth century inevitably shaded into discussion of historicity, posing questions about the chronological divisions within French history and about how influences seeped from one era to another. The period also

27. Sainte-Beuve, *Portraits de femmes*, 2:1134 (Madame Roland).
28. Sainte-Beuve, *Oeuvres*, 2:957, 959, 960.
29. Sainte-Beuve, *Nouveaux lundis*, 9:189; on de Bonald and other reactionaries, 9:180–89.

posed questions about social class: how (Sainte-Beuve asked) did French elites interact with the ordinary people of the nation, and which in fact represented the true France? Both sets of questions only became more acute as the nineteenth century advanced, bringing social tumult and a growing sense of national weakness, both exemplified in the events of 1870–71. The urgency that these questions had for nineteenth-century writers is suggested by the example of Hippolyte Taine, in the generation after Sainte-Beuve. Like Sainte-Beuve, Taine placed reflection on the seventeenth century at the center of both his first major work and his last, his investigation into what he called "the origins of contemporary France.

In defining his approach to history, as we have seen, Taine emphasized his debt to Sainte-Beuve. But he also presented himself as a follower of Stendhal, a remarkable choice in that few midcentury intellectuals took the novelist seriously. His own method, he wrote in an early work, viewed history as "at bottom, *a problem of psychology*," and in this he had only one precursor: "one man, Stendhal, through a certain turn of mind and a peculiar education, has attempted it, and even yet most of his readers find his works paradoxical and obscure. . . . [H]e brought scientific processes to bear on the history of the heart. . . . [H]e was the first to point out fundamental causes such as nationalities, climates, and temperaments; in short, he treated sentiments as they should be treated, that is to say, as a naturalist and physicist." This included teaching how historical documents themselves should be understood: "in his writings, as in those of Sainte-Beuve and the German critics, the reader will find out how much is to be derived from a literary document."[30] Late in life, he claimed to have read Stendhal's novels at least sixty times.[31] Conversely, another of Taine's early works sharply criticized Victor Cousin.[32]

But for Taine, the trouble with the seventeenth century was its poisonous influence on modern life, rather than its irrelevance. This theme dominated his first major work, his 1853 dissertation on La Fontaine. There he described French society in terms familiar from Sainte-Beuve, as divided between two cultures. "There have always been [in France] . . . two orders of men and of things, depending on whether the Gallic or the Latin culture has prevailed. We have only an artificial civilization, which covers us without penetrating." During the late Middle Ages a truly popular culture

30. Taine, *English Literature*, 1:23, 24; see also Talbot, *La critique stendhalienne de Balzac à Zola*, 220.

31. Taine, *Sa vie et sa correspondance*, 2:67.

32. Taine, *Les philosophes classiques*.

had begun to develop, but it failed to mature fully. France "has never had its Dante or its Boccaccio, . . . no national poet like Shakespeare," and the seventeenth century finally killed off any chances that a popular high culture might survive. "Finally, the classical centuries arrive: familiar words disappear, language becomes ennobled, the theater takes as its public and its subject matter the *gens de salon* and the great lords. It's the literature of Versailles." "Our literature, like our religion and our government, is posed atop the nation, rather than rooted in it." As a result, most French literature failed in the task of understanding human life. "Our style, so clear and so exact, says nothing beyond itself; . . . it is too artificial and too correct to open any passages to the depths of the inner world."[33]

Hence the importance of La Fontaine, as one of the tiny number of French writers who managed to cross these social and cultural divisions, bringing together nature and culture. "La Fontaine is our Homer," wrote Taine, because in his work all social classes appear, "each in its situation, with its emotions and language, with none of the details of human life, trivial or sublime, left out in order to reduce the account to a uniform and smooth tone." The most important human realities are addressed, but "nowhere is one crammed into the proprieties of high [*noble*] literature." Only a handful of French writers share this willingness to address reality, Taine argued, the most important of them Rabelais. "La Fontaine is a relative of Rabelais, and their heroes have a family resemblance." Like Rabelais, La Fontaine could disengage himself from contemporary notions of propriety. In the seventeenth century, "contemporary tastes pushed writers to wit, eloquence, the classical rules, the imitation of Latin; he yields again and again, but always returns to his senses"—and to his Rabelaisian taste.[34] For Taine even more than for Sainte-Beuve, then, the Rabelaisian tradition mattered for French cultural history. As the seventeenth century erected its standards of good taste and order, only Rabelais's few descendants continued to address the nation's real life.

Taine's analysis and even his language echo Stendhal and Sainte-Beuve, but with an important difference: rather than see French classical culture as a mere museum piece, he stressed its enduring presence in the nation's life. This remained his position throughout his career, and as a result the seventeenth century plays a surprisingly large role in his last great work, *Les origines de la France contemporaine*, whose first volume appeared in

---

33. Taine, *La Fontaine et ses fables*, 56, 59, 60, 61, 69.
34. Taine, *La Fontaine et ses fables*, 46, 61, 97, 39.

1875. The book presents itself as an extended reflection on the traumas with which the 1870s had begun: military defeat, which called into question the capacity of French thought to deal with the modern world, and the Paris Commune, which suggested that a democratic society might descend into chaos. Before 1870 Taine had been considered a dangerously radical thinker, but the book's appearance immediately transformed him into an icon of conservatism. Yet Taine's thought in fact had changed little after 1870. In the 1870s as in 1853, he saw the seventeenth century as the turning point in French cultural history, and he continued to stress the divide between Rabelaisian and neoclassical France. "Between Amyot, Rabelais, Montaigne" in the sixteenth century and his own nineteenth century, he wrote in *Les origines*, there had come the force of classicism, rationalizing language and thought. This was "a historic force, of the first order. . . . It established itself at the same time as the monarchy and polite conversation, and not by accident."[35] The classical spirit of the seventeenth century demanded regular sentence structures and a limited vocabulary; French came to have many fewer words than English, and in consequence the French could think fewer thoughts, understand less of the world.

In describing this failure, Taine recycled his language from the 1850s. French neoclassical style, he continued to argue, "is incapable of depicting or registering completely the infinite and irregular details of experience. . . . With this style, one cannot translate the Bible, or Homer, or Dante, or Shakespeare," nor could the realities of contemporary life be captured: "it's astounding to what degree art can overcome natural instinct." Classicism deformed even science, by insisting that all writing be accessible to the nonspecialist *honnête homme*; and how could science progress in a society that admired a suave chatterer more than an ill-socialized researcher?[36] If in 1870–71 France's technology lagged behind Germany's and if it fell prey to radical ideologies, the simplifications of seventeenth-century culture were ultimately to blame. *Les origines* offered a critique of democracy that was equally a critique of monarchy; France's troubles originated in the era of monarchical grandeur, when Louis XIV and his advisors enshrined the ideals of literary classicism.

From Stendhal forward, then, we can see a line of critical reflection on the seventeenth century's place in the nation's life. This line of thought

35. Taine, *Les origines de la France contemporaine*, 1:140, 141.
36. Taine, *Les origines de la France contemporaine*, 1:145, 103, 146.

had complicated political overtones. None of the writers considered here was a democrat, but all spoke scathingly of the French monarchy and of the aristocratic society around it; and Sainte-Beuve and Taine both regretted the seventeenth century's destruction of popular literary traditions, exemplified in writers such as Rabelais and La Fontaine. I suggested in the previous chapter how radical Sainte-Beuve and Taine seemed also for their atheism, which separated them from those (such as Cousin and Michelet) who believed that history moved toward a clear destination, a progress guaranteed by God's ordering of the universe. (That question will receive further exploration in the chapter that follows.) Their questions about the seventeenth century formed part of a larger interrogation of contemporary certitudes. In revising French chronology, they raised questions about France's historical destiny, its advance from the chaos of the Wars of Religion, through the age of monarchical grandeur, to the postrevolutionary present.

But by the time of Taine's death in 1893, with the Third Republic solidly in place, French historical destiny had acquired a new look for many intellectuals, and especially for those in the recently reformed and reinvigorated university. The continuity of historical progress seemed clearer than it had during the Second Empire, and the questions raised by Stendhal, Baudelaire, Sainte-Beuve, and Taine seemed less pertinent. Hence a striking intellectual shift, as writers of all political persuasions settled into a consensus on the constructive influence that the seventeenth century had had on the nation's development. René Descartes became the republic's semiofficial philosopher, taught and celebrated in all the country high schools,[37] and seventeenth-century statesmen were celebrated. In 1893 itself Gabriel Hanotaux, historian, diplomat, and twice minister of foreign affairs, introduced his *Histoire du Cardinal de Richelieu* with a ringing statement of the topic's contemporary relevance. Reading about Richelieu, he hoped, would give his fellow citizens "a new occasion for confidence in the destiny of their country" and would help demonstrate "to the statesmen of the Republic the effectiveness of the tradition" of diplomatic activity that Richelieu embodied and that Hanotaux saw himself continuing.[38] From the far Right, there was the voice of Charles Maurras, founder of the

37. Azouvi, "Descartes," 4475–519.
38. Hanotaux, *Histoire du Cardinal de Richelieu*, 1:vi, viii. Christian Jouhaud has drawn attention to this point, and more generally to the eagerness of republican historians to see in Richelieu a precursor of contemporary political choices. Jouhaud, *La main de Richelieu, ou le pouvoir cardinal*, passim.

Action Française. "A deplorable error," he wrote, "has led our master Taine to describe as classical the outlook that prepared the Revolution."[39] In fact, it was "La vieille France" that had "l'esprit classique," and "even in their most libertine tales, its writers submitted to the rule of reason."[40]

And on the political left there was Jean Jaurès, both professor and politician. His *Histoire socialiste de la Révolution française* likewise defended French classicism against Taine's criticisms, presenting it as an important part of the nation's move toward modernity, and as central to republican identity. "By what misguided surgery can Monsieur Taine have separated modern science from the classical spirit? These are two tightly linked forces, or indeed altogether merged." Jaurès defined classicism in much the same way as did Taine himself, stressing the importance in it of abstraction and simplification. "Always and everywhere, beneath the infinite and overwhelming diversity of particular facts, science sees and disentangles, by a daring operation, a few great, decisive, profound characteristics. . . . It is with the same method that the classical mind constructed its [literary] works"; and Jaurès pointed for examples to Descartes, Pascal, and the seventeenth-century tragedians. All this required a specific form of language, "a language that is streamlined [*rapide*], sober, and forceful," one that did without "the excesses of sensation, the contortions, the systematic picturesqueness that Monsieur Taine would like to impose on it." Only a language thus modernized could break through "that old, outmoded, confused world."[41]

The modes of thought that have been traced thus far provide an important framework for understanding the work of Lucien Febvre. Cofounder of the *Annales* school of historical thought and the director of its postwar expansion, Febvre can reasonably be called the most influential historian of the twentieth century, and his book *Le problème de l'incroyance au XVIè siècle: La religion de Rabelais* can be counted among the century's most important historical works.[42] For in this work Febvre drew together ideas that would remain paradigmatic for French historical culture during the remainder of the twentieth century: ideas about mental structures and their relations to lived experience, about the practices of daily life, about the need for a new kind of history that would explore the full range of

39. Maurras, *Trois idées politiques*, 279.
40. Maurras, *Romantisme et révolution*, 245.
41. Jaurès, *Histoire socialiste de la Révolution française*, 1:98, 99, 100.
42. Febvre, *Le problème de l'incroyance*.

human experiences and at the same time respect the discipline's scientific standards. In keeping with the book's significance for France's intellectual future, Febvre dedicated it to "Fernand Braudel, en espérance." He had already come to view Braudel as his successor in leading the *Annales*, extending a trust that Braudel would brilliantly justify.

Febvre's great work appeared in 1942, under the difficult circumstances of war and German occupation, and he faced personal difficulties in these years as well. By this point his associate Marc Bloch had moved first to the relative safety of southern France, and then into hiding and active resistance. In order to keep the journal alive, Febvre had pressured Bloch into renouncing his share in its management, though Bloch continued to publish in it under an easily decoded pseudonym. Febvre's assistant (and mistress) Lucie Varga was equally in danger and eventually would die from the privations she suffered as a Jew in occupied Paris. But Febvre seems already to have understood that the journal and the historical movement surrounding it faced new possibilities, as well as terrible challenges. Soon after the Liberation, he relaunched the journal, with a new subtitle and a strong statement of its new editorial mission, titled "Manifesto of the New" (These issues receive further discussion in Chapter 5.) The confidence implied by this step derived partly from Febvre's already imposing presence in French academic life; *Le problème*'s author was no outsider, but a central figure in the French academic establishment. Since 1933 he had held a chair at the Collège de France, the nation's leading institution of higher education, and his publisher's preface to *Le problème* described him as "one of the greatest historians of the twentieth century."[43] In the decade before his death, in 1956, Febvre translated this academic standing into impressive institutional achievements. He established the Maison des Sciences de l'Homme and became president of its formal base in the École Pratique des Hautes Études; after his death, under Braudel's leadership, this would become an altogether autonomous, degree-granting institution. He participated regularly in government commissions on higher education and, through UNESCO, acquired even some measure of international influence.[44]

Le problème thus appeared at a moment of crisis, a moment that combined terrible difficulties with an intense awareness of the future. But in fact the book had dominated Febvre's thinking for much longer, in fact

43. Paul Chalus, introduction to Febvre, *Le problème de l'incroyance*, 10.
44. For a summary of Febvre's career, see Müller, *Bibliographie des travaux de Lucien Febvre,* 27–28.

since 1924, well before the foundation of the *Annales*. In the summer of that year, he wrote to the eminent Belgian medievalist Henri Pirenne, whose support for their new journal he and Bloch were seeking to secure: "I've spent the last few weeks studying the difficult [*délicats*] problems that Abel Lefranc has raised—in a somewhat boisterous way, as I see it— concerning Rabelais's religion, Probably I'll squeeze two or three large articles out of these studies, possibly a monograph." Three years later he wrote to Pirenne that the planned articles had definitively evolved into a book, now almost complete. "It will be a somewhat bizarre book, in fact a study on the conditions of religious life in sixteenth-century France, perhaps original in parts, in any case interesting for me." But the project dragged on, and in 1930 it was still far from finished. "I'm still with Rabe-lais," he wrote Pirenne, "(who is not really Rabelais, you understand, but the enormous problem of the conditions and limits of atheism [*libre pen-sée*] in the sixteenth century). It's at once fascinating and infinite."[45] Its difficult gestation made *Le problème* a unique exception among the writ-ings of a fast-working and prolific author; a recent bibliography includes more than two thousand items.[46] The book's subject matter, it seems, en-gaged him at an especially deep level, posing difficult intellectual questions and demanding a wide range of research and reflection.[47]

When it finally appeared, *Le problème* had become a consideration of the nature of historical difference. It argued that different eras had differ-ent mental structures, which allowed only specific ways of thinking about the world. The book had thus become "a study of historical psychology, at least as much as a work of historical erudition." "To each civilization its mental tools . . . , valid for the civilization that was able to forge them, for the era that used them."[48] Whether consciously or not, such comments echoed Stendhal, Sainte-Beuve, and Taine, who (as seen in Chapter 1) had also used a language of historical psychology and who had stressed the degree to which cultures adapt to the needs of the societies around them. But Febvre's understanding of the contours of French history differed markedly from theirs. In Febvre's chronology, Rabelais stood with the

45. Lyon and Lyon, *Birth of Annales History* 80 (24 June 1924), 87 (2 January 1927), 120 (7 January 1930). Peter Burke incorrectly suggests that the book was a wartime project. P. Burke, *French Historical Revolution*, 27.

46. Müller, *Bibliographie des travaux de Lucien Febvre*.

47. Cf. Fink, who, in *Marc Bloch*, 143, suggests that the administrative demands of the newly formed *Annales* delayed Febvre's work; this is not convincing for a writer of Febvre's celerity.

48. Febvre, *Le problème de l'incroyance*, 100, 140–41.

Middle Ages, Descartes with a modernity that extended to his own times. However free a spirit, Febvre's Rabelais was caught within a world of limited epistemic possibilities: "what clarity, what penetration, in the end what effectiveness (by our standards, of course) could men—Frenchmen—have who for their speculations did not yet dispose in their own language of any of those characteristic terms" that moderns automatically use when they undertake philosophy, whose absence "implies not merely difficulty, but actual deficiency or lacuna of thought?"

For Febvre, it was Descartes who began the process of freeing French thought "from all these difficulties"; and Febvre contrasted "the fatal sterility of traditional thought" with "the revolutionary fecundity" of Cartesian reasoning. Language played a crucial role in Febvre's account, as in Taine's, but Febvre's seventeenth century was one of linguistic creativity, rather than restriction. A new philosophical vocabulary emerged, allowing Descartes and his contemporaries to reason in a newly systematic way. In their attempts "to conquer the secrets of the world," earlier thinkers "had nothing, no arms, no tools, no overall plan."[49] In tracing this failure, Febvre offered a strong, even radical view of historical progress, contrasting "the fatal sterility of traditional thought, enclosed in its Latin straitjacket," with the "revolutionary fertility" of the new philosophy represented by Descartes. This was in fact a divide between civilizations: "the men of the sixteenth century continued attentively to follow the path of the men of the twelfth, thirteenth, fourteenth centuries," whereas the science of Descartes represented the beginnings of modern life itself. Even sixteenth-century philosophy "is only opinions. A chaos of opinions, contradictory and floating. Floating, because they lack a solid and stable foundation. The solid foundation that will consolidate them. Science."[50] Just as the sixteenth century participated in the world of the Middle Ages, then, the seventeenth century formed part of the same historical civilization as Febvre's own twentieth century.

Finally, *Le problème* insists on the connectedness between daily experience and intellectual life. The book's third part begins with a section on "private life," and throughout Febvre stresses the ways in which innumerable intimate experiences made the men of the sixteenth century different from those of modernity. "Their very structure was not ours. I have said this before," he wrote; "we're hothouse plants; they lived in the open air.

49. Febvre, *Le problème de l'incroyance*, 328, 340, 341, 360.
50. Febvre, *Le problème de l'incroyance*, 341, 340, 350.

Men near the earth and rural life. Men who, even in their cities, found themselves in touch with the country, its animals and plants, its smells and noises."[51] Understanding sixteenth-century ideas about religion thus required extended consideration of the basic conditions of sixteenth-century life—the workings of familial rituals, the sounds and smells, the relative force of the visual and the other senses. Ultimately, material and cultural life are shown to be two aspects of a single whole.

Febvre wrote within an academic context that gave considerable attention to these issues. As his initial comments to Pirenne indicated, he wrote partly in response to the literature professor Abel Lefranc, his colleague at the Collège de France and the author of standard works on Rabelais; Lefranc had strongly argued for Rabelais's position as a precursor of the Enlightenment. Less explicitly, though, he also argued with the economic historian Henri Hauser, who taught at the Sorbonne until 1936—when Marc Bloch succeeded him in the position. (Hauser will receive brief attention in Chapter 4.) In a series of lectures on *La modernité du seizième siècle*, presented in 1929 and published the following year, Hauser argued that modern thinking about the world and expectations from it began in the late fifteenth century. These advances were followed "by a regression, by a victory during the course of the seventeenth century, of the forces of conservatism over those of progress."[52] In vigorously denying the sixteenth century's modernity, Febvre intervened in an important contemporary academic debate. But he was also intervening in a much larger discussion that French intellectuals had carried on since the Revolution itself. For all its immense learning and its use of anthropological parallels, *Le problème de l'incroyance* in important ways simply restated the chronology that Victor Cousin had developed in the 1820s, while using the ideas of historical difference developed by Stendhal and Baudelaire. Like these last two writers, he sought to implement an historical psychology, a term that Taine had employed. Like Cousin, he celebrated France's Grand Siècle as the period in which modern thought first became possible.

From 1815 through the mid-twentieth century, I argue here, French intellectuals continued to think about their nation's chronology within the limits of a stable discursive framework. That framework allowed for numerous

---

51. Febvre, *Le problème de l'incroyance*, 394 (I have eliminated a paragraph break in this citation).
52. Hauser, *La modernité du XVIe siècle*, 12.

specific ideas about the shape of French history and wildly divergent judgments about different periods. If the answers varied, however, the questions themselves changed little. They centered on defining the relationship between the modern present and the premodern past, and on dating the shift from the one to the other. For the writers considered here, both sets of questions led to reflection on the seventeenth century, the age of Richelieu, Louis XIV, and the other great architects of the French state. Intellectuals asked whether the culture of that age had produced a fundamentally new outlook on the world, or whether the upheavals that began in 1789 had rendered it irrelevant. The debate cut across the basic divisions of French intellectual life, chronological, professional, and political. Mid-twentieth-century university scholars such as Lucien Febvre returned to the same issues that had preoccupied the novelist and man-about-town Stendhal a century earlier; the socialist professor Jean Jaurès saw the problem in much the same terms as did the right-wing nationalist essayist Charles Maurras.

These debates proved so tenacious partly because they touched on the sociology of French history, as well as on its chronology. To define the seventeenth century's place in the nation's life was to comment on the location and character of its identity. Those who argued that Descartes, Racine, and Louis XIV had laid the bases for modern French life tended (like Febvre) to see a dichotomy between a modernizing elite and a tradition-bound population; the enlightened alliance of kings and writers had given the French new tools for understanding and mastering the world, and these eventually made their way from the nation's political and intellectual leadership to its ordinary people. Those who (like Stendhal and Taine) viewed seventeenth-century culture as irrelevant or pernicious described it instead as a rickety superstructure atop the deeper realities of French popular culture. To them the real France was that described by Rabelais and La Fontaine, the world of canny tricksters and bawdy jokers. On this view, neoclassical culture and its state sponsors constituted a mainly repressive force, not a creative one. The terms in which these questions were discussed changed little between the 1820s and the 1940s because the questions themselves were not merely historical. They concerned the present as much as the past, and as a result they were posed with particular urgency following moments of political crisis, when national identity itself appeared to have been threatened: following the revolutionary era, the debacles of 1870–71, and the German occupation that began in 1940.

For the same reason, the politics of these debates cannot be summarized by simple party labels. Despite their violent political differences, differences that produced real deaths, Charles Maurras, Jean Jaurès, and Lucien Febvre all celebrated the constructive value of French classicism and the monarchy that sponsored it. Conversely, Hippolyte Taine denounced democracy, but also sought to valorize Rabelaisian popular culture as the core of Frenchness; and he dismissed the supposed leaders of French politics and culture as a destructive influence on the nation. It makes little sense to divide these intellectuals between "progressives" and "conservatives," at least in respect to their historical thought, for the ideological impact of their debates worked at deeper levels. Nor is it appropriate to divide the professional practice of history from the larger currents of French intellectual life. Febvre's *Le problème de l'incroyance* is a masterpiece of historical erudition, and its influence on postwar scholarship has been immense. But in writing the book, Febvre also participated in an old cultural debate, which used the markers of French chronology to argue about the essence of French national identity, in the present as in the past.

3

GOD AND THE HISTORIAN:
SAINTE-BEUVE'S *PORT-ROYAL*

"Port-Royal has come into fashion," as a topic that "reverberates everywhere," noted Charles-Augustin Sainte-Beuve in 1848.[1] His assessment mixed surprise, gratification, and annoyance. He had begun his own book on the topic in complete isolation, he claimed, believing that the public would find Jansenist practices strange and repellant. In fact the public responded with enthusiastic interest. The 1840 publication of *Port-Royal's* first volume (there would eventually be five) led quickly to Sainte-Beuve's election to the Académie française, and by 1843 he was complaining about imitators. In the draft of a letter that was apparently never sent, he accused Victor Cousin of unacknowledged scholarly borrowing on the topic, "behavior that, despite all I owe you, I cannot help but find distasteful and improper."[2]

1. Saint-Beuve, *Port-Royal* (hereafter *P-R*), 2:34.
2. Sainte-Beuve, *Correspondance générale*, vol. 5, part 1, 193–94, 12 July 1843; quotation at 193.

Sainte-Beuve himself took the project seriously enough to devote twenty years of mature scholarly effort to it, and it was by far his most important work. When its last volume finally appeared, in 1859, it had already been recognized as one of the century's literary landmarks.

Port-Royal is a complex book that deals with an overlapping set of themes. It centers on the convent of Port-Royal itself, whose nuns from the 1620s on sought to establish newly severe forms of Catholic devotion, and it follows the enthusiasm that these efforts evoked in Parisian high society and the suspicion with which the government viewed them, suspicion that eventually led Louis XIV's government to disperse the nuns and raze the convent's buildings. But Sainte-Beuve was as much concerned with the cultural background to these struggles as with the nuns' own story. His book thus explores the theological guidance that they sought from the Belgian bishop Jansenius and the French abbé Saint-Cyran, who together developed a theology (eventually labeled Jansenism) that emphasized human depravity and divine predestination and denied individuals a role in achieving their salvation. It traces the intellectual life that grew up around the convent, as figures such as Blaise Pascal found themselves attracted to its combination of practical and intellectual rigor; and it compares their ideas with those of other seventeenth-century intellectuals, both religious thinkers (for example, François de Sales) and secular (Michel de Montaigne and François de la Rochefoucauld).

Because of its range of topics, in the end *Port-Royal* had come to constitute the nineteenth century's most substantial effort to come to terms with early modern culture and the society that produced it. At the same time, Sainte-Beuve's comments and complaints draw our attention to some historical problems surrounding that encounter. Why did a topic of apparently marginal significance attract such passionate engagement, from both Sainte-Beuve and his audience? What concerns did the nineteenth century's interest in Port-Royal, Jansenism, and the broader currents of seventeenth-century piety express? How did nineteenth-century intellectuals define their relationship to these early modern ancestors, whose values differed so sharply from their own, and what did that understanding suggest for nineteenth-century historical practice? In previous chapters, I have argued that Sainte-Beuve played a central role in the development of nineteenth-century historical thought, with regard to both the century's interest in social history and its understanding of French chronology. For these reasons his impact on twentieth- century historical thinking matches that of more commonly discussed historians like Leopold von Ranke and Jules Michelet. Considerable importance thus attaches to understanding the explicit arguments and broader implications of his most important historical work, a work to which he devoted the central years of his career.

I shall suggest that a great deal was in fact at stake in *Port-Royal,* and that the text should be read as part of an effort to define the nature of modernity itself.[3] Like others of his generation, Sainte-Beuve had to cope with the intellectual fallout of the French Revolution of 1789. Within the new world that the Revolution had made, the historical study of religious practices offered a way to think about the distance between the Old Regime and the new. The history of religion posed basic problems about what modernity was and how it had come into being.[4] *Port-Royal* deserves attention for a second, closely related reason. As a historical exploration of Christian belief, the book inevitably posed questions about the historian's own religious commitments and approaches. This was a difficult issue for nineteenth-century scholars; as noted above, most of that century's leading historians viewed some form of religious belief as a necessary foundation for making sense of societal development. In this context, *Port-Royal* mattered for its atheism. It was a forceful effort to establish history as an altogether secular discipline, not only without need of religious commitments, but actually antithetical to them. *Port-Royal* posed the problem of the historian's own modernity.

Among *Port-Royal*'s striking features is its author's insistence on his subjects' distance from nineteenth-century ideas about human nature—and thus their apparent irrelevance to an understanding of the modern world. Pascal, for instance, believed passionately in miracles and in the power of relics. "The Jansenists saw in this the triumph of their cause," Sainte-Beuve notes sadly; "I see in it above all the abasement of the human spirit."[5] The group's penitential practices raise what Sainte-Beuve calls the "hateful topic of *uncleanliness,* the most genuinely shocking" aspect of its behavior; "that is what revolts us," he says in reference to Pascal's use of

3. In my focus on Sainte-Beuve as a historian of modernization, my approach here differs sharply from that taken in the important recent work of Wolf Lepenies, *Sainte-Beuve*; Lepenies stresses Sainte-Beuve's critical views of modern morality and of the modern intellectual and sees the idea of vengeance as the crucial theme running through Sainte-Beuve's work.
4. Early modern religion has remained central to more recent explorations of the modernization process. Especially influential examples include M. Weber, *Protestant Ethic and the Spirit of Capitalism,* and Febvre, *Le problème de l'incroyance.*
5. *P-R,* 2:179. Further references to the work appear parenthetically in the text.

a studded iron belt next to his bare skin, before going on to describe the unwashed clothes of Mother Angélique and others (*P-R*, 2:298, 296, 297). The Jansenists' doctrine of predestination amounted to a "spiritual terrorism," "a permanent attack on the tenderness of human imaginations," "enough to make one's hair stand on end" (*P-R*, 2:910, 333). Such strangeness encouraged Sainte-Beuve to describe his task as essentially anthropological. Rather than a history of how modern France was made, he suggests in his conclusion, he has produced "the exact description of a tribe, a holy race." Knowledge of such men and women could serve only to illuminate "the variety of the species, the diverse forms of human existence [*l'organisation humaine*]" (*P-R*, 3:673, 674).

Sainte-Beuve's younger friend Ernest Renan stressed this aspect of the work still more emphatically. In a review of *Port-Royal*'s final volume, Renan suggested the oddity of Sainte-Beuve interesting himself in a topic so distant from his normal preoccupations. As explanation, Renan pointed to the critic's interest in subjects that showed "human nature in its rarest, strangest manifestations [*accès*]." But such interest could have nothing to say about the development of modern France. "Everyone has in the past his ancestors, and ours are in fact not to be found in Port-Royal," partly because Port-Royal's thinkers had contributed little to the development of modern science. He concluded in ringing terms: "Port-Royal cannot be compared to the Italians of the sixteenth century for freedom of thought, nor to Protestantism for important intellectual and religious achievements. Here, I hasten to add, are our ancestors."[6] Jansenism represented a historical dead end. It had not contributed to the evolution of modern France. Its study offered insights into human nature's endless possibilities, but said nothing about modern humankind.

Sainte-Beuve reinforced this argument for Port-Royal's irrelevance to the long-term march of history by stressing its oddity even within the context of seventeenth-century piety. Commentators have expressed surprise at the book's lengthy discussions of figures who had little or nothing to do with the convent or with Jansenist thought; and these digressions include discussions of such religious figures as François de Sales, Vincent de Paul, Bishop Bossuet, the abbé de Rancé, and a variety of others.[7] But

6. E. Renan, *Nouvelles études d'histoire religieuse*, "Port-Royal," 453, 454, 459, 460.

7. See Wellek, *History of Modern Criticism*, 3:43: "The book has been criticized for artificially dragging in literary subjects that are only remotely connected with Port Royal and for overrating the literary influence of the movement in 17th-century France. But Sainte-Beuve is well aware that he uses Port Royal as a kind of thread or point of reference and even pretext for

their presence helps buttress one of the book's principal arguments, for the specificity of the Jansenists' ideas within their own times. (At a later point I will consider the significance of the book's digressions on secular figures.) Even the great religious reformers among their contemporaries, Sainte-Beuve shows, retained a fundamental respect for the social world around them and an affectionate interest in ordinary life. Bossuet, seeking the implementation of Christian ideals, "praises the powerful of the earth with an eye to [achieving his] practical objectives, lofty and desirable no doubt," but nonetheless incompatible with complete faith in Christian truths. Sainte-Beuve's François de Sales emerges as constantly alert to the beauties of the natural world and concerned with giving literary pleasure to his readers, lacking the real Christian's indifference to sensual pleasure. More seriously, this Saint François lacks a deep sense of the distinction between Christian and non-Christian—and thus holds out hope for the salvation of virtuous pagans and unbaptized infants. Unlike the Jansenists, he expresses a powerful feeling for the charms of childhood and cannot avoid presuming children's innocence, despite clear Christian teaching to the contrary. Vincent de Paul, a third example of seventeenth-century saintliness, has so much personal humility that he glorifies the aristocrats among whom he moves, and speaks as if Christian virtues matter less than social grandeur (P-R, 1:362, 276–79, 262–63, 498). In all of these examples, Sainte-Beuve takes pains to stress his subjects' isolation within seventeenth-century culture, their unrepresentative standing.

In these ways, *Port-Royal* seems repeatedly to undercut its own significance, showing its subjects to have been both atypical of their times and insignificant in the larger development of modern society. Yet Sainte-Beuve gives these arguments a series of unexpected twists. First, *Port-Royal* suggests that in their very oddity the Jansenists in fact expressed central truths about Christianity itself. Their apparently suicidal disregard for society's concerns represented authentic Christianity; in their apparently sensible readiness to accommodate their teachings to ordinary life in the social world, their rivals in fact unwittingly worked for the destruction of their faith. "This is harsh," Sainte-Beuve writes of Saint-Cyran's statement that only one soul in a thousand will be saved, "but one must

---

literary history. One must rather admire the skill with which he succeeds in enhancing the appeal of a subject that appears so specialized and remote from imaginative literature."

admit that for a Christian [*chrétiennement*] it is true; all those who disguise the fact either forget Christianity or transform it. And if one is not careful, Christianity transforms itself so as to fit with [human] nature. Nod off, and you awaken more or less Arian or Pelagian"—believing, in other words, either that Jesus was a human prophet rather than an aspect of God, or that salvation can be attained through unaided human effort, both heresies according to the Catholic Church (*P-R*, 1:367n). Hence religious choices like those made by Port-Royal's penitents, who renounced prosperous careers, would always evoke the baffled anger of even pious contemporaries. "This is the mark that Christian heroism carries in all times . . . everything great and holy has been carried out despite the world, despite its indignation and its insults" (*P-R*, 1:395). In this respect, the Jansenists' radical pessimism about human nature was especially important. "Far be it from me," he writes in argument with Joseph de Maistre, "to claim that there is only one way to be a Christian. But one of the most direct ways to become one, surely, is to view fallen human nature exactly as Hobbes, La Rochefoucauld, Machiavelli did. . . . Otherwise, if one accords so much goodness to contemporary man, one becomes accustomed to thinking of him as not so very fallen; little by little one arrives at [Rousseau's] Savoyard vicar, in other words, at Pelagius; for it was hardly necessary that God Himself die to reclaim man from so little" (*P-R*, 2:229–30).

Hence the real threat to Christianity as Sainte-Beuve describes it is not Jansenist pessimism, but the optimism that social progress has occasioned over the past few centuries. Living better and interacting more rationally, humanity can no longer understand itself in the terms that genuine Christian practice requires. Sainte-Beuve thus concludes his assessment of Jansenist ideas about fallen human nature: "It's not merely the theme of Jansenism, note, but rather the theme of Christianity itself. . . . If Jansenist pessimism were to become completely unacceptable today; if, thanks to a degree of social progress, human nature were to appear too sound to be described in terms of fundamental misery— . . . then Christian thought [*argumentation*] itself would have weakened" (*P-R*, 2:231).

Such arguments lead Sainte-Beuve to a materialist interpretation of Christianity's history, which sees Christianity's appeal as directly dependant on societal conditions. In eras of fear and uncertainty, pessimistic readings of human nature will naturally prevail, and Christianity will offer powerful consolations; but "the day that . . . because of the progress and triumph of the physical sciences and of industry, there no longer remain terrifying hidden corners in the world, the universe, or (more difficult still) in the human heart," then Pascal's point of view would lose much of its force (*P-R*, 2:362n). In fact, much of this had already happened by the time of Voltaire, a result of "the perfection of life, the elegance [*la douceur*] of eighteenth-century civilization" (*P-R*, 2:363). *Port-Royal* thus presents its heroes as men and women keenly aware of the coming onslaughts of modernity, who sought desperately to warn their fellow Christians and shore up Christian belief. "From the heights of their tower," Sainte-Beuve writes of Jansenius and Saint-Cyran, "they already saw far beyond the seventeenth century; they foresaw the great invasion arriving and spreading, if no steps were taken, and they cried out, as it were, in terror and formidable opposition" (*P-R*, 1:624). Their doctrines, in so many ways incompatible with a commonsensical, humane life in the contemporary world, in fact expressed an authentic Christianity; their opponents, who argued for adapting religion to new ethical standards, in fact failed to see the nature of that world, and in particular failed to see the directions in which it was evolving. For Sainte-Beuve, to study Jansenism was to study the encounter between traditional European culture and the modern world, which would prevail in the eighteenth century and after.

This line of thought, reappearing discreetly throughout *Port-Royal*, rendered it, in important respects, an anti-Christian book. Although Sainte-Beuve admired much about his subjects, he repeatedly stressed the ties between their beliefs and the social conditions of a backward, vanished world; at the same time, these beliefs in fact embodied the authentic message of Christianity, demonstrating the inappropriateness of that message within an advanced society such as his own. Given its connections to a specific social world, real Christianity of this sort could not survive under the conditions of modernity, which had succeeded in eliminating so many of the fears and uncertainties on which faith had rested in previous centuries. It is not surprising that the papacy responded by placing the book immediately on the Index of Prohibited Books.

Its view of the logic of Christian belief attached *Port-Royal* directly to the Enlightenment, and in other ways too Sainte-Beuve stresses his book's affinities with eighteenth-century criticisms of conventional religious values. At the outset, Sainte-Beuve draws the reader's attention to these issues by giving the work a physical setting in the present. He had arranged with friends that this material receive its first public exposition as a series of lectures in Lausanne, during the academic year 1837–38, and his introduction stresses the ideological implications of this beautiful yet melancholy setting. In the background lurked Swiss Protestantism. More prominently, he notes, over the previous century the region had welcomed a long series of intellectual rebels, whose relations to Christianity of all forms had been mainly hostile: "There, I told myself, the young Rousseau had passed," he writes in the original preface, followed by Voltaire, Madame de Staël, Byron, and Gibbon—the last a parallel to which Sainte-Beuve drew particular attention (*P-R*, 1:88). *Port-Royal* thus opens with strong affirmation of its ties to both the Enlightenment and to Romantic libertinism. These connections imply the writer's essentially conflictual relations with convention, and consequent homelessness; all five of the authors whose presence in Switzerland prefigured Sainte-Beuve's own were exiles, voluntary or involuntary. Reflection on French religious culture is here presented as a further step in the Europe-wide tradition of philosophical contestation. Later in the book as well, Sainte-Beuve describes himself "in a time of voluntary exile" visiting sites of Jansenist refuge in Holland (*P-R*, 3:284).

But again, the apparent simplicity of this contrast—on the one side, seventeenth-century believers, on the other, Enlightened skeptics and romantic wanderers—tends to break down in the course of its elaboration. Sainte-Beuve suggests resemblances as well as differences between the Jansenists and the exiles who had preceded him through Switzerland, and such patterns of resemblance become a recurring theme in the book. The resemblance begins with the isolated convent of Port-Royal des Champs itself, which Sainte-Beuve repeatedly describes as a site of romantic isolation and melancholy, both before and after the nuns' expulsion.[8] "For those of us who love Port-Royal," he wrote, "our true homeland will always be Port-Royal des Champs"; and of course both the nuns and the male *solitaires* who lived among them shared with the famous writers whose inheritance Sainte-Beuve claimed the experience of exile and solitude. Sainte-Beuve suggests the point directly in his description of "the Pascal of the *Pensées*," who "managed to unite melancholy, almost Byronic passion with a kind of strength and geometrical precision, which gave an incomparable vigor to his style [*accent*]" (*P-R*, 1:347, 2:133). In images like these, the Jansenists have ceased to represent a pure resistance to modernity. They have become instead precursors of a distinctively nineteenth-century

8. The convent of Port-Royal had two houses, one in Paris, the other in the countryside south of the city. The movement's center of gravity shifted from one to the other, depending on the external pressures to which it was subject.

sensibility. The Byronic Pascal recalls our attention to the Byronic recol-
lections that Sainte-Beuve himself experienced during his Swiss sojourn.

The presence of Romantic melancholy in Port-Royal's story points to
a larger paradox in Sainte-Beuve's account: despite their determination to
resist modernity, his book suggests, the Jansenists were in fact among
its primary agents, as much cultural revolutionaries as reactionaries. *Port-
Royal* thus offers a troubling double message. Those most appalled by
modern culture find themselves contributing to it in fundamental ways,
even as they seek to halt its encroachments; deeply committed to preserving Christian belief, they contribute to its destruction. To some extent,
Sainte-Beuve presents the Jansenists' modernity as accidental, a result of
their peculiar circumstances. As victims of papal and monarchical persecution, they necessarily acquired some skepticism about the justice and
good sense of the political order around them, and they were compelled
to organize themselves in innovative ways. These were the terms that the
archbishop of Paris used in 1679 to explain the king's persecution: the
movement had developed as a *corps* independent of the king, and (as
Sainte-Beuve summarizes the complaint) "it was this republic of Port-
Royal that was to be suppressed." The Jansenists' successful manipula-
tions of public opinion only added to this impression that the group could
not really fit within the limits of monarchical obedience; and in fact some
of its principal leaders published underground. Its political theory stressed
obedience, but as an illegal movement relying heavily on pamphleteering,
its practices were necessarily threatening (*P-R*, 3:170, 176).[9]

This political modernity was in some sense an accidental aspect of Port-
Royal, imposed on the convent and its supporters by the monarchy's persecutions. But alongside the modernities that its situation required, the
movement displayed others, which were more clearly matters of intellectual choice. Among these, Sainte-Beuve placed particular emphasis on
the Jansenists' receptivity to science. Descartes in particular elicited their
enthusiasm: "'It was these Messieurs who made philosophy fashionable
among the ladies,'" as a late seventeenth-century source claimed. The
Grand Arnauld responded warmly to Descartes's ideas at their first appearance; he and his collaborators studied Descartes's writings carefully,
discussed them, and used some of them in their own logical treatises.
They were equally enthusiastic about the study of nature and by midcentury, were dissecting dogs in order to study the circulation of the blood

9. For recent emphasis on the political modernity of Jansenism, see Van Kley, *Religious
Origins of the French Revolution*.

(*P-R*, 1:758, 3:320, 326, 1:752). In this instance, Sainte-Beuve presents the Jansenists as blind to the consequences of their intellectual involvements. Only "Pascal had some feeling of alarm" at the implications of Cartesianism, "a sublime anxiety, that the future justified" (*P-R*, 1:326).[10] In contrast, Arnauld (like Bossuet) was misled by the ease with which Cartesian doctrines could be fitted into Christian teachings, and thus (as Sainte-Beuve presents the case) he ignored the dangerous implications in Descartes's method. For "it was from Descartes's method itself, once abroad in the world and fashionable, that the danger came. . . . Descartes contributed more than anyone else to making the human mind a *precision instrument,* and that leads far." For himself, Arnauld could sustain the distinction between doctrine and method, and thus could view Cartesian method as harmless. But "these compartments exist only in a mind that respects them; they collapse at the slightest forward movement of a less respectful spirit." And so to Sainte-Beuve's categorical conclusion: "Every philosophy, whatever it may be in its origins and in the hands of its creator, becomes anti-Christian or at least heretical in the second generation: this is the law, and one must recognize it" (*P-R*, 3:324). Unlike Pascal, most of the leading Jansenists failed to understand the consequences of their enthusiasms. In promoting Descartes, argues Sainte-Beuve, they unwittingly undermined their own Christian project.

Such ironies of misperception matter considerably in Sainte-Beuve's account, but they are less important than a third aspect of Port-Royal's modernizing impact. Although enthusiasms like Arnauld's reflected individual personalities and specific intellectual encounters, there were also more basic affinities between the Jansenists and the modernity against which they struggled, affinities that were structural rather than personal. In their very efforts at Christian reform, Sainte-Beuve's Jansenists were part of a seventeenth-century cultural revolution, playing their role in rendering Europe's inherited culture irrelevant. Sainte-Beuve develops this argument partly through a long series of apparently offhand analogies, between the impact of Jansenist theologians within their field and that of other seventeenth-century cultural figures. Arnauld's *Frequent Communion,* thus, "brought about the reform in both style and method of French theology, such as Malherbe and then Boileau achieved in verse, Corneille in tragedy, Descartes in metaphysics, Pascal for genius itself and for the

10. It should be noted that Sainte-Beuve was not necessarily correct in thus linking Jansenism to enthusiasm for Descartes and for science more generally: cf. Nadler, *Arnauld and the Cartesian Philosophy of Ideas.*

perfection of prose, Mme de La Fayette for the novel, Domat for jurispru-
dence. When Boileau expressed so much admiration for Arnauld, he in
fact owed him this much, as a potent forerunner and contributor to the
improvement of taste" (P-R, 1:637). Arnauld's work, Sainte-Beuve had
argued earlier, was in fact far more modern than that of François de Sales,
despite François's apparent ease with the real world (P-R, 1:285). In this
case, Port-Royal fitted within the modernizing seventeenth century both
through analogies of form—Jansenism resembled other movements for
change—and as a powerful influence: its teachings helped to create change
in cultural areas that ostensibly had little to do with theology.

In the same way, Sainte-Beuve presents Jansenius as a precursor of
La Rochefoucauld, indeed as a more serious and coherent presenter of La
Rochefoucauld's ideas: "[H]ere, it seems to me, we have the essence of
La Rochefoucauld, not in detached, ironic maxims, without root or connection to one another, but rather in the form of truths attached to the
tree, in which one can follow everything." He also presents Jansenius as
a philosophical statement of the ideas that John Milton had "painted" as
a poet. More broadly, even the school texts that Port-Royal produced, its
methods for studying logic and language, reshaped the practices of French
intellectual life: "Port-Royal's literary function, in fact, was to spread [vul-
gariser] certain sound habits of reasoning and writing, and to introduce
them little by little to the public domain" (P-R, 1:612, 608, 2:242).

Pascal represents the most important of these ironic linkages between
the Jansenists' antimodern beliefs and their modernizing impact. Pascal's
relations with Montaigne were especially significant in this respect, for
Montaigne (Sainte-Beuve is at pains to show, in another lengthy digres-
sion) represented all that Port-Royal disliked: genial paganism, acceptance
of the world as it is, praise of sensual pleasures. Yet "in vain does [Pascal]
trample him, reject him; the trickster returns each time. [Pascal] worries
about [Montaigne], cites him, even occasionally copies him into the fabric
of his own Pensées, misleading his friends in the edition they prepared:
there are sentence of Montaigne left in as having come from Pascal. Montaigne had fixed himself within him, while pretending to be a passing
guest." "The Pensées . . . properly understood, are only [Montaigne's] Apo-
logie de Sebond redone with self-control. In this one sees the intention and the
unifying thread of our study" (P-R, 1:826, 860; my emphasis). Seeking to
combat Montaigne's ideas, Pascal has become their transmitter—and this
connection between the would-be saint and the good-humored sensualist,
Sainte-Beuve here acknowledges, represents a central theme in Port-Royal.

In a similar way, Sainte-Beuve stresses Pascal's overlap with Boileau and Molière, the latter still more bluntly pagan than Montaigne, because of their common approach to the problems of moral behavior in the social world. "Pascal was the first," he writes of the commentaries on modern manners that culminated in Boileau. "Pascal and *les Précieuses ridicules,* these are the great modern precedents" of the attitudes that ended the vogue for such dreamy novels as those of the Scudérys. "Pascal was only Molière's predecessor" (*P-R,* 3:436). This relationship between Pascal and Molière renders Pascal a principal founder of modern ethical behavior and reasoning. "The *Provinciales* killed off scholastic theology in the domain of ethics, as Descartes killed it off in metaphysics; they did a great deal to secularize wit and the idea of the *honnête,* as Descartes did in institutionalizing philosophical thinking." This modern morality, as Sainte-Beuve describes it, is above all a matter of good sense, moderation, sound education, good manners, and propriety. It altogether lacks moral heroism, and in that sense it represents a falling off from the high moral standards of seventeenth-century Christianity. But whatever its limitations, this morality had become an essential fact of modern society. "Since the fall of the old society and the old classes, since the rise of the middle class, this morality has predominated among the leading strata of our modern society (I speak here of France)."

Without wanting to, possibly without even imagining such an outcome, Pascal had helped create the moral foundations of nineteenth-century middle-class society. This morality of *honnêtes gens* would receive its full elaboration by Molière and La Bruyère, in the following generation, when both protested against the false piety of Louis XIV's later reign. But "both did so by taking up again, reforging for their own needs and according to their own genius, the arms that Pascal had invented and made famous." They were in this regard "the direct successors and heirs of the Pascal of the *Provinciales*" (*P-R,* 2:246–48, 250). In comments such as these, Sainte-Beuve altogether inverts his earlier suggestions of the Jansenists' irrelevance to the development of the modern world. Far from irrelevant, they now appear as leading creators of modernity, in their politics, their prose, their science, their vision of human nature, their ideas of the good itself.

This ironic view of the Jansenists' place in history—emphasizing their contributions to a modernity that they believed themselves to be combating—points to the influence of Hegelian ideas in mid-nineteenth-century

France. The German philosopher G. W. F. Hegel had taught that individuals "develop themselves and their aims in accordance with their natural tendencies, and build up the edifice of human society; thus fortifying a position for Right and Order *against themselves*. . . . [I]n history an additional result is commonly produced by human actions beyond that which they aim at and obtain—that which they immediately recognize and desire. They gratify their own interest; but something further is thereby accomplished, latent in the actions in question, though not present to their consciousness, and not included in their design."[11] Such ideas enjoyed a significant vogue in Sainte-Beuve's Paris, largely thanks to the efforts of Victor Cousin. During his exile in the 1820s Cousin traveled extensively in Germany, establishing ties with Hegel's disciples, and on his return from exile he presented himself as an interpreter of these and other recent German contributions to philosophy.[12] Modern scholars have noted the deficiencies in Cousin's actual knowledge of German philosophy, but his enthusiasm and powerful institutional role nonetheless ensured that Hegelian ideas would influence mid-nineteenth-century French intellectuals. Hippolyte Taine commented that "I read Hegel every day, during an entire year, while I was in the provinces [in 1851–52]; probably I will never again experience such powerful impressions as he gave me." Enough members of Taine's generation shared his enthusiasm that the university authorities sought to discourage students from reading Hegel.[13]

But Sainte-Beuve's differences from both Hegel and Cousin were equally striking, and in the end more important. Sainte-Beuve diverged first in his apparent indifference to the state and to larger ideas about national development. Political power in *Port-Royal* shows itself above all as a malign influence, which tends quickly to pointless brutality. The book shows both Richelieu and Louis XIV dealing with even mild-mannered dissent in ways that served no rational interest and caused great suffering. The interrogations that Richelieu's men carried out on the Jansenist theologian Saint-Cyran "were at once ridiculous and nauseating, acts of vicious and cruel stupidity; it's only just that they besmirch Richelieu's grand reputation." Sainte-Beuve notes the absurdity of Louis XIV, having just gloriously fought the whole of Europe in the Dutch War, declaring "war

11. Hegel, *Philosophy of History*, 27.
12. Kelley, *Descent of Ideas* 14–23.
13. Quoted in Bourget, *Essais de psychologie contemporaine*, 132. See also Leger, *La jeunesse d'Hippolyte Taine*, 113, 133. Recent historians who have explored the ironic tendencies of nineteenth-century French thought have perhaps underrated Hegel's influence and have given more weight to Alexis de Tocqueville's influence than seems warranted.

on a house of poor nuns." Elsewhere, he describes a line of tyranny that extended from Richelieu through Louis XIV to Napoleon (and by implication to Napoleon III), all of them "masters of the earth" who inevitably find any independence of thought inherently suspect, even in the absence of questions about the established order (*P-R*, 1:489, 3:153, 2:244).[14] Sympathetic study of Port-Royal, Sainte-Beuve makes clear, implies emphasis on the brutalities and costs that political powers exact and the frequent irrationality of their objectives. But the critique of absolutism implies no corresponding defense of centrist nationalism, of the sort that Cousin himself warmly endorsed. Sainte-Beuve quotes with tepid approval the "emotional peroration" with which Cousin closed one of his lectures, then notes that "a naturally skeptical spirit like my own" can take no real position on Cousin's views.[15] Set within the context of Cousin's philosophy and influence, *Port-Royal* seems a deliberate rejection of national sentiment and of confidence in the state as a force for good.

A second area of divergence concerns the end point of historical development, the modern world itself. Sainte-Beuve's views of that world were complicated and in many ways contradictory. Thirty years after his death, Charles Maurras argued that he had first developed the ideas that would culminate in his own right-wing movement, the Action Française—but in his last years Sainte-Beuve was viewed as a liberal hero for his opposition to the Second Empire.[16] In fact precisely this ambivalence about the modern world, the end point of the history that *Port-Royal* traces, separated him from Hegel and Cousin. Sainte-Beuve viewed modernity as unavoidable, in many ways admirable, but also as a disturbing condition. His most famous expression of this disturbance comes in his essay "De la littérature industrielle," published in 1839, in the midst of his first public presentations of the material from *Port-Royal*.[17] Sainte-Beuve's choice of title is itself striking, raising as it does (a decade before *The Manifesto of the Communist Party*) an image of the Industrial Revolution transforming European cultural life. To be sure, Sainte-Beuve insisted that "industrial literature" had always existed, at least since the invention of printing;

14. It is important to note the radical implications of Sainte-Beuve's political assessments. In contrast, though staunch republicans, the Sorbonne historians of the late nineteenth and early twentieth centuries tended to invert this critical view of absolute monarchy, seeing in Richelieu and Louis XIV heroic builders of modern France; see Jouhaud, *La main de Richelieu*, and the brief discussion in Chapter 2, above.

15. Sainte-Beuve, *Portraits littéraires*, 1021–22.

16. As discussed in Chapter 1, above.

17. In Sainte-Beuve, *Pour la critique*, 197–222.

rather than industrial modes of production, he wrote, it resulted from the readiness of authors to write purely for money, without regard for the lasting value of what they produced. Modern conditions, however, had enormously intensified the flow of such writing. "We must resign ourselves to the new modes, to the invasion of literary democracy as to all the other democracies. . . . Writing and getting oneself into print will be less and less a mark of distinction. With our electoral and industrial customs, everyone, at least once in his life, will have had his page, his speech, his prospectus, his toast—in short, will be an author."[18] One might resign oneself to this postrevolutionary order, and even admire its achievements; certainly Sainte-Beuve offered no defense of the society of the Old Regime. But he could not accept the vision of triumphal progress announced by Hegel and Cousin.

The detached, divided view of what history had produced allied in Sainte-Beuve with a final, distinctive commitment: his absolute secularization both of the processes of history and of the historian. In defining *Port-Royal*'s significance, it is important to recognize how radical this step seemed to Sainte-Beuve's contemporaries. They worried both about the threat that atheism represented to society as a whole and about what godlessness meant for historical understanding. In 1863 the bishop of Orléans published a pamphlet violently denouncing Renan, Taine, and Émile Littré, all close associates of Sainte-Beuve, asking that they either express their belief in God or "publicly accept the name of atheists or materialists, from which they recoil." As a result of these suspicions, all three found their elections to the Académie française blocked until the fall of the Second Empire.[19] To such figures as the bishop, Sainte-Beuve and his circle menaced the social order itself.

Such ideas echoed within French academia. From the start of his career, Cousin defined his task as a philosopher as that of preserving religious belief in a postrevolutionary world;[20] and in his 1828 lectures at the Sorbonne he repeated Hegel in proclaiming God's role in history. "It is because Providence is in history that humanity has its necessary laws and history its necessary course," he told an enthusiastic audience. "History is the demonstration of God's providential design for humanity; history's

18. Sainte-Beuve, *Pour la critique*, 206.
19. Quoted in Casanova, *Sainte-Beuve*, 414.
20. Kelley, *Descent of Ideas*, 15.

judgments are God's own judgments."[21] Although with more attention to historical details and documents, this was essentially the position of the great German historians of the nineteenth century as well, among them Leopold von Ranke and Johann Gustav Droysen; without some form of divinity acting as guarantor, they believed, the movement of history would collapse into a story of meaningless brutality.[22] "History recognizes something infinite in every existence," proclaimed Ranke in the 1830s: "in every condition, in every being, something eternal, coming from God; and this is its vital principle. . . . This is the religious foundation on which our efforts rest."[23] Religious belief founded the idea that all states have "spiritual bases" and that their development is not a matter of mere accident and power, but rather the emergence of something essential about the world. Only with this understanding could the world retain a rational appearance.

In France, Michelet had more complicated views, but (as Lionel Gossman has shown) Christian imagery and ideas were fundamental to his philosophy of history, structuring his views about the development of France and about the Revolution's place in that development.[24] Even Tocqueville, whose ironic sensibility and pessimism in some ways resembled Sainte-Beuve's, readily invoked God as an aid to historical understanding. In a letter to Arthur de Gobineau, Tocqueville argued for the impossibility of believing in "the greatness and growing prosperity of our modern societies" were religion to disappear; a godless society would experience only "a long moral decrepitude and a vicious, troubled old age," whose only possible cure would lie in a new spiritual awakening.[25]

In contrast, Sainte-Beuve presented himself in *Port-Royal* as a religious skeptic, interested in the phenomenon of belief but incapable of sharing in it. He is, he says, "this skeptic, respectful and saddened" by the Jansenist vision of the world. Elsewhere he describes himself as "an unbeliever [*profane*], and once a poet, seeking poetry in everything, even (need I add?) in religion" (*P-R*, 1:845n, 2:719). These occasional remarks in *Port-Royal* itself received amplification in other essays. Late in life, for instance, Sainte-Beuve described the varied belief systems through which he had passed: from "the most advanced ideas of the eighteenth century . . . my

21. Quoted in Gossman, *Basel in the Age of Burckhardt*, 219–20.
22. Gossman, *Basel in the Age of Burckhardt*, 215–16; Megill, "'Grand Narrative' and the Discipline of History," esp. 158–59, 161.
23. Ranke, "On the Character of Historical Science," 38.
24. Gossman, *Between History and Literature*, 201–24.
25. Tocqueville, *Correspondance*, 68 (22 October 1843).

true core," through engagements with Saint-Simonianism, Catholicism, and Protestantism. But "I never engaged my faith" in these spiritual flirtations; rather, they constituted "only a long course in moral physiology."[26] In a review of 1864 he offered a description of the intellectual that reinforced this vision of absolute spiritual detachment, a position from which religious beliefs were as much objects of study as any other scientific or historical topic. The review concerned a profession of faith by the historian and onetime government minister François Guizot. Guizot's faith, like his politics, stressed limits and proprieties; it sought "to reaffirm . . . certitude" in contemporary minds much shaken by critical thought. Sainte-Beuve summarizes Guizot's view: "He says to criticism and science, as once he said to democracy and the Revolution, you will go so far and no farther." Guizot presented the intellectual as socially useful, responsible for sustaining order and belief in the world around him.[27]

No argument was possible against such moral self-confidence, wrote Sainte-Beuve, only the counterexample of "the perfect image of the critical spirit," an alternative vision that Sainte-Beuve developed as something of an autobiographical fable. Rather than Guizot's stress on the intellectual's societal integration and responsibilities, he presented an intellectual who lived "alone, without family, without children," in rooms "where the noises of the street do not reach, . . . beyond all social ties, free of all that comes with familial bonds, social duties, public proprieties and rhetoric." Thus socially isolated, the intellectual, combining attributes of the scientist and the literary critic, explores the large questions of human existence, and above all "what is today the principal question, the one to which lofty minds devote their most serious efforts, the question of origins."

This was a stance of intellectual skepticism, but also of a deeper pessimism about the order and character of the world itself. "The intellectual has learned that destruction is life's perpetual law and condition, necessary to its growth and progress; some are invariably sacrificed to others, without which they cannot thrive; life thus constructs itself on death itself and on large foundations of sacrifices; the strong eat the weak, and that necessity recurs everywhere, in history as in nature; disguise it as one may, it nonetheless survives." Killing marks even the intellectual's own activities. His rooms are blood-stained from experiments concerning the nature of life, and in the corner "a poor skinned animal testifies

26. Sainte-Beuve, *Portraits littéraires*, 1073–74 ("Pensées," XV).
27. Sainte-Beuve, *Nouveaux lundis*, 9:90.

to a sated curiosity about physiology";[28] the image refers back to *Port-Royal* itself, where the Jansenists' "ruthless" fascination with vivisection had been described (*P-R,* 1:758), yet another way in which they are revealed as accomplices in modernity's construction. In the long run, the critic's activities may serve humanity, yet (so runs Sainte-Beuve's fable) no guarantee of utility accompanies these efforts, nor is it even certain that the ideas will reach the larger public; for the most part, the public would only find the critic's discoveries frightening.

Sainte-Beuve's imaginary descriptions suggest the destabilizing impact of the intellectual's work, indifferent as it is to society's values and needs. Yet the force of the description is ultimately positive. No pious moralizing of the sort that Guizot offered can stop the development of new knowledge and critical understanding, and the intellectual is heroically devoted to seeing things as they are. This effort requires the destruction of old verities, but this only reflects the nature of change in the world itself, which renews itself only through conflict and destruction. This emphasis on the intellectual's rootlessness and isolation echoes in a darker mode the imagery of *Port-Royal*'s opening, in which Sainte-Beuve traces his connection to other intellectual exiles; and the book's conclusion likewise refers to the vision of the intellectual as pure scientist, concerned only with understanding, indifferent to societal orthodoxies. He had attempted, he writes, only "to see things and men as they are," to write "as a servant of science" (*P-R,* 3:674). Sainte-Beuve thus offers a novel idea of historical interpretation itself: his historian is to become a scientist, indifferent to limits that conventional values and virtues might place on his narration and to the social uses of what he writes. These expectations have particular force because he applies them to the investigation of religious belief itself. For the historian who treats religion itself as a branch of "moral physiology," no sacred topics remained.

Port-Royal, I have suggested, offers a sustained exploration both of the modernization process and of the historian's place in the world that modernization has produced. Sainte-Beuve's ideas on these topics were not systematic, or even free of contradictions, naturally enough, given the twenty years that he devoted to *Port-Royal.* Nonetheless, the coherence of his vision remains striking. Modernity as he presented it had little to do with industrialization or urbanization. To some extent it reflected

28. Sainte-Beuve, *Nouveaux lundis,* 9:98, 100, 101, 104–5, 106.

changes in how people live, but it resulted primarily from cultural rather than material changes, a series of changes in how men and women thought about science, manners, ethics, the arts, and the purposes of life. Taken together, these changes in outlook amounted to a new mode of life, a new world. For all its concern with antiquated theological disputes, *Port-Royal* ultimately focused on the boundary separating modern from premodern societies.

Much of *Port-Royal* concerns the complex process by which France crossed this boundary. As in the rest of his work, Sainte-Beuve's approach in *Port-Royal* is microhistorical, a series of close examinations of individuals, their biographies, and the texts that they produced. In an 1840 note in his private journal, Sainte-Beuve explained his belief in this approach: "It has become a commonplace to say that literature is an expression of society, but it is no less true to add that society is also the expression of literature. Every influential author creates a world that copies him, continues him, and often goes beyond him."[29] The Jansenists of *Port-Royal* were "influential authors" of this sort, and in fact (the book argues) they changed the world; they are shown to be at the center of modernizing trends across the spectrum of French culture.

But underlying this focus on the particular was a larger conception of the movement toward modernity. Despite their variety, Sainte-Beuve's case studies amount in the end to a vision of modernity as a single movement, whose manifestations in various domains closely parallel one another. This essential unity of the modernizing process is partly sociological, in that many of the same cultural actors participated in its diverse developments, and partly analogical: developments in theology, for instance, show structural resemblances to those in philosophy, poetry, science, and rhetoric. More important, however, are the intricate causal linkages that render so many of the Jansenists unwitting and unwilling modernizers. The force of these connections was such, so *Port-Royal* ultimately suggests, as to justify speaking of modernization as a single process, touching all areas of French culture, so pervasive that even its avowed enemies in the end furthered it. *Port-Royal* thus illustrates one of this book's fundamental arguments: Sainte-Beuve and the writers around him centered their historical reflections on the problem of modernity. Their histories ultimately concerned societal transformation—even as they wrote about nuns, theologians, and philosophers.

29. Sainte-Beuve, *Les cahiers*, 183, no. 575.

A final element in the modernization process looms over the whole of *Port-Royal:* for Sainte-Beuve, the decline of Christian belief is at the center of modernity itself, and real Christianity is almost impossible amid the conditions of modern life. The ruined convent of Port-Royal des Champs, razed at Louis XIV's insistence, of course tidily symbolizes this image of decay, but *Port-Royal* includes another representation of the destruction of faith, in the person of the historian himself. Sainte-Beuve inserts himself often into his text, as an exemplar of the incapacity for belief that modernity has produced. In the end, *Port-Royal* suggests, the historian who can best understand the passionate faith of the vanished premodern world is the one who himself has no faith of any kind.

4

LOST WORLDS:
LUCIEN FEBVRE AND THE ALIEN PAST

In this chapter I explore an idea that was central to French historical writing in the twentieth century: the idea that fundamental differences of experience, feeling, thought, and personality divide contemporary society from what came before it, making the past so unlike the present as to constitute a "world we have lost."[1] I seek here to understand how this idea came into widespread use and to explicate some of the discussions that it has occasioned. A vision of the past as alien territory, I argue, was central to the development of French historical thought during the first half of the twentieth century, and it prompted some of the century's most innovative research. It remains important in much contemporary scholarship. Inevitably, however, developing and documenting this idea of difference have

1. The term derives, of course, from the British historian Peter Laslett, whose *The World We Have Lost* offered an especially forceful articulation of this view.

required historians to step beyond the limits of mere science. These questions call forth historians' assumptions about their own modernity and demand that they make claims about what we are, we who differ in such basic ways from the men and women of earlier times. Exploring the gap between modernity and its antecedents has thus implicitly meant exploring the modern self, and as such it has drawn on cultural resources well outside the discipline of historical research, on ideologies, experiences, and literature.

Ideas about historical difference thus reveal with particular clarity interactions between historical knowledge and its cultural surroundings. In this chapter I develop four arguments about the character of that interaction in twentieth-century France. First, I want to show the importance of the question itself in the process by which distinctive historical approaches defined themselves in the early twentieth century. Far more than any differences about the value of social history, the differing views of the otherness of the past that were held by rival historical schools served to set them apart, and in particular served to define the *Annales* school, the century's most influential group of historians. Second, in this as in the other topics investigated in this book, twentieth-century historians worked in a complex but mostly tacit dialogue with their predecessors, a dialogue that included borrowing, adaptation, and criticism. In this domain as in others, *Annales* historians reused old ideas, while fitting them to new demands and addressing new circumstances in the contemporary world. Third, I argue here for the importance of these contemporary circumstances in shaping the scholarship of twentieth-century historians. For French historians, this meant above all the presence of colonialism, and I seek to show here the strong presence of colonial imagery in their writings about the history of their own nation. The twentieth-century colonial world supplied them with metaphors for understanding the social structures of preindustrial Europe, and it supplied incentives for doing so, because the urgency of contemporary colonial encounters encouraged viewing historical data as knowledge that had real-world uses. Finally, I suggest that the force of such contemporary concerns encouraged French historians to reflect on the boundaries between their own practices and those of other intellectual disciplines. Precisely because their scholarship touched on the ideologies and experiences of contemporary life, they found themselves forced to define the specificities of their own form of knowledge.

As throughout this book, my approach here is primarily textual, with little reference to the backgrounds or personal lives of the scholars I consider, and indeed with little reference to any but their published work. This method obviously precludes some lines of inquiry—and may seem perversely ill suited to an investigation of social history, which has so often sought to link private life with public utterance.[2] Yet an approach via the history of ideas and images serves one of my primary aims throughout the book, that of understanding how intellectual traditions, interacting in complicated ways, have shaped professional historical practices, in some instances despite the practitioners' own plans. My refusal of intentionality applies especially to the historian on whom the inquiry focuses, the sixteenth-century specialist and *Annales* school cofounder Lucien Febvre. Febvre almost inevitably occupies this focal role, for the problem of anachronism, of differences between past and present, concerned him during much of his career; and his reflections on it have continued to shape French historical thought—not surprisingly, since he published abundantly and exercised immense institutional powers.

From early on Febvre insisted on the originality of his scholarship and scholarly programs, which he vigorously differentiated from the academic traditions around him, and despite some nuances, recent scholarship has almost entirely accepted his self-presentations.[3] My purpose here is partly to undercut such rhetoric and to reinsert Febvre (against his will) within a series of partially overlapping intellectual backgrounds, elements of which he both adopted and modified. The point is not to diminish Febvre's accomplishments, but to interpret them in terms different from those that are usually employed. Questioning some of Febvre's claims to methodological innovation, I want to suggest, clarifies another side of his work: in this respect as in others previously examined in this book, we can see him as intervening in debates that had preoccupied French intellectuals throughout the nineteenth and early twentieth centuries.

Images of social history as a venture into unknown, unmapped territory, in which new rules and reasoning would be necessary, have been among the genre's enduring themes. Already in 1930 Marc Bloch described himself at the opening of *French Rural History* as "an explorer making a rapid survey of the horizon before plunging into thickets from which the wider view is no longer possible."[4] In 1949 Fernand Braudel opened his work

---

2. For a very different approach, stressing the interconnectedness of historians' social positions with their thought, see Kaplan, *Farewell, Revolution.*

3. See Chapter 1, above.

4. Bloch, *French Rural History,* xxiii.

on the Mediterranean with a similar self-depiction: beginning his project had "all the charms but undoubtedly all the dangers of a new departure."[5] Two generations later, the medievalist Georges Duby used comparable language to introduce the five-volume *History of Private Life,* though Bloch's colonial explorer had now morphed into a (less politically troubling) adventuresome archaeologist.[6] This imagery has sometimes been understood as tactical, a part of that academic maneuvering by which new disciplines position themselves in a competitive environment, a sales pitch in the marketplace of ideas.[7] But claims to have received little guidance from the scholarly past also had important implications concerning the sources of historians' own knowledge: as wanderers in unmapped territory, they needed to draw on intellectual resources from the culture at large and from a knowledge of "life" itself. Bloch and Febvre made these implications explicit, each calling on historians to turn from the hermetic study of parchment and paper to the study of how life actually was lived, in the present as in the past.

Febvre made this idea the centerpiece of his 1933 inaugural lecture at the Collège de France: young scholars, he complained, were "molded in their thinking by a culture based entirely on texts"; their historical writing was inevitably a "sedentary labor, a labor of the office and of paper, the windows closed, the curtains drawn." What was needed instead was a history that sought to "restore life to bygone societies, all their life, material and spiritual, political, economic, and social."[8] This task required the historian to draw on his (and masculinity was explicitly invoked here) own knowledge of "life," as Febvre made clear in a later reflection, his 1944 work on Marguerite de Navarre. "All these labels," he wrote of interpretations of Marguerite's writing that differed from his own, "of no interest to the man who knows life [*l'homme qui sait la vie*], either produce atrocious anachronisms, or else claim to encapsulate in a few words the entire life and the infinitely varied work of a woman who lived for fifty years the fullest, the richest of lives."[9] In one sentence, Febvre here managed three uses of *la vie* and one of *vivre.* His scholar was to learn from life, rather than from books alone.

Bloch was equally emphatic. "This faculty of understanding the living

5. Braudel, *Mediterranean and the Mediterranean World,* 1:18, 19.
6. Discussed in Chapter 5, below.
7. See, for instance, Hunt, "Does History Need Defending?" 241–49.
8. Febvre, "De 1892 à 1933,"
9. Febvre, *Amour sacré, amour profane,* 205.

is, in very truth, the master quality of the historian," he wrote in 1941. This faculty was to be kept sharp, he suggested, "by keeping in constant touch with the present day," since "here, in the present, is immediately perceptible that vibrance of human life which only a great effort of the imagination can restore to the old texts."[10] A decade earlier, he had applied the same language to his scholarly specialty, rural history. "Deliberate refusal to notice and investigate these changes" in the structure of land-holding, he argued at the start of *French Rural History*, "is tantamount to a denial of life itself, since all life is change."[11] In the following generation, in his own inaugural address to the Collège de France, Fernand Braudel made much the same point: historical study had changed, he told his audience, because of "life itself. I have said it elsewhere, *la vie est notre école.*"[12]

Febvre repeatedly sought to define more specifically the life experiences that had shaped his own scholarship and that of others in his generation. In his inaugural lecture he noted the significance of World War I, which had disrupted historians' pious certainties along with those of so many others. But he also noted the much broader array of intellectual changes that had marked his young adulthood, starting well before 1914: "[T]he repeated shock of new ideas, . . . the bankruptcy of old ideas, old doctrines thrust into the void by the new"—all this had produced a "crisis of everything that surrounded and framed historical thought."[13] In 1942 he spoke in more somber terms, invoking "all the tragedies and collapses" of the previous forty years, which had forced him to revise his understanding of the Renaissance.[14] The end of World War II occasioned another such reflection, as he announced the beginning of a *"new Annales"* and sought to understand its place amid the ruins the war had left. At that time he described yet another element in the historiographical caesura he believed his generation had lived through, the shockwaves produced by increasingly intense interaction between different regions of the globe; like war and intellectual change, globalization demanded new kinds of history.[15]

Bloch and Braudel offered similar diagnoses. "Our mental climate has changed," wrote Bloch in 1941. "The kinetic theory of gases, Einstein's mechanics, and the quantum theory have profoundly altered that concept

10. Bloch, *Historian's Craft*, 43, 44.
11. Bloch, *French Rural History*, xxx.
12. Braudel, *Écrits sur l'histoire*, 31 (delivered 1950).
13. Febvre, "De 1892 à 1933."
14. Febvre, *Le problème de l'incroyance*, 13.
15. I discuss this essay later in this chapter.

of science which, only yesterday, was universally accepted. . . . For certainty, they have often substituted the infinitely probable; for the strictly
measurable, the notion of the eternal relativity of measurement."[16] Writing after the war, Braudel was more somber: "[I]f [history's] methods,
programs, the answers that yesterday seemed most solid and sure—if its
concepts have suddenly all fallen apart, it is because of the strength of
our reflection and work, and even more because of our lived experiences.
Those experiences, over the past forty years, have been especially cruel for
all men; they have forcibly pushed us to look deep within ourselves and,
beyond that, to the common destiny of humanity, that is, to the crucial
problems of history. . . . [W]hy should the fragile art of historical writing
escape the general crisis of our era?"[17]

The rhetoric of scholarly innovation, then, insisted on historians' openness to the world around them, drawing attention to the presence in their
work of extrahistorical materials and ideas; the historian thus depicted was
a participant in the larger culture. That culture was a rapidly changing one,
which repeatedly confronted historians with the challenges of a modernizing world, requiring them to address new topics and use new methods.
Until World War II Bloch and Febvre's journal *Annales* gave concrete
embodiment to these views: a large percentage of its articles concerned
the recent past, and the editors themselves regularly offered reflections on
current conditions.[18] But we need to be more suspicious of this rhetoric
than historians have usually been. For one thing, despite his references
to twentieth-century crises, Febvre's rhetorical opposition between life and
book-learning recycled images long used by French writers, among them
Stendhal in the nineteenth century, Rousseau in the eighteenth, and Montaigne and Rabelais in the sixteenth. More important, the history of society was no uncharted wilderness even in the 1920s, let alone when Duby
introduced the *History of Private Life,* in 1985. That collection, as shown
in the following chapter, had vigorous antecedents in the twenty-odd
volumes produced by the Parisian librarian Alfred Franklin titled *La vie
privée d'autrefois* starting in 1887. Several of Franklin's intellectual contemporaries had similar interests. Albert Babeau, for instance, opened
his *La vie rurale dans l'ancienne France* (1885) by describing his subject as
"the private life of the inhabitants of the countryside," and he eloquently

16. Bloch, *Historian's Craft,* 17.
17. Braudel, *Écrits sur l'histoire,* 15.
18. Dosse, *New History in France,* 48–50.

stressed the importance of the task. "Political history," he wrote, "must be supplemented by what . . . Herbert Spencer calls the natural history of society. To describe the homes, clothing, food, habits, mores, pleasures, the conditions of work and leisure; to penetrate the daily and the real, not forgetting to study religious feeling, intellectual development—to study all of this among the country-dwellers of France during the past three centuries, is this not a task well worth attempting?"[19]

Lacking university positions, Franklin and Babeau in some ways stood at the margins of an increasingly professionalized historical discipline, but the story was similar among the professionals at the Sorbonne: there too discussion of social history was vigorous and lively early in the twentieth century. The issue emerged in 1901, for instance, at the founding meeting of the Société d'histoire moderne, called together under the joint presidency of Alphonse Aulard, Ernest Lavisse, and Gabriel Monod—three figures who exemplified the nineteenth-century preoccupation with positivist political history, pillars of the old Sorbonne about which Lucien Febvre so often complained.[20] Henri Hauser presented to the group the place of social history within its future work: "We will all readily agree, I believe, that the study of the social sciences can be useful to historians. History has always been a social science. . . . Since the nineteenth century, the social perspective has been increasingly dominant in our ways of seeing history, as it been in reality itself. . . . There exists a historical school that claims that history ought to be reduced altogether to the history of economic and social facts. . . . Without going so far, . . . we have to acknowledge that political and intellectual facts are themselves conditioned by economic facts."[21]

For Hauser, the difficulty lay not in the historians' responses to social science, but rather in social scientists' indifference to historical dimensions of their own subject matter; their disciplines (he suggested) had originated in studies of the law and continued to be influenced by the law faculties' present-mindedness. Other early twentieth-century historians echoed Hauser's bland assumption that social questions would receive a warm welcome among academic historians. Bernard Monod opened a brief review essay in the same year by noting that "at a time when social

19. Babeau, La vie rurale dans l'ancienne France, 1, 2.

20. As evidence both for the nuances of Febvre's own views and for the Sorbonne's openness to social history, it is worth noting that Febvre dedicated his thesis on the Franche-Comté "à mon maître Gabriel Monod."

21. Revue historique 77, no. 2 (1903): 323.

questions have assumed growing importance in the eyes of the public . . . , we must welcome with pleasure works that, illuminating in new ways the development of these problems, allow us to understand how they were posed and how men tried to resolve them in the past."[22] A common theme thus marks these expressions of the university's welcome to social history, that of the linkages between past and present. Hauser and Monod stressed the usefulness of the past, the relevance of its social arrangements to "the social question" of their own day, and Hauser returned to this theme throughout his long career. In a 1930 lecture series pointedly titled *La modernité du seizième siècle,* he noted the sense of kinship that his generation felt toward the sixteenth century; "most of the problems that interest us today were posed then." "Everywhere one looks," he concluded, "the sixteenth century seems to us a prefiguration of our own time."[23] This emphasis on connecting society's past to its present fitted within the orientations of university-centered political history-writing, which in the late nineteenth century called attention to such connections in a variety of domains—viewing Richelieu and Louis XIV, for instance, as architects of the modern French nation.[24] These were strong endorsements of a social history that sought to minimize the gap between past and present. For Hauser, the history of society needed to be written precisely because past resembled present.[25]

But as shown in previous chapters, antiquarians and professors were not the only intellectuals concerned in these years with the history of society, and theirs was not the only vision of how past and present fitted together. Literary critics shared these interests, but suggested other directions in which it might develop. Early in the twentieth century, Marcel Proust described this sociological interest as in fact the dominant motif of the previous century's literary criticism. As the preeminent critic of the era, Sainte-Beuve offered Proust his particular target, for he believed (according to Proust's critique) that one understood literature only by understanding the writer as social being, by examining his wealth, relations with women, "his daily manner of living." Proust's point was the inadequacy of this vision, which failed to understand that the writer bore no relation

22. "Bulletin historique," *Revue historique* 75, no. 1 (1901): 134.

23. Hauser, *La modernité du XVIe siècle,* 11, 105.

24. See, for example, Jouhaud, *La main de Richelieu,* 10, 26, and passim, and the discussion in Chapter 2, above.

25. For an insightful analysis of Hauser's vision of connections between past and present, see also Descimon, "Declareuil (1913) contre Hauser (1912)," 1615–36.

whatsoever to the external man, "the one we show in our habits, in society, in our vices."[26] Fastening this critique on Sainte-Beuve was perhaps unfair, if only because Sainte-Beuve sometimes presented himself as a skeptic with regard to an ambient interest in exactly this sort of sociological explanation. "In our days," he complained already in 1829, "a lofty and philosophical method has introduced itself into all branches of history. In judging the life, the actions, the writings of a famous man, one begins by thoroughly examining and describing the era that preceded his arrival, the society that welcomed him, the general movement of mind."[27] But here Proust's fairness to Sainte-Beuve matters less than the assumption that the two shared: that sociological criticism was a dominant motif in the intellectual world around them and risked submerging the individual writer in the visible realities of social existence. Each presented this sociological interpretation of culture as the commonplace assumption of nineteenth-century intellectuals.

A generation after Sainte-Beuve, the sociological method received less ambivalent exposition from his younger friend Hippolyte Taine. Taine made the contextual the basis of literary understanding. "Always," he wrote in an essay on the seventeenth-century novelist Madame de Lafayette, first published in 1858, "language copies life; our habits in the world form the expressions of our books; one writes as one acts. . . . Almost always, habits of the mind express [*annoncent*] those of the heart." From these mild observations, focused on issues of language, Taine advanced to a startling conclusion: seventeenth-century style and sentiments "are so distant from our own that we understand them with difficulty. They are like oversubtle flavors: we no longer perceive them; so much delicacy seems to us coldness or pallor. A transformed society has transformed the soul. Man, like all living beings, changes with the air that nourishes him. This is so from one end of history to the other: each century, with its own conditions, produces feelings and beauties particular to it; and as the human race advances, it leaves behind forms of society and kinds of perfections that are no longer to be met with."[28] A concern with literary understanding had led Taine to an essentially structuralist view of historical time. Unlike sociologically inclined university historians such as Hauser, his point was not the usefulness of the past but its distance, a distance so great as to preclude aesthetic or moral judgment. "No age has the right," he concluded,

26. Proust, *Contre Sainte-Beuve*, quotations at 126, 127
27. Sainte-Beuve, *Portraits littéraires*, 7, 8 (portrait of Boileau).
28. Taine, *Essais de critique et d'histoire*, 243, 251, 255.

"to impose its beauty on its predecessors; no age has the right to borrow its beauties from its predecessors. One must neither sneer nor imitate, but invent and understand. It is necessary that history be respectful, and art original."[29]

Taine presented himself as undertaking a study of systems, by which "every natural grouping of human events" would reveal its inner unity, which "composes a totality from which nothing can be removed without the rest perishing." His purpose was to bring together the multiple levels of human experience, "the three great works of human intelligence, religion, art, and philosophy; the two great works of human association, the family and the state; the three great works of human labor, industry, commerce, and agriculture." To study these systems implied changing the nature of historical thought itself. "History's aim is not to drown us in detail, as it is commonly thought today," but to understand the "master forces" that govern each era, uniting the diversity of its surface manifestations. Only when thus pursued "will history cease being a compilation and become a science."[30] Contemporaries recognized what these ideas meant for historical practice. In 1883 the conservative novelist Paul Bourget commented admiringly on the breadth of social practices that Taine's conception of history embraced, all of them ways for the historian to get at what he termed the individual's "intimate being."[31] Taine's readers clearly understood what his work implied for the practice of history itself.

Many of the same ideas could be found in the work of Taine's contemporary, the medievalist Numa Fustel de Coulanges. Like Taine's, Fustel's work was immensely popular, and it too stressed the magnitude of differences between past and present.[32] His 1864 *La cité antique* opened with a ringing statement of "the radical and essential differences that once and for all separate those ancient peoples from modern societies." These differences, he believed, should put an end to the use of ancient examples in thinking about the modern world, a practice whose dangers had been illustrated by the French Revolution. In fact, human nature itself changed from one century to the next, "almost always" (he believed) for the better.[33] Also like Taine, Fustel believed that these differences resulted from the fact

29. Taine, *Essais de critique et d'histoire*, 255.

30. Taine, *Essais de critique et d'histoire*, ix, x, xi, xvi (Preface to the first edition).

31. Bourget, *Essais de psychologie contemporaine*, 145, discussed in Chapter 1, above.

32. *La cité antique*, published in a tiny initial printing, by a young and unknown author, reached its twenty-second edition in 1912: see François Hartog's preface to Fustel de Coulanges, *La cité antique*, vi–vii.

33. Fustel de Coulanges, *La cité antique*, 1, 2.

that human societies functioned as structures, whose parts reinforced one another, creating systems that the historian had to understand. History was thus primarily the study of social structures in the past. Late in life, Fustel commented to a student: "'In the past few years they've invented the word sociology. . . . The word history had the same meaning and referred to the same thing, at least for those who understand it properly. History is the science of social facts, that is, sociology itself.'"[34]

Such figures as Sainte-Beuve, Taine, Bourget, and Fustel de Coulanges indicate the broad interest that a social history focused on the otherness of the past had for nineteenth-century intellectuals and their readers. But they also suggest that history's uncertain disciplinary moorings. It interested literary critics and "psychologists," among whom Taine was sometimes grouped, more than professional historians. It also had complicated political overtones, as has also been suggested in previous chapters. This seems worth underlining, because both admirers and critics of social history have stressed its interest to the political Left and its challenges to long-established cultural traditions.[35] In his inaugural lecture, Lucien Febvre spoke of "demography replacing genealogy, in exactly the degree to which the Demos on its throne has replaced kings and princes."[36] But the view that a history of society inherently suited a democratic social world applies only to some of the writers described here. The professors of the late nineteenth-century Sorbonne, whose attentiveness to "the social question" Henri Hauser so readily assumed, can indeed be described as leaning toward the political Left. They resolutely supported the newly founded Republic and worked to strengthen the traditions of 1789, if not those of 1793; these remained contentious issues in the late nineteenth century, as French society debated the institutional powers of the Catholic Church and as the Dreyfus affair raised questions about military and societal authority. But these were precisely the academics whose historical aims and methods Febvre most vigorously dismissed. Sainte-Beuve, Taine, Bourget, and

34. Quoted in Grenier, *Camille Jullian*, "L'héritage de Fustel de Coulanges," 130.
35. See, for instance, Steven Kaplan's summary: "The waning of social history was much more closely associated in Germany with the end of the intellectual hegemony of the left than in France, where social history had never been confined to a red base. There were French echoes to the German conservative argument that social history was intellectually unsatisfactory, . . . as well as to the argument that social history was in some way dangerous either because it gave primacy (and thus succor?) to the class struggle or because it implicitly or expressly espoused social engineering." Kaplan, *Farewell, Revolution*, 14. For the influence on Febvre of Jean Jaurès and Marx, see also P. Burke, *French Historical Revolution*, 13–14.
36. Febvre, "De 1892 à 1933," 101.

Fustel de Coulanges had more complicated relations with the society around them, sufficiently so that neither conservative nor progressive seems an adequate label for any one of them. Sainte-Beuve's career was marked by recurring political vacillations, broadly tending from youthful conservatism toward elderly radicalism. Taine and Fustel began their careers further to the left, but were shocked by the Paris Commune into conservative positions; Bourget was a conservative from the outset, but his opinions became more firmly monarchist with age.

Likewise, the political implications of these intellectuals' legacies continued to fluctuate even after their deaths. The nationalist anti-Semite Charles Maurras attempted to assimilate both Sainte-Beuve and Fustel into his movement, claiming of Sainte-Beuve, for instance, that in his writings "one would find the first indications of that resistance to the ideas of 1789 that, later, would bring honor to such figures as Taine and Renan."[37] Yet when the Action Française (the political movement that Maurras founded in response to the Dreyfus affair) sought to use the anniversary of Fustel's birth as the occasion for political demonstrations against the republic, both his family and his students protested;[38] and the movement's celebration of Sainte-Beuve interested almost no one. As for Taine, in appearance so straightforward a conservative, Maurras expressed suspicion, introducing a 1922 collection of his most important essays by complaining of Taine's misreading of French cultural history.[39] The idea of otherness, it seems, appealed to writers who were uncertain about the contemporary world. They could not share the Sorbonne historians' confident interest in watching the past build toward the present, but their ideas included enough ambiguities to prevent wholehearted annexation by right-wing political movements. Such uncertainty encouraged the eventual use of these ideas for altogether different purposes.

In 1935, Febvre published a study of the Rhineland, in collaboration with a geographer colleague. It opens with an epigraph from Montesquieu: "[T]ransporting into centuries of the distant past all the ideas of the century one lives in—of all sources of error, this is the most fruitful." The quotation announced both a broad sympathy for the Enlightenment and

37. Maurras, *Trois idées politiques*, 259.
38. Hartog, *Le XIXe siècle et l'histoire*, 168–94.
39. Maurras, *Romantisme et révolution*, 3 ("préface de l'édition définitive"). It is worth noting that this edition came from the Nouvelle Librairie Nationale, official organ of Maurras's Action Française; Maurras intended his opinions to be those of his political movement.

a preoccupation with the problem of anachronism, which would be central to Febvre's thinking until his death two decades later.[40] Begun while Febvre taught at Strasbourg and underwritten by a local bank, the book explicitly sought to apply scholarship to the political questions that loomed over the region. It also formed an extended plea for taking Montesquieu's advice seriously, arguing that current assumptions about geographical boundaries had no basis in the past. No geopolitical structures rendered Franco-German conflict over the Rhineland inevitable; in fact the essence of Rhenish geography lay in the connections it permitted between peoples.[41] *Le Rhin* thus argued that history might serve the present, but that it did so by demonstrating how loosely past and present were connected. History unmasked "pseudodestinies [*fatalités*]," the assumption that current conflicts over the region were rooted in the past or in geography. The otherness of the past affirmed political freedom and possibility.[42]

Febvre developed the theme of anachronism at greater length a few years later, in his two great wartime works on the sixteenth century, *Le problème de l'incroyance* (1942), on the question of Rabelais's religiosity, and *Amour sacré, amour profane* (1944), on the princess-poet Marguerite de Navarre.[43] Both works deal with literature, and both address questions of disciplinary limits, insisting on the specificity of the historian's approach to literary materials. The issue had long concerned Febvre. In 1932, reviewing the work of Ernst Cassirer, he had spoken of "two outlooks [*esprits*], the philosophical and the historical. Two outlooks that are altogether distinct [*irréductibles*]."[44] In another article in the same journal issue, he offered a similar reading of the line dividing social history from literary history.[45] A few years earlier, he had devoted even stronger criticism to the idea of mixing psychoanalysis and history: "A Freudian Luther is so easy to imagine that one feels not the least curiosity or wish to [pursue] the acquaintance when an investigator undertakes to delineate him."[46] In studying Marguerite de Navarre, he wrote in 1944, he would seek to link religious

40. Febvre and Demangeon, *Le Rhin*, vii.

41. Febvre and Demangeon, *Le Rhin*, 293.

42. For another, equally emphatic statement of Febvre's belief in human freedom from geographical constraints, see his *Geographical Introduction to History*, 342–57 and passim.

43. These works are discussed from a somewhat different perspective in Chapter 2, above.

44. Febvre, "L'histoire de la philosophie et l'histoire des historiens," 97–103, quotation at 103.

45. Febvre, "Histoire sociale ou histoire littéraire," 39–50.

46. Febvre, *Martin Luther*, 35. Cf. P. Burke, *French Historical Revolution*, 11; Burke sees *Annaliste* anticipations of Erik Erikson's *Young Man Luther*.

beliefs "to the conceptions, the institutions, the moral practices of an era; a problem that does not belong to literary history; a problem that justifies the historian's intervention."[47] It clearly mattered to Febvre to close off the boundaries between historical study and other disciplines, even as he stressed the inadequacy of history's own disciplinary traditions.

Le problème de l'incroyance represents Febvre's most extended discussion of this kind, for it is organized around a quarrel with literary history itself. A rigorously historical approach to Rabelais and his contemporaries, so runs Febvre's famous argument, reveals the limited freedom that any artistic creator, indeed any historical actor, might enjoy. The literary historian Abel Lefranc believed that Rabelais had broken free of medieval categories and could view the world in materialist, atheistic terms; his Rabelais is a cultural revolutionary. For Febvre no such freedom was available, to Rabelais or any other intellectual. Even a Rabelais (apparently the most irreverent figure of his era) had only its "mental tools," and these left him incapable of certain basic thoughts—notably of thinking a world without God. Febvre thus presented mentalities as structures of mind that no individual could altogether evade.[48] In 1949 Philippe Ariès (then working quietly in the government's Institute of Applied Research for Tropical and Subtropical Fruits, with no personal connection to Febvre or the *Annales* group) described Febvre's conception of history as "a succession of total, closed structures, irreducible one to another. . . . There exist between two civilizations essential oppositions. In the movement from one to the next, something new occurs, something like a biological mutation. . . . A society appears to him as a complete and homogeneous structure, which expels foreign elements, or reduces them to silence."[49]

What created and sustained an era's "mental tools?" Much in Febvre's account stressed the weight of daily life. Innumerable small, ordinary experiences convinced thinkers of God's existence and of the utility of religious

47. Febvre, *Amour sacré, amour profane*, 18–19.
48. Febvre's intellectual biography raises questions that extend well beyond the scope of this chapter. However, it is worth noting that his work of the 1930s and 1940s asked very different questions from those of his doctoral dissertation, of 1912. That work starts from an interest in "une individualité politique," that of a specific province, and seeks to understand that individuality through studying "the struggle, the violent combat between two classes: nobility and bourgeoisie. Struggle for power, for influence, for political domination, no doubt; but the deeper causes of antagonism, are they not elsewhere? It is in the analysis . . . of contemporary conditions of existence that we will seek to find them." *Philippe II et la Franche-Comté*, 7, 9. The place of class conflict of this sort in the work of both Febvre and Marc Bloch is discussed in Chapter 6, below.
49. Ariès, *Le temps de l'histoire*, 300.

belief; new beliefs would require new modes of life, indeed a near reconstruction of human nature itself. "Man is not Man," Febvre wrote; "men
vary much more than we imagine, and much faster."[50] Febvre gave particular attention to the violent impulses that marked Rabelais's world,
and he distinguished that world from that of the twentieth century. "Let's
imagine François Rabelais's contemporaries," he wrote, "their violence
and capriciousness, . . . the extraordinary volatility of their moods. . . .
[These were] the natural results of a life dominated by contrasts, and far
more than we can imagine. Contrasts between night and day, unknown
to us in our electrically lighted homes; between winter and summer, softened for us—in normal times—by a thousand inventions: these they endured, practically without attenuation, for weeks and months at a time.
Evening out of conditions of life, evening out of temperaments—the two
go together."[51] Febvre shared this view with Marc Bloch, whose *Feudal
Society* in 1939 similarly explained the violent moods of earlier eras in
terms of their unstable conditions of life: the "perpetual insecurity" of
medieval life, Bloch wrote, explained "the emotional instability so characteristic of the feudal era."[52]

This readiness to situate physical and emotional violence in the past,
comfort, order, and stability in the present, deserves our attention partly
because it is not so obviously true as might be imagined, even at the level
of empirical research, and partly because of the circumstances in which
Febvre and Bloch wrote. Both men had served the entire four years at the
front during World War I, amid untold horrors, and both had watched
with alarm the rise of National Socialism; alert to what anti-Semitism
might mean for France, in 1935 Bloch had already confided to Febvre his
fear of ending in a concentration camp,[53] and in 1944 he was in fact tor-
tured and executed for his part in the resistance. Students of the twentieth
century have encouraged us to see in the violence of the trenches an
experience that unsettled and finally destroyed Victorian self-assurance;
Febvre, Bloch, and Braudel, we have seen, all referred to the impact of
warfare on their thinking. Yet these effects remain invisible in Febvre
and Bloch's analysis of the division between past and twentieth-century
present. In their texts, knowledge of twentieth-century violence has been
repressed in favor of an exactly opposite interpretation, with only the phrase

50. Febvre, *Le problème de l'incroyance*, 142.
51. Febvre, *Le problème de l'incroyance*, 99.
52. Bloch, *Feudal Society*, 1:73.
53. Fink, *Marc Bloch*, 185.

"en temps normal" acknowledging the step. Their twentieth century remains an era of peace, stability, personal self-control, and predictability, and
their twentieth-century "man" differs from his predecessors, simply, in living at a different level of civilization. Gender-specific terminology is appropriate here, for Febvre saw these processes of change in explicitly gendered
terms: the civilizing process centered on maleness itself, in turn linked to
animality and violence. The sixteenth century, he wrote, "continued the
long effort, the double effort of religion and courtesy, seeking to render
less violent, less tense, less crude the brutal, uncontrolled male soul."[54]

Febvre's somewhat startling introduction of gender at this point in his
analysis alerts us to a further intellectual choice underpinning his ostensibly empirical formulations, for the 1940s had available an altogether
different understanding of the linkages among violence, gender, and
modernity. In 1949, Simone de Beauvoir presented potential violence as
central to gender distinctions in modern societies, indeed as central to
constituting modern social roles: "It is around age thirteen that boys undertake a genuine apprenticeship in violence, and that their aggressiveness,
sense of power, liking for challenges all develop. . . . To be sure, in normal
times brute force plays a small role in the adult world—but it pervades
that world; much masculine behavior starts against a background of
possible violence. . . . [V]iolence is an authentic test of one's congruence
with oneself, with one's passions, with one's own will."[55] For de Beauvoir,
the refusal of violence, its systematic eradication in the course of childhood training and societal experience, signified exclusion from modern
society, rather than adaptation to its norms. Thus nonviolence characterized modernity's subject groups: women, to be sure, but also blacks
in the American south and the French themselves during the German
occupation.[56]

Febvre's wartime writings, I have suggested, include an ambiguous argument about historical time. On the one hand, he seems visibly to have
adopted notions of otherness developed by Taine and Fustel, treating each
society as "a complete and homogeneous structure," with a peculiar combination of sensibilities and modes of life. But ideas about cultural multiplicity ultimately yielded in Febvre's thought to a large and fundamental
contrast, between earlier and later, less and more modern, less and more

54. Febvre, *Amour sacré, amour profane*, 286.
55. Beauvoir, *Le deuxième sexe*, 2:91–93.
56. Beauvoir, *Le deuxième sexe*, 2:93.

civilized societies. Modernity's control of violence is central to the distinction; and Febvre's interpretation (I am suggesting) insists on large, eminently debatable assumptions about both his own world and the early modern past. In developing these arguments, Febvre and Bloch participated in a reclassification of Western chronology to which both William Bouwsma and Clifford Geertz have recently drawn attention. Periodization in terms of medieval, Renaissance, and Reformation has declined in importance and has increasingly been replaced by the broader division between modern and premodern eras. The distance between the modern world and earlier periods, on this view, is so great as to render other categories secondary.[57]

Why divide time in this way? Characteristically, Febvre stressed the originality of his own thoughts, which came (he suggested) from properly applying the historian's craft, seeing the past in its own terms, avoiding the modernizing preconceptions that shaped the work of literary scholars like Lefranc and philosophers like Cassirer. Previous chapters have revealed the extremity of these claims. Yet Febvre's failures to cite antecedents renders all the more interesting the one acknowledgment that he did offer, to the philosopher and anthropologist Lucien Lévy-Bruhl. Lévy-Bruhl had invented the term *mentalité* itself, as a tool of spatial rather than chronological analysis; he wrote of *Les fonctions mentales dans les sociétés primitives* (1910) and *La mentalité primitive* (1922), as ethnological categories. Like Febvre, he saw different peoples as inhabiting essentially different intellectual and emotional worlds; "man" was a variable category, and the range of possible differences was enormous. In his *L'âme primitive* (1927), for instance, he argued that "le primitif" does not "feel himself as a 'subject'" and cannot distinguish "between his own identity and others'." In this respect "the obvious analogies, so often pointed out, between the primitive and the child," he argued, were "singularly striking."[58] Hence in "primitive societies" "the true living being is the group: individuals exist only through it."[59] These conditions implied a fundamental sameness in primitive societies around the world. Lévy-Bruhl occasionally acknowledged differences between the societies he cited, but they mattered far less than the common patterns.

Febvre's *Le problème de l'incroyance* drew explicitly on Lévy-Bruhl. "No

57. Bouwsma, *A Usable Past*, "The Renaissance and the Drama of Western History," 348–65; Geertz, *After the Fact*, 136–37.
58. Lévy-Bruhl, *L'âme primitive*, 2.
59. Lévy-Bruhl, *L'âme primitive*, 2.

one (Febvre wrote) who has lived long with the men of the sixteenth century fails to be struck, when he studies their ways of thinking and feeling, by all in them that evokes that 'mentalité primitive' that the philosopher has so completely restored for us. We see the fluidity of a world where nothing is strictly delimited, where beings themselves lose their boundaries."[60] Two years later, his book on Marguerite de Navarre added some suggestive metaphors. The book opens with Febvre's suggestion that those who see "foundations of modernity" in sixteenth-century writers resemble "all those good-hearted missionaries who used to return in wonder from the Americas [the *îles*]: for all the savages they met believed in God; just a small further step, and they would become true Christians." Much later in the book, he speaks of these same historians placing "the brain and heart of a white man of the twentieth century on the body of an imperfectly evolved animal [*bête mal évoluée*]."[61] As in *Le problème de l'incroyance*, here too his vision of sixteenth-century selfhood seems to have drawn heavily on Lévy-Bruhl's ideas: when we consider "the ego [*le moi*] of men living under such conditions, can we believe that it was unified, and that the extent of its variations was simply what we see in ourselves—ourselves who have been stabilized, equalized, softened?"[62] Febvre believed that the modern ego was so solid that it could resist even the savageries that he himself had witnessed.

Febvre's adoption of so confident a view of the modern mind represented yet another distinctive intellectual choice, for both the science and the literature of his young adulthood made available alternative views. Hippolyte Taine had argued that modern rationality constituted an always tentative achievement, constantly subject to both societal and individual disruptions; there was nothing especially solid about the modern ego.[63] Taine's younger friend Paul Bourget had opened his 1883 *Essais de psychologie contemporaine* by presenting melancholy and "a universal nausea in the face of the insufficiencies of this world" as basic conditions of "our century, in which so many conditions of life have been perfected."[64] To

60. Febvre, *Le problème de l'incroyance*, 404.

61. Febvre, *Amour sacré, amour profane*, 298, 14, 320.

62. Febvre, *Amour sacré, amour profane*, 306. Writing for a nonspecialist audience, Febvre was still more decided in presenting these views: "[L]e sentiment du moi, qu'on nous donnait comme primitif, manque à bien des stades de l'évolution psychique; . . . les sentiments de différenciation personnelle restent rudimentaires chez les membres des sociétés encore peu évoluées." Febvre, *Encyclopédie française*, vol. 8, avant-propos, 2–4.

63. Taine's psychology is discussed in Chapter 1, above.

64. Bourget, *Essais de psychologie contemporaine*, 9.

the preceding generation, the modern mind was characterized precisely by its divisions and instabilities, its vulnerability to illness and disruption. Following Lévy-Bruhl, Febvre inverted this widely accepted tradition of thought, vigorously affirming the value of modernity itself, as a bringer of psychological as well as material ease. He had a deep commitment to this position, moreover. In his study of human geography (begun before World War I but completed during its immediate aftermath), he emphasized "how much more primitive man appears to be curbed by nature, harassed by traditional customs and tied down by prejudices and foregone conclusions than civilized man. The savage is above all a creature of habit, and habit chiefly governs his movements." These were above all habits instilled by fear, for in primitive societies anxieties surrounded all encounters with nature and explained much of the poverty of primitive life. "There are prohibitions, restrictions, taboos on all sides," he wrote, that prevented men from making full use of even the most readily available natural products.[65] In contrast, modern man "shows himself as a being essentially endowed with initiative, so well armed that he can confront the forces of nature without fear, and with the certainty of succeeding in the end. . . . Man, civilized today, banished from geography as the patient, reappears in the very forefront of it as dominant agent."[66]

After World War II, Febvre returned to these issues more systematically, at an especially critical moment: his editorial reopening and reorienting the *Annales*. In his 1946 "Manifesto of the New *Annales*" he sought to position the journal within the postwar world. This was, he acknowledged, a world in ruins, and a world now under the greater threat of atomic ruin. Yet for Febvre the war was essentially a secondary phenomenon, which posed no special problems of historical understanding. His manifesto did not mention extermination camps or issues of wartime complicity, nor did it suggest that the war had raised new questions about human guilt or European cultural traditions.[67] Rather, he described the postwar crisis as centering on relations between peoples, a crisis of globalization. "More serious than the ruins," he wrote, was the increasing rate of contact between groups previously isolated by distance. This "prodigious acceleration" of travel between continents now "brings into sudden contact human groups charged with contrary electricities—those who have

65. Febvre, *Geographical Introduction to History*, 162–63, 164.
66. Febvre, *Geographical Introduction to History*, 356–57.
67. Febvre, "A nos lecteurs, à nos amis," 1–8.

had most cause up to now to keep their distances, morally as well as physically. . . . That is how our world has been destroyed. . . . All the drama
is there, in the drama of civilizations. It was visible in 1932. It is playing
itself out in 1946."[68]

The reference to 1932 pointed to an earlier article on these same issues,
which Febvre had written in response to the Paris International Colonial
Exposition of 1931. Then too he had spoken of the "frightening collision
of continents" that aviation implied, but in 1932 he envisioned mainly one
direction of influence, from the west to the colonial world. "One looks
anxiously at those yellow, black, brown faces, which our airplanes can
reach in a few hours—and with our airplanes, our ideas, our newspapers,
our books, the direct, almost instant echo of our political discussions, our
social or diplomatic conflicts."[69] He had seen these faces both in the photographs that the exposition presented and in its colonial villages, in
which groups who had been taken from French and other colonial territories were installed in the Bois de Vincennes for the six months that the
event lasted, to display for visitors their customs and handicrafts.[70] Such
transplantations had been common during the high colonial era, but they
ceased after 1931, for already both the exhibition's specific format and its
larger purposes raised painful questions among European intellectuals.
Writing in the *Revue des Deux Mondes,* a passionate defender of the exposition acknowledged that "the sedition of the colonized races" now confronted Europeans with the anger of more than a billion subject people;
and he complained that in response, French elites either displayed indifference or "yield[ed] in advance to what they saw as inevitable," Europe's
renunciation of colonial authority.[71] Left-wing writers denounced the very
idea. A manifesto from André Breton, Louis Aragon, Paul Éluard, and
others was titled "Do Not Visit the Colonial Exposition" and described the
event as camouflage for the brutal violence of colonial occupation.[72]

Febvre's article barely hinted at this anger. He spoke instead of the event
as "une fort belle oeuvre," "un harmonieux ensemble," whose organizers

68. Febvre, "A nos lecteurs," 2. Febvre's silence on the fate of the Jews is of course especially striking in view of his relations with Marc Bloch during the previous decade. Cf. Dosse,
New History in France, 80; Dosse stresses the impact of knowledge of the Holocaust. For a
different view, stressing the Holocaust's limited impact on postwar intellectuals, see Judt,
"The Believer," 40–47.

69. Febvre, "L'histoire économique et la vie," 1–10; quotations at 7, 8.

70. Greenhalgh, *Ephemeral Vistas,* 89–90.

71. Gouverneur Général Olivier, "Philosophie de l'Exposition Coloniale," 285–86.

72. The text is available in Erik Orsenna's novel *L'Exposition Coloniale,* 352, which also
describes the anger that ordinary left-wing activists felt about the exposition.

had "aimed just right and thought big."[73] In the heated atmosphere of 1930s Paris, such language carried its own political messages. In the article Febvre did not praise colonialism, but he did take seriously the ethnic, economic, and cultural assumptions behind it; and elsewhere he had offered more straightforward endorsement of these.[74] Febvre's concerns about colonialism lay not with its justice but in its implications for the direction of world history. Passing before the exposition's photographs of colonial schoolrooms, he wrote, one wonders "behind those foreheads, what is going on? What extraordinary mixture of new ideas and old traditions? What chaos?" The historian, he concluded, is left to reflect on "the masses of men, unequally spread among the continents, among countries that formerly knew nothing of each other; now here they are, next-door neighbors. Yesterday, closed off from one another, today in contact. Yesterday, small and isolated battlefields, where the White Man triumphed easily, one against one hundred. Today—need one spell out the sectors along an immense front that the White Man himself equips, materially and morally, against the White Man?"[75] By 1946, he had come to view this exchange between peoples as still more directly a threat to France itself— and a far more frightening prospect, for now France would find itself in an endless cultural and material competition. "To live, for ourselves and our sons tomorrow, this will mean—already means today—adapting to a perpetually changing [glissant] world." "Time is passing, hurrying. . . . The world is pushing you, you can feel its fevered breath. No, you will not be left in peace. . . . The world of yesterday is finished. Finished forever. If we French have some hope of succeeding in these circumstances, it is in understanding—faster and better than the others—this basic truth."[76]

The complexity of Febvre's language here reflected his sense of the multiple problems that globalization posed. Decolonization brought one set of threats, but the rising influence of the United States brought equally grave ones, which became clearer in the postwar years. In 1948 Febvre wrote privately to Raymond Aron, protesting against Aron's warnings about the Soviet Union. "Alas! our French culture [is] so strongly attacked, contested, persecuted by the 'American influence.'" Febvre represented France at UNESCO, and at every meeting "we are obliged to oppose, we French, the brutal intentions of 'our American friends' in matters of

73. Febvre, "L'histoire économique et la vie," 1.
74. Febvre, Geographical Introduction to History, 356–57.
75. Febvre, "L'histoire économique et la vie," 8, 9.
76. Febvre, "A nos lecteurs," 3, 5, 6.

science, culture, and education. For the past three years we have encountered the most consistent, systematic policy of crushing our language and
ideas. . . . We need to look straight on at both [Soviet and American] per-
ils. In the final analysis one is as bad as the other. And we need to fight
both with the same seriousness, if we are French and aware of what France
means. . . . it is not on one but on two fronts that we must struggle, to
save for the world a small quantity of spiritual liberty and critical intelligence, if there is still time."[77]

Philippe Ariès drew a simple lesson from the circumstances of the postwar world: early modern Europe and the contemporary underdeveloped
world could directly illuminate each other. In a 1958 article he wrote that
"the breakup before our eyes of those traditional societies [in Africa] under
the impact of our colonization reproduces directly, though at a more rapid
pace, the splintering of our own Old Regime society between the late eighteenth and late nineteenth centuries."[78] Febvre's reading of this chronological break showed a similar sense of the analogies between his own
world and that of early modern Europe, but his interpretation was ultimately more complicated: though material changes counted heavily in his
understanding of modernization, he viewed the process as ultimately an
intellectual one, resting on new ways of understanding the world rather
than on new modes of production or other economic relations. Indeed,
he presented his work as correcting nineteenth-century assumptions that
"exalted material forces over intellectual ones."[79] In understanding the
twentieth century, this meant stressing the effects of "our ideas, our newspapers, our books," on the colonial world, rather than noting material
changes there. Likewise for the sixteenth century: his chapter on "mental
tools" begins by his describing the intellectual confusions that the French
experienced in the age before modern philosophical tools became available.[80] Material conditions mattered in Febvre's account, but language
and conceptualization mattered much more. Only when they could think
clearly about the realities of their existence could individuals begin to control the world around them.

Those mental tools (as shown in Chapter 2) were primarily French, the

77. Aron, *Mémoires,* 401–2.
78. Ariès et al., *Écrits pour une Renaissance,* 204.
79. Febvre, *Le problème de l'incroyance,* 281.
80. Febvre, *Le problème de l'incroyance,* 328. These issues receive more detailed discussion
in Chapter 2, above.

work of René Descartes and his successors. Asserting in this way the value of French philosophy and *philosophes,* of course, was anything but a neutral scientific choice in the 1940s. Febvre's works affirmed French traditions at a time of national humiliation under the German occupation, and of potential marginalization, in the increasingly interconnected world that his 1946 editorial described. Less overtly, the works also continued Febvre's silent dialogue with Taine and other nineteenth-century intellectuals. Taine also had seen the arrival of classical language as a critical moment in French cultural history, but he had viewed the process as almost entirely destructive: classicizing purists had cut away the linguistic richness inherited from the Middle Ages, producing an intellectual impoverishment that helped explain the Enlightenment's fatal inability to ground its social theories in human realities.[81] We may read Febvre as directly inverting Taine's complaints: affirming continuities between the modern republican order and long traditions of French thought, stressing the value of these traditions against other ways of seeing the world.[82]

Lucien Febvre's historical project, I argue in this chapter, included a complex process of intellectual appropriation and adaptation, in which questions of historical difference played a central role. For Febvre, sixteenth-century society was fundamentally unlike his own, and societal differences allied with basic differences of human psychology to create an essentially new kind of human being. These were not new ideas in the 1920s, when Febvre began writing what, twenty years later, would become *Le problème de l'incroyance.* On the contrary, like the idea of social history itself, ideas about the otherness of past societies had been developed and debated in the circle around Sainte-Beuve and Taine during the later nineteenth century. Febvre brought a new scholarly depth to these debates, but his principal innovation was interpretive. He redirected what had been mainly conservative ideas to support a positive conception of modernity itself. I have sought to show here how resolutely Febvre adopted this modernist perspective, which celebrated the seventeenth- and eighteenth-century rationalists as creators of the modern world and stressed the inadequacy of other modes of thought, those of sixteenth-century France and twentieth-century Africa alike. He offered a modernist vision of personality as well. Modern conditions of life had "stabilized, equalized, softened"

81. Taine, *Les origines de la France contemporaines,* 1:145.
82. For an important reading of the political implications of Febvre's wartime thought, see Davis, "Rabelais Among the Censors" and "Censorship, Silence, and Resistance."

personalities, permitting new forms of self-control and autonomy and erad-
icating the fears that dominated traditional life. Indeed, only with the
modern era could one speak of an authentic self, for only then was there
sufficient predictability in the outer world to allow individuals to respond
in consistent, integrated ways to it.[83]

Politics contributed to these scholarly formulations, for Febvre's scholarship (like that of his predecessors) responded to his concerns and
assumptions about the world around him. He and Bloch both called for
a history that did exactly this. Historical writing that failed to engage with
the contemporary world, they argued, could hope neither to illuminate the
past nor contribute to the present. But this engagement with the present
led to complex political stances, which can neither be reduced to party
labels nor dismissed as immediate responses to passing events; the questions that Febvre raised in *Le problème de l'incroyance,* after all, preoccupied
him over the last thirty years of his career. In that book and in the studies
that derived from it, I have argued here, he explored a division that he
saw in the present as well as in the past, the division between premodern
and modern. In both past and present, he found evidence for the depth
of this difference, which, he believed, showed itself in the most basic elements of human personality. There was smugness in this celebration of
European selfhood, but also anxiety. The increasing rate of contact between peoples, he believed, had entailed more frequent conflicts between
them. Globalization had helped produce World War II, and it would ultimately threaten France's own place in the world. The need to defend that
place became a recurring theme in Febvre's work. Against the march of
globalization and the more direct interventions of German and American power, he offered the vitality of French intellectual life. *Le problème
de l'incroyance* presented French philosophers as central agents in creating the modern world; his postwar reflections stressed the importance of
French intellectuals in the present as well.

History's importance as a means of responding to the contemporary
world seems to have encouraged Febvre to reflect on its character as a discipline. Febvre's historian needed to consider all manner of topics, including even ephemeral contemporary events like the Colonial Exposition, and
for that very reason it was important to define the specific approaches
that she or he brought to these universally interesting materials. Febvre's

83. For recent reflection on these issues, see Chartier, *Cultural History,* "Intellectual History and the History of *Mentalités,*" 19–52; Lloyd, *Demystifying Mentalities*; Buckley, *At the Origins of Modern Atheism*; and Lowenthal, *The Past Is a Foreign Country,* 199.

conclusions were severe. He stressed the differences between history and the numerous modes of thought that adjoined it, and the inadequacy of many historical approaches as well. There was another dimension to his interest in disciplinary boundaries, however. In his touchy insistence on the specificity of historical method, an insistence surprising in a scholar who had such wide interests, Febvre continued his silent dialogue with the intellectuals of the nineteenth century. They had pointedly ignored generic boundaries, writing fiction, philosophy, psychology, and literary criticism as well as history, and often producing hybrids that shared features of all of these; the Goncourt brothers even turned to painting and drawing. Febvre's emphasis on history as a distinctive science can be read as, in part, another of his ways of coping with these overmighty intellectual ancestors.

5

PRIVATE LIVES AND HISTORICAL KNOWLEDGE

 "Our project was fraught with peril. The ground we hoped to explore was untouched. No one had sifted through or even identified useful source materials, which at first sight seemed abundant but scattered. We had to clear away the brush, stake our claim, and, like archaeologists approaching a site known to contain riches too great to be systematically explored, settle for excavating a few preliminary trenches."[1] With these bold words, the medievalist Georges Duby introduced the monumental *A History of Private Life,* five volumes tracing the European experience from ancient times to the present, first published in 1985 and in 1987 translated into English. With contributions from many of the greatest French historians of the postwar era, the volumes offer an important vantage point for reflecting

---

1. Duby, foreword to Ariès and Duby, *History of Private Life* (hereafter *PL*), 1:vii.

on French historical writing of the later twentieth century. Duby's images of discovery and appropriation express a position taken throughout *A History of Private Life*, an emphasis on the novelty and risk of the undertaking. Roger Chartier summarizes this stance in his conclusion to volume 3, on the early modern period. He describes the volume as "but the first fragments of a new kind of history, which has yet to be written."[2]

Its editors' stress on innovation makes *A History of Private Life* an especially relevant case study for the present book. As they suggest, an interest in the private has been characteristic of twentieth-century historical practice, which has so often turned away from the narrative methods and high political subject matter of earlier centuries. I have tried here to complicate contrasts of this kind, and to suggest that contemporary practice be viewed in terms of dialogue with the nineteenth century, rather than departure from it. Study of private life provides a useful domain from which to explore this view, because the study of private life was not in fact uncharted territory when *A History of Private Life* was planned. Especially prominent on the intellectual landscape were the twenty-seven volumes that the librarian and amateur historian Alfred Franklin devoted to *La vie privée d'autrefois, arts et métiers, modes, moeurs, usages des parisiens, du XIIe au XVIIIe siècles*. Franklin's first volume came out in 1887, and later volumes appeared at an astounding rate over the following decade. By the turn of the century, he had produced studies of early modern clothing, cleanliness, eating, child rearing, shopping, health care, and dozens of other topics. Franklin was a careful and energetic scholar, with considerable breadth of vision. He used the documents that have continued to supply the foundations for much study of private life, and, although he interested himself mainly in Paris, he had as much to say about ordinary people as about the higher ranks of society.

My purpose in confronting *A History of Private Life* with its century-old predecessor is not to diminish what Duby, Chartier, and their collaborators have achieved. Nor is the confrontation intended to reveal unacknowledged influences on their work—though it is striking that Franklin's name does not appear in the indexes or bibliography to *A History of Private Life*. On the contrary, I shall argue that the more recent volumes take a radically different approach from Franklin's. Rather, the comparison allows us to pursue a series of questions at the core of the present inquiry: What are the relations between amateur and professional scholarship? How

2. Roger Chartier, epilogue to *PL* 3:609.

exactly does intellectual innovation take place in the study of history? How have different historians coped with some central traditions in French culture, and what have been the implications of their choices? The task of this chapter is to understand some of the alternative ways in which the history of private life has been written, so as to understand more clearly the choices and rejections that underlie historical writing.

For this purpose it is helpful to start with the figure of Alfred Franklin himself. Franklin's career unfolded almost entirely within the quiet confines of the Bibliothèque Mazarine, which Charles-Augustin Sainte-Beuve himself had directed between 1840 and 1848. Born in 1830, the son of a successful lawyer, like most of the other figures in this study Franklin attended a leading Parisian lycée. He joined the library in 1856 as one of three unpaid librarians that its staff of ten normally included. Such men were expected to move on to paid positions elsewhere, but thirteen years later, entirely satisfied with the institution's resources and minimal demands, Franklin remained at the same rank; his superior introduced him to the French minister of education as "the oldest unpaid functionary in France." Thereafter he began a slow ascent through the library's paid positions, and in 1885 he became its director, enjoying a substantial salary and (like Sainte-Beuve) an apartment in the building. Despite his apparently lackadaisical attitude to his career, his direction of the library drew praise from bureaucratic superiors. "An enormous amount of work has been accomplished," noted an inspector general in 1895. His successor was even more emphatic. "In the past fifteen years or so," ran a report from 1898, "the Mazarine has finally emerged from the torpor in which dozed the previous several generations of officials attached to the establishment."[3] Yet Franklin never renounced his role as an easy-going society figure. "Homme d'esprit, brilliant causeur" (the words of an obituary), he moved easily within Parisian high society, to which his voluminous writings gave him entry. He died at his country home in 1917, having unwillingly retired from the library at the age of seventy-six.[4]

Contemporaries viewed positions like Franklin's as sinecures, with irritation and (as he himself acknowledged) complete justice. Few readers visited the library, and little was expected of its officials. The ministry determined in 1875 that librarians serve at least two days each week, and

3. Archives Nationales, Paris, F17 3488, reports of 16 July 1895 and 21–23 December 1898.
4. Franklin, *Histoire de la Bibliothèque Mazarine*, viii–xix, 322, 325; and *Bulletin de la Société de l'histoire de Paris*, 24–25.

in 1880 they insisted that the library remain open five hours daily. But even these requirements were little enforced until 1887—when the ministry moved to a three-day work week and workdays of six hours. Rather than librarianship, the Mazarin library offered a home, revenues, and scholarly resources to a succession of well-known writers. Sainte-Beuve was followed as director by Silvestre de Sacy, editor of the *Journal des Débats* and member of the French Academy, and Franklin's colleagues included other well-known writers.[5] As director, Franklin himself appointed another such figure to one of its unpaid positions: Marcel Proust began work there in 1895, but could not meet even the library's modest demands and, having failed to appear for several years, in 1900 was deemed to have resigned.[6] Franklin was particularly bewildered, since his own projects thrived in this atmosphere. In addition to his twenty-seven volumes on private life, he produced at least as many volumes on other historical topics and one historical novel.

To Franklin, life within the library seemed in many ways a continuation of the seventeenth century itself. The institution "had resisted the invasion of modern ideas; it kept the cult of the past, and, confined within its traditions, remained unchanging in the midst of a world in transformation"; surrounded by seventeenth-century books and architecture, most of the personnel shared a "cult of the seventeenth century,"[7] and (as has been seen) Sainte-Beuve and others became famous for works on the period. Yet this rootedness in the past encouraged in Franklin and his colleagues an easygoing tolerance for cultural and political diversity. In 1901 Franklin praised de Sacy (the first director under whom he worked) for de Sacy's complete absence of anti-Semitism—a significant statement at a time when the Dreyfus affair continued to send aftershocks through Paris society; a fervent Catholic, de Sacy was equally tolerant of Protestantism. Tolerance extended to socialists as well. Franklin himself could speak with good humor of the worker-intellectual, "a fine fellow, by the way," sent by the Paris Commune in 1871 to direct the library. Franklin explained his attitudes in terms of his researches in the library's holdings. "While going through those soporific collections," he wrote of his efforts at cataloging seventeenth-century pamphlets, "where sleep so many burned-out passions, I reflected that the same fate awaits most of the writings

5. Among them were Philarête Chasles, a literary historian and Academician, and the novelist Jules Sandeau, yet another Academician, who became a close friend of Franklin's.
6. Painter, *Marcel Proust*, 1:169, 250–51.
7. Franklin, *Histoire de la Bibliothèque Mazarine*, xi, xvii.

generated by our present-day political and religious controversies. Each century is fascinated by ideas, doctrines, on which the future of the world seems to depend—and which the next century will carelessly abandon, wondering how so many words and so much ink could have been devoted to them."[8] In late nineteenth-century Paris, to be of the seventeenth century entailed a skeptical stance toward contemporary disputes, and in this Franklin was at one with his colleagues.[9]

Just before his death, Franklin described himself to his physician. According to the physician's report, Franklin "[believes] neither in God nor in the devil; confesses himself very happy and has always been so"; and acknowledges "four passions, women, dogs, tobacco, and sugar."[10] Yet alongside this happy paganism Franklin displayed a sustained commitment throughout his career to the history of French Protestantism—at a time when such a choice counted for a great deal within the historical profession.[11] In 1865 he became treasurer of the recently established Société de l'histoire du protestantisme français and as such a member of its governing committee; over the years he made donations to the society's library, wrote occasional pieces for its journal, and helped supervise at least two of its publishing projects.[12] Although not a Protestant himself, he thus enjoyed some degree of contact with leading figures in the professionalizing discipline, including Gabriel Monod, Charles Waddington, and François Guizot himself, all of them also important members of the society.

His 1875 novel *Ameline Dubourg* illustrated the cultural implications of his religious stance. The book tells a tale of Huguenot martyrdom and resistance in the mid-sixteenth century. It is populated with stock characters of nineteenth-century historical fiction: a handsome and quick-witted young student, a bigoted and villainous cleric, a pious printer, and two heroines, the one dark, intense, and persecuted, the other blond and rich. It can easily be read as a case study of the interlocking evils of

---

8. Franklin, *Histoire de la Bibliothèque Mazarine*, x–xiv, 327.

9. Thus Chasles, though speaking from very different presuppositions from Franklin's: "I have held for a long time the most profound indifference to the movements of modern society; . . . setting against the civilizing hopes of my best friends not just an ironic skepticism, but serious doubt." *Études sur les hommes et les moeurs,* 28.

10. Mollard, "Alfred Franklin," 89.

11. His interest apparently derived from his mother's Protestant background. Carbonell, *Histoire et historiens,* places the religious divide at the center of historical debate during these years; see esp. 409–51.

12. For examples of his activities, see *Bulletin de la Société de l'histoire du protestantisme français* 14 (1865): 69; 16 (1867): 208; 22 (1873): 204; 30 (1881): 49–56; 33 (1884), 197.

monarchical and clerical power during the Old Regime. The novel describes royal persecution of Protestants in its rawest, most brutal forms, and royal hypocrisies (the king and his mistress watch decent Protestants burn at the stake) receive abundant attention. Even the Parisian crowds "in the depth of their heart, blamed these useless barbarities." The novel also includes a powerful description of the nature of societal progress, set in the mouth of the magistrate and Protestant martyr Anne Dubourg: "God, in sending us into this world, has given us the mission of organizing it; that is the heavy task which generations transmit one to another, and pursue slowly throughout the ages. The state of civilization at which we have arrived is the result of severe and incessant labor, for, from the humble inventor to the martyr for great social ideas, man never wrests from God one atom of creative power, except by force of courage, will, perseverance, and energy—every birth costs blood or tears."[13] Franklin's novel offers a rather complex vision of the relations between past and present. On the one hand, injustice and force mark much life in Old Regime society. On the other, this regime is no single entity, for according to the novel human progress and inventiveness have an ongoing history. Because of human efforts, the sixteenth century already enjoys an advanced state of civilization. These ideas seem to have had broad resonance in the late nineteenth century, well beyond Franklin's Protestant milieu. The Académie française awarded him a prize for the novel, as tending to promote French patriotism; the award citation describes it as "extraordinarily moving . . . , to be recommended as well for its charming and distinguished style."[14] Franklin appears to have exemplified in a small way the large influence that Protestant historians had on nineteenth-century French thought about the past.

Despite occasional ventures of this kind, Franklin devoted most of his energies to his monumental history of private life, which can be seen as a lifelong obsession loosely paralleling Sainte-Beuve's *Port-Royal*. Each of its volumes focuses on a specific question about conditions of daily existence. Five consider the marketplace, asking what goods were sold and how they were presented to consumers, stressing the range of objects that middle-class men and women bought in early modern markets, and exploring in detail the processes of retailing. Education and the workplace receive less attention, only one volume each. Aside from these seven volumes

---

13. Franklin, *Ameline Dubourg*, 13, 84.
14. Quoted in *Bulletin de la Société de l'histoire du protestantisme français*, 25 (1876): 568.

dealing with essentially public spaces, *La vie privée* concerns itself essentially with life inside the home, and chiefly with the most intimate aspects of that life. Thus, six volumes deal with medicine and hygiene, asking what medical treatments ordinary Parisians underwent, what sanitary facilities they had available to them, how they cleaned and dressed themselves. Two volumes deal with childhood and its rituals; four with eating and drinking, asking what items were available and how Parisians ate. These volumes shade into a history of civility: for Franklin the history of food was intimately bound up with the rituals around its consumption, hence with the history of manners. Time-keeping receives a volume, animals two. Four volumes present Franklin's gleanings from mid-eighteenth-century courtroom rhetoric, which reveals the private conflicts dividing Parisians, and a last volume consists simply of "variétés parisiennes."

Franklin offered no programmatic statement explaining this organization of his work. As a result, understanding its guiding principles requires some close reading of the text. But despite its meanderings, important principles organize this history. Although it rests on an impressive documentary apparatus, worthy indeed of late nineteenth-century scientific history, from his opening pages Franklin inserted himself and his readers into his text, through repeated authorial interventions—in this respect also paralleling Sainte-Beuve. This rhetoric serves an intellectual strategy, undercutting intellectual complacency by demonstrating the problems of acquiring knowledge.[15] Historians, Franklin repeatedly suggested, cannot fully understand the past, or indeed the present. Hence their work undermines other forms of cultural certainty. Having followed the complicated history of relations between surgeons and physicians during the early modern period, for instance, he concludes: "Whence the moral that we should resist holding our opinions too stubbornly, and that we must as far as possible persecute no one. Let us tell ourselves that what to us seems obvious truth to our grandchildren will perhaps seem obvious error. All human history can be summed up in these two lines."[16]

15. In speaking of late-medieval doctors, thus, Franklin begins by confessing his ignorance of fourteenth-century Parisian population: "Mais pour effacer la mauvaise impression que doit causer à mon lecteur ce double aveu d'ignorance," he continues, "je vais m'empresser de lui fournir une preuve de savoir destinée à provoquer son admiration." A new avowal, on the problems of monetary conversion, follows almost immediately: "[C]eci m'amène à confesser encore une fois les lacunes de la science." Franklin, *La vie privée d'autrefois*, 2–3, 5. Hereafter, Franklin's collection is referred to as *VP*, with more specific indications for individual volumes.

16. *VP, Les chirugiens* (1893), 4–5.

The historian's skeptical, mocking presence within his text is a first mark of Franklin's interest in attaching himself to sixteenth- and seventeenth-century modes of thought. A second is his interest in the physical realities of life, which seems deliberately to attach his work to the Rabelaisian tradition in French culture—a tradition that, as seen in Chapter 2, carried heavy ideological implications in the literary debates of the nineteenth and twentieth centuries. Franklin's vision of private life gives a central place to the history of the body, and especially to the least dignified aspects of bodily life. This readiness to confront physical existence in the past goes very far. He does not shy away from the history of urination and defecation, and he pursues the implications of his findings for a history of cleanliness: "Let us sketch broadly the history of cleanliness in France," he writes, opening his very first volume.[17] His history of food includes an extended discussion of table manners. He presents extensive documentation of the fact that all classes ate with their hands into the seventeenth century. He explores the barriers that early modern men and women needed around their bodies. Like Norbert Elias, he notes that they had little need of privacy when urinating and defecating;[18] like Georges Vigarello, he notes that even in the eighteenth century, high-society ladies had no qualms about bathing before their servants, whom they regarded "as animal[s] in whose presence even the most delicately modest could act with complete freedom."[19]

His focus on the body leads Franklin to further reflections on the complexity of historical chronology and progress. His history of cleanliness supplies him with especially complex patterns of development. Thus he finds more cleanliness in the Middle Ages, "outside the Church," which regarded bathing as an unacceptably sensual pleasure, than in the Renaissance. Before 1500, public bathhouses were scattered throughout Paris and the rest of the country. The wealthy had private baths and retained the Roman habit of bathing before dining. In the sixteenth century these habits died out because of specifically religious opposition, for the medieval bathhouses were also "places of pleasure." Denounced by Catholics and Protestants alike, the baths closed and the "habit of water" was lost, even in private homes. "Morality gained, that much is certain,"

17. VP, Les soins de la toilette (1887), 3.
18. Elias, History of Manners, 123–43.
19. VP, Les soins de la toilette, 121. Cf. Georges Vigarello, in Le propre et le sale, 105; and Sarah Maza, in Servants and Masters in Eighteenth-Century France, 187, use the same example to support similar arguments about upper-class women's indifference to their servants.

but cleanliness lost out.[20] For Franklin, the example illustrated the non-linear movement of history and the tenuous connections between the elements of historical change. History did not progress in one direction only. Closer attention to morals might mean decline in other elements of civilized behavior. Brilliant culture in the sixteenth century came with a growing acceptance of personal filth—though Franklin also noted the century's obsession with clean white linen, a finding that complicated even a model of simple decline.

Underlying such specific observations on the mixed nature of historical development is a broader stance toward change that runs through Franklin's work. Franklin saw resemblances between past and present, and he proves extremely reluctant to accord privileged standing to the present. "The nineteenth century," he writes, "is certainly as good as any other. My own view in fact is that it is better than its predecessors, and that, had one given me the choice, I would have delayed for several more centuries my entry into this world." But (he continues) the reality of progress should not lead one to presume the backwardness of the late medieval and early modern periods.[21] Repeatedly, he stresses the complexity of life and sentiment in the past; though he views the late nineteenth century as superior to earlier eras in comfort and manners, he defines the differences in terms of degree rather than of kind. The stance is especially clear when Franklin turns to the marketplace and workplace. Even in the thirteenth century, thus, in Parisian shops he finds signs of consumers' hunger for novelties and a readiness of shopkeepers to appeal to it.[22] "Those clever merchants who in the last few years have so successfully created our great department stores certainly believed themselves to be innovators," he writes in opening his volume on shopping. "I am sorry to dispel this illusion. The concept that they believe they have invented is at least six hundred years old." For Franklin, the medieval and early modern periods included complicated market relations, oriented to the varied desires of middle-class consumers.

His treatment of labor relations is similar. "From the thirteenth century," he writes, "the organization of labor, to be sure still very imperfect, had been studied with intelligence, and in many ways it rested on more liberal bases than nowadays." Franklin was aware of the political stakes in any such praise of the Old Regime's corporate organization: "Almost

20. *VP, Les soins de la toilette*, 9, 16, 20, 21, 25.
21. *VP, La cuisine* (1888), 3.
22. *VP, Les magasins de nouveautés*, vol. 1 (1894), 1–2, 5 ff.

always, an author [of studies on the guilds] is satisfied either to defend these institutions, or to exaggerate their vices, depending on what serves his own political or religious views." Franklin is not an apologist for the Old Regime's corporate life, whose disappearance (he adds) we should not regret. Rather (he suggests) empiricism leads naturally to certain forms of social criticism of the present. "My sole concern has been . . . to paint the milieu in which workers lived during more than six centuries. Such a subject provokes reflections and parallels at each step."[23]

The same impulse seems to lie behind Franklin's treatment of civility and manners. On the one hand, as we have seen, Franklin is eager to show the filth and disorder that characterized much premodern life. Yet he is also highly sensitive to the complexities of medieval and early modern practices. Thus he stresses the passion for education in the medieval and early modern periods, despite the often deplorable conditions within which it took place. Although unsystematically, he attempts to chart the dimensions of this early learning, and he finds them surprisingly wide; as one example, "men had no monopoly on education." The widely mentioned ignorance of medieval nobles and kings is convincingly dismissed as a legend. Franklin offers no statistics on literacy, but he carefully traces the development of schools for the lower classes.[24] This early history of literacy allies with an emphasis on the early development of elegant manners and of the self-control that these required. The early fifteenth century already employed "a highly detailed code of etiquette and precedence" and thus constitutes an argument against attributing the rise of good manners to Francis I or Louis XIV.[25] In sum, Franklin repeatedly takes up, tests, and rejects hypotheses about the otherness of earlier historical periods. He stresses the achievements of daily life in the past. Rather than barriers between past and present, he tends to see commonalities and linkages.

As one result, Franklin's history has noticeable political implications. The critique of existing social arrangements, he suggests, naturally follows acquaintance with the functioning of the past. An equally powerful message comes from Franklin's treatment of the great of the early modern world, and especially of its kings. For Franklin, the history of private life is partly an act of unmasking—literally so, for stripped of their public costumes, the great display all the flaws of ordinary human beings,

23. VP, *Comment on devenait patron* (1889), 2, 5.
24. VP, *Écoles et collèges* (1892), 141–42, 135, 144.
25. VP, *Variétés gastronomiques* (1891), 197.

and suffer all the indignities as well. Louis XIV serves as Franklin's favorite lesson in this regard. He uses the abundant documentation surrounding the king's ailments to explore the troubles that life might bring in the seventeenth century and to explicate their social context. His discussion starts with the king's lack of cleanliness, the habitual failing of seventeenth-century high society: "It is known . . . that the fistula that Louis XIV suffered sometimes results from a lack of cleanliness, and that lice often troubled the Sun King's sleep."[26] He recounts tales of the filth at Versailles, and mockingly notes its re-creation in the St. Cloud of Louis XVIII, "for the traditions of Versailles were scrupulously kept there."[27] His treatment of kings' private lives begins with ridicule.

Ridicule becomes stronger as Franklin follows Louis XIV's medical history, for that history abundantly illustrates the disparity between the grandiose pretensions of power and the realities of human frailty. "No human glory seemed equal to his. If, as Bossuet claims, He who rules in the heavens rules over kings, in truth He could find no better occasion for proving His power. He yielded to the temptation." Franklin then follows the details of Louis's fistula and its treatments. For a year, the doctors experimented with alternative remedies on other unfortunates; meanwhile, Louis's chief surgeon improved his skills by himself operating on all those in the Paris hospitals suffering from the affliction. Louis submitted to the operation with exemplary courage and calm and greeted his court almost immediately afterward; Franklin is appropriately impressed by this display of self-control. But he then undercuts his praise by describing the financial outcome of the operation. "The *great operation,* as it was called, cost France at least a million in our currency," he concludes, having added up the rewards that Louis lavished on his two surgeons, two physicians, four pharmacists, and one surgeon's apprentice. In Franklin's treatment, the episode suggests not only the despotic quality of Louis XIV's monarchy, but also the burden that it represented to "la France."[28]

By thus stressing kings' physical frailties and their cost to the nation, Franklin deliberately undermines the grandeur and creative power of monarchy. He does the same in discussing the history of civility, which he largely detaches from the king's influence. The court remained largely indifferent to hygiene through the eighteenth century, he finds; "salvation came from the hotel de Rambouillet, which . . . had the glory of spreading

26. VP, *Les soins de la toilette,* 37–38.
27. VP, *L'hygiène* (1890), 32 (quoting Viollet-le-Duc).
28. VP, *Les chirugiens,* 134–35, 141–42.

through France elegance, manners, urbanity, savoir-vivre."[29] Not the monarchy or court, but what Franklin would probably have described as the upper middle class, played the essential role in this civilizing process. The Church played a still less glorious role, actively discouraging cleanliness and good manners.

This political argument, that society's leaders ultimately have little impact on its most creative and significant developments, underlies Franklin's theory about the subject-matter of history itself. His text repeatedly stresses the significance of the history of private life—and the corresponding inadequacy of a history centering on the public and the political. His declaration opening a volume on cooking is characteristic: "[H]istory, as it is still understood today, never gives us a fully exact idea of the epoch that it seeks to depict. The political events that it registers so carefully in reality are only accidents in a people's existence and trouble less than one imagines its intimate life, up to now too little investigated."[30]

For Franklin as for the other nineteenth-century writers examined here, political events obscure rather than reveal the actual course of historical development. He finds an especially telling example in the history of the sixteenth century. The century was dominated by "the hateful dynasty of the last Valois," five kings who included "a child, a fool, and three gentlemen who together combined every vice, shame, and crime"; despite this political leadership, in the sixteenth century French culture and society flourished.[31] His own century will require a similar understanding, he suggested. Later historians will doubtless recoil in horror at the list of invasions, coups d'état, and revolutions that France suffered between 1815 and 1871. Yet (he argues) these events have proved essentially irrelevant to the improving texture of nineteenth-century life and will probably give future historians a misleading vision of nineteenth-century society.[32]

His historical researches brought Franklin respectful attention from the intellectual establishment of his day. Seven of his volumes received prizes, from the Academy of Medicine, the Academy of Moral and Practical Sciences, and the French Academy. Gabriel Monod, founder of the *Revue Historique* and a leader of the movement to create a scientific political history in France, praised one of the early volumes as "a collection that will be favorably received by all those interested in the social and

29. *VP, Les soins de la toilette,* 43.
30. *VP, La cuisine,* 1–2.
31. *VP, Les repas* (1889), 2.
32. *VP, La cuisine,* 2.

economic history of Old Regime France."[33] Already in 1868 a review in the *Journal des Savants*—journal of the Institut—likewise suggests the sympathetic context within which Franklin pursued his researches. Franklin had contributed a volume on early Parisian libraries to an *Histoire générale de Paris*, a project overseen by Baron Haussmann himself and supported by the Paris city council. Franklin received praise for his erudition, but the reviewer was most enthusiastic about another volume, devoted to Parisian chroniclers of the fourteenth and fifteenth centuries. The reviewer quoted with approval the editors' description of what the chroniclers offered: "We see them . . . strolling freely through the streets, . . . penetrating those houses of which the old maps show only the outlines, minutely depicting the interiors and showing us the residents. . . . [T]hey bring the reader into shop and church and make him see a whole world working, praying, teaching, suffering, or joyously taking its pleasures. It is the society of the times in full life."[34]

But more important than such official endorsements, Franklin's project fitted well with the intellectual preoccupations of writers like Sainte-Beuve and Taine, still at the height of their influence as he wrote. Like them, he sought to valorize the Rabelaisian tradition in French culture, and like them he looked with suspicion on the elites of the Old Regime. He shared their reluctance to view French history as a straightforward march of progress, their skeptical vision about the official pieties of contemporary life, and their belief that the real history of France consisted in its social experiences, rather than its politics. Clearly he had not thought so hard about these matters as they, and, however insightful, he remained an antiquarian, more concerned with striking details than broad interpretations. But he nonetheless offered a coherent vision of the historian's task, and it closely paralleled theirs. The historian was to explore the evolution of society, and in doing so force readers to think critically about their own world. Franklin was not a lone pioneer or eccentric, but a characteristic product of his times.

A History of Private Life appeared almost exactly a century after Franklin's first volume.[35] It is a collective enterprise, and nowhere more so than in volume 3, on the early modern period: fifteen authors—well-known

---

33. Monod, "Bulletin historique, France," 103.
34. *Journal des Savants*, February 1868, 126–27.
35. In the following section, page references to Ariès, *A History of Private Life*, vol. 3, are given parenthetically in the text.

specialists on the period, with distinguished work of their own—participated in the project. The number and distinction of the participants give
the work a complex tone and diverse interpretive stances. The contributors, however, are united in that all specialize in French history, and the
volume's conclusion frankly acknowledges that this is essentially an exploration of French private life, with brief comparative glances elsewhere
(609–11). Similarities of time and place justify comparing at least this
volume with Franklin's.

More important than its Frenchness, a clear thesis unites *A History of
Private Life*. The work argues for a sharp demarcation between modern
and the premodern worlds. Through 1789, so runs the argument, these
worlds overlapped in complicated ways. Modernity triumphed in some
domains of life, struggled in others; it touched some social classes more
decisively than others. Yet such complications did not diminish the essential conflict between these two modes of living and thinking. Philippe
Ariès opens the volume by stressing these programmatic themes and the
importance of the division that they imply. "From the central Middle Ages
to the end of the seventeenth century," he writes, "there was no real change
in people's fundamental attitudes." What changed thereafter was in fact
the attitude to private life itself. Before the eighteenth century, Europeans
lived mainly in collectivities; since then, they have lived alone or in very
small groupings. For the historian of private life, Ariès concludes, the
central question becomes, "How was the transition between these two
historical periods made?" (2). In the program thus sketched, private life
has a history rather than merely a past. It emerged at a specific moment,
through the working of specific causes. It has not always existed, and will
not necessarily continue to exist in the future.

This interpretive program, with its dichotomous vision of worlds in
conflict, recurs throughout the substantive sections of the book, despite
the complexity and subtlety of the material that these present. The conflict affected the most basic domains of life. In the seventeenth century,
thus, "the cyclical image of time gradually gave way to a more linear,
more segmented view of existence. . . . The individual, no longer in the
shadow of the family, acquired a distinctive personality of his own" (316).
Social class further limited the place of individualism in the premodern
world. Nicole Castan writes: "[F]or those who lived humbly, and especially
for the masses of peasants scattered throughout the countryside, there was
no freedom. Family and work imposed constraints that left little room

for innovation, except for those willing to risk uprooting themselves and enduring the attendant uncertainties. Few who renounced the certainties of tradition survived" (444). In turn, a weak sense of the individual's significance diminished attachment to children. Only after about 1700 did there emerge a new "will to keep [children] alive" (314).

Similar terminology dominates the book's discussions of early modern cultural practices. Having explored popular festivals, Daniel Fabre describes "a debate between tradition and ritual on the one hand and legal and bureaucratic modernity on the other" (564). Maurice Aymard writes that "a new, more inward and autonomous view of the individual gained prominence, opening the way to new forms of friendship" (470). Roger Chartier opens his discussion of reading patterns by speaking of "the fundamental tension between two cultures: one increasingly based on recourse to the written word in both the public and the private spheres; the other based on nostalgic and utopian esteem for a society without writing, governed by words that everyone could hear and signs that everyone could understand" (123). Jean-Marie Goulemot adds the example of literary production: "Medieval literature was oral and public. . . . [It] was for the most part anonymous. Writers belonged to the community." Even apparently individualistic writers convey "not so much the inner life of the individual as the unhappy consciousness of having violated the rules of the community. Unhappiness is born of separation" from the community (363). This dependence on the community diminished in the seventeenth century, when a "new importance attached to the individual subject at the expense of the collective subject," an "emphasis on the individual at the expense of the collective" (382).

The list of early modern transformations is thus a long one. It includes visions of time, childhood and the family, space, communication. Ultimately, the history of private life thus seen adjoins the history of individualism. "To be sure," writes Chartier in introducing one section of the book, "the history of private life should not be confused with the constitution of the individual as subject. . . . But the new concept of the individual had an important influence on the definition of private space in the early modern era" (165). If this history is not limited to "the constitution of the individual as subject," it nonetheless treats that development as a fundamental theme in early modern history.

Hence certain omissions in this history of private life, subjects whose neglect is especially striking in view of the fascination they held for

Franklin. *A History of Private Life* largely dispenses with a history of the body and leaves bodily indignities almost untouched. Only one of the fourteen chapters deals with food and drink. Sexuality and medicine appear only as tangential topics in chapters devoted mainly to other questions; homosexuality is never mentioned. In his conclusion Chartier describes one element in this relative inattention to corporeal matters: "[P]rimary importance was accorded to sentiments and values rather than to the history of material culture" in such matters as housing and dress (610). But the exclusion extends further than this comment would suggest, to the bodies and bodily practices that figure so largely in Franklin's account.

A similar orientation appears in the patterns of causation that the volume presents. Given the book's commitment to exploring how Europeans moved from one cultural world to another, explanatory mechanisms necessarily play a crucial role within it. *A History of Private Life* offers three engines of change: the state, the Reformations (Catholic and Protestant alike), and the development of literacy (15). In this account, causes are mainly cultural and political. Noticeably absent are the market or workplace; indeed, economic arrangements and changes play scarcely any role in the book. Very little is said about urbanization. Nor do changes come from oppositional groups or from tensions about normative practices. Rather, norms themselves—jointly produced by church and state—play the crucial role in creating the modern world.

This is perhaps most evident in the volume's treatment of the royal court. Again and again, the contributors stress the primacy of the courtly aristocracy in the transitions that they depict. "Fashions in manners were inaugurated by the entourage of the king and the leading nobles," writes Jean-Louis Flandrin (269). He refers mainly to cuisine, but his emphasis on the cultural leadership of the great recurs throughout *A History of Private Life.* "The court and the city led the way, the provinces followed," writes Castan (428). Old Regime society "was dominated by a privileged minority capable of thinking in new ways about the division between the public and the private. For the favored few, protected by law and social institutions, access to private life was a sign of freedom" (444). Here and throughout, modern culture tends to trickle down from elite to masses. The contrast with Franklin is stark. He stressed the freedoms of the marketplace, with its long tradition of myriad offerings. His successors stress the formative powers of the court, with its insistence on self-control, and the chances for psychological development that affluence offered the great.

The distance from Franklin shows up even in relatively small matters.

Thus, like Franklin, Madeleine Foisil examines Louis XIV's medical troubles. Unlike Franklin, she presents these not in a separate section on medicine and hygiene, but rather as an example of the "literature of intimacy"; here the body's experiences are subordinated to the culture of self-reflection. Foisil uses scholarly sources that Franklin did not, including the manuscript diary of the king's physician, whereas Franklin used only the less-informed comments of courtiers and other observers. Yet there is a price for this scholarly perspective, for Foisil unquestioningly adopts the perspective of her sources. "There is no splendor in this document, only the misery of an afflicted body," she writes (358). But a form of greatness in fact emerges from the catalog of Louis's sufferings, for in this account suffering resulted from the king's devotion to duty. "Pain and suffering did not exempt the king from performance of his duties. . . . Public events affected the king's health. Military campaigns were fatiguing. . . . His diligent attention to affairs of state brought Louis XIV the usual host of problems associated with the sedentary life. . . . Private sorrows inevitably affected the king physically, despite what Fagon [Louis's physician] called his 'unshakeable courage in pain and peril'" (360–61). No mention is made of lice or the other forms of uncleanliness that Franklin so relished describing. Nor does money enter her discussion: we hear no echo of Franklin's calculations of how much Louis's troubles cost "la France." Franklin too admired Louis's courage, but ultimately the king's maladies taught other lessons: about the frailties of those in power, about the disparity between their grandiose claims and their personal habits, about the cost of maintaining the powerful. Foisil emphasizes instead the burdens of power, stoically assumed.

A History of Private Life thus inverts several of the themes running through Franklin's La vie privée. Franklin stressed the presence of modern elements in even the thirteenth century, and he underlined the radical implications of focusing on private life. Above all, he stressed a corporeal vision of private life, as an alternative, even antithetical past to be set alongside the lofty claims of political and religious history. His successors have emphasized instead the disjunctures of past and present, and they direct attention to the dominant role of political and religious history: the state and the Church perform the task of "constituting the individual as a subject."

A generation ago, such a finding would have surprised critics of French historical writing. Even sympathetic historians saw the Annalistes and their associates as insufficiently attuned to issues of political power,[36] and crit-ics saw them as lacking sympathetic understanding for the workings of Old Regime society. Such expectations might suggest that *A History of Private Life* constitutes a radical departure from previous *Annales* school practice; later in this chapter I will explore this possibility in detail and suggest grounds for rejecting it.

But understanding *A History of Private Life* must begin with its more immediate intellectual background, and with the individual whose thought dominates much of the book. Philippe Ariès in fact planned the project and with Georges Duby served as its general editor. He died in 1983, be-fore it could be completed, but his influence remains visible throughout. The work's dedication spells out this influence: "This book was willed, conceived, and prepared by Philippe Ariès. . . . We, the contributors, have written it with his goals and thoughts of his friendship in our minds." Chartier repeats the point in concluding Volume 3: "[W]e have tried to keep faith with the intentions of the man whose idea this series was—Philippe Ariès" (611).

Ariès had a complex career. Born into a Catholic and royalist family, he studied at the Sorbonne during the late 1930s and participated as an Action Française activist in the street clashes of Popular Front era.[37] Although a serious student, like Hippolyte Taine before him he failed the orals for the *agrégation*, the highly competitive examination that admit-ted one to French academic life. After brief military service in 1940, in 1943 he entered government service, at the Institute of Applied Research for Tropical and Subtropical Fruits. He remained there for the following thirty years, but combined this career with an extraordinary series of pub-lications. A first book appeared in 1943, on French regionalism. This was followed by important works on demography, historiography, the history of childhood, and attitudes to death. Ariès in short occupied a situation not unlike Alfred Franklin's. Both were amateur historians who worked on the margins of Parisian academic life, and both were strongly marked by their religious milieus.

Also like Franklin, Ariès was never a real outsider on the Parisian intel-lectual scene, despite his occasional readiness to claim the role and call

36. Hunt, "French History in the Last Twenty Years," 209–24. Such reservations are of course entirely inappropriate to the most recent developments within the *Annales* school, which have seen an impressive turn toward studies of the state and of politics.

37. Ariès, *Un historien du dimanche*, 30–36, 61–71, 121, 210; E. Weber, in *Action Française*, 53–55, describes the role of the student movement, the *camelots du roi*, in the 1930s.

attention to his unusual professional position. From the outset he took a critical, superior stance toward the intellectual life of the universities. In 1949 he wrote of the "radical isolation of university history," its inability to interest anyone but specialists. The professors' writings were dry and dull because the professors themselves were outsiders, drawn either from religious minorities or from the lower orders of society.[38] Although outside the university, Ariès thus could confidently assume a prominent role in Parisian cultural debates. From the late 1940s he had an editorial role in one of the major French publishing houses, and there he eventually directed one of the country's best-known series on history and social science. His 1948 work on French population placed him in contact with specialists in the developing field of historical demography. In 1955 he helped to found a conservative weekly newspaper, and he produced for it a series of brilliant columns, on topics ranging from labor conflicts at Citroën to recent performances of Racine. Only with the 1960 publication of his book *L'enfant et la vie familiale sous l'Ancien Régime* did he become widely known among historians. The work was soon translated into English, and for a time Ariès was better known among American historians than in France. But his works received increasing attention there too: already in 1956 he had addressed the Académie des Sciences Morales on the Old Regime family.[39] In 1980 these efforts received an additional form of official recognition: he was invited to join the École des Hautes Etudes en Sciences Sociales, the center of the *Annales* school itself.

In a series of interviews late in his life, Ariès reflected on the sources of his intellectual interests and development. Some of these he located in the work of the early *Annales* historians themselves. While at the Sorbonne he read Lucien Febvre and Marc Bloch, and he cited Bloch with approval in his first published work, in 1943—despite the risks of praising a Jewish scholar in occupied Paris.[40] But Ariès also made it clear that a different kind of influence marked him earlier and more profoundly, that of the royalist Action Française, the movement founded by Charles Maurras. His family had belonged to the movement, and he married within it.[41]

38. Ariès, *Le temps de l'histoire*, 274–75; I have discussed this view in Chapter 1. For a recent restatement of this view, that university historians have lacked the cultural breadth of their nineteenth-century predecessors, see Kaplan, *Adieu '89*, 752–59, analyzing the views of François Furet.

39. *La Nation Française*, 7 March 1956.

40. In his work *Le temps de l'histoire*, written in the late 1940s, Ariès praised Bloch and Febvre for having revitalized a nearly moribund French academic historical writing.

41. Ariès, *Un historien du dimanche*, 70, 121.

La Nation Française, the weekly newspaper to which he contributed, demonstrated both the intensity and the complexity of those influences.[42] Its title deliberately recalled Maurras's *L'Action Française*; its editor, Pierre Boutang, had served as Maurras's secretary;[43] and the journal took pains to sustain Action Française positions. It regularly celebrated the royal family, and it continued to defend Pétain and Maurras himself in the unpropitious circumstances of the late 1950s. The parliamentary politics of the Fourth Republic evoked the journal's unremitting scorn. "The idea of counting votes to determine sovereign power will make our grandchildren laugh, if it does not first destroy our race," opened a commentary in 1955; a front-page editorial in 1956 described "democracy, that mad queen," as having "drawn to our fields and cities the miseries that Charles VI's madness brought upon them. Again foreigners have become powerful in Paris, as during the time of Bedford," during the English occupation of the Hundred Years War. Other of the journal's commentaries developed this xenophobic thread, and occasionally added to it an allusive anti-Semitism—at least where the rival journalists of *L'Express* were concerned. A lead editorial in 1957 in *Nation Française* addressed Jean-Jacques Servan-Schreiber: "You are, sir, . . . *mendès-français* in nationality"; another in 1955 spoke of Françoise Giroud, "whose name is not Giroud and who comes to us from the Carpathians," as appealing only to those "who enjoy being insulted by shameless immigrants."[44]

Although he shared his colleagues' admiration for monarchy in general and the French royal family in particular, Ariès seems to have been genuinely immune to such angry tribalism. He disagreed in print with some of his fellow writers on issues of national identity and strongly denounced instances of racial intolerance.[45] His journalism in fact resembled his scholarship and often made use of it. But the incendiary Boutang remained a close friend, and Ariès shared with all his fellow editors an intense concern about the spiritual and social dangers of modern life. Thus, in a 1958 book that he wrote jointly with them, he spoke of the "grand vide" of the modern world, in which "there remains only an overdeveloped professional and work life, and a reduced and lifeless private existence." Technocratic individualism, the true heir of the Enlightenment, had produced

42. For an excellent overview of *La Nation Française*, see Verdès-Leroux, *Refus et violences*, 455–65.
43. For a brief sketch of Boutang and his place in French political life, see Lévi, *Adventures on the Freedom Road*, 149–54
44. *La Nation Française*, 20 March 1957, 14 December 1955, 2 November 1955, 9 May 1956.
45. For examples, see *La Nation Française*, 8, 22 February 1956, 1 October 1958.

"une solitude humaine désolée" as the characteristic mark of modernity. Materialistic excess was one manifestation of this societal breakdown: French highways, wrote the editors, were clogged with "voitures trop neuves," whose occupants concerned themselves only with private inter-ests.[46] For Ariès, the confrontation between old society and new was a daily reality rather than an episode in the vanished past—hence its significance to discussions of current politics. His contribution to the volume opened with a ringing invocation of how recently the old world had died: "The generation of 1880, that of our fathers, even of our own early childhood, knew in France the last traces—living traces—of a very old, complex, care-fully constructed society." That society still survived in the underdeveloped world—"[T]oday," he suggested, "there is no better way to bring back to life our medieval and early modern ancestors than travel through the cities of northern Africa or the countryside of central Africa"—but there too modernity threatened. "The breakup before our eyes of those traditional societies under the impact of our colonization reproduces directly [tout simplement], though at a more rapid pace, the splintering of our own Old Regime society between the late eighteenth and late nineteenth centuries. This millennial world disappeared in a single century in the most advanced parts of the West."[47] For Ariès, old and new regimes represented antithet-ical modes of thinking and living, and the difference had ethical overtones. For that reason, understanding the difference formed an important task of contemporary social and political thought.

Late in his life, Ariès described his intellectual development in terms of a dual process of liberation, from both the conventional history of the Sorbonne and from some of the values of the Action Française. Each tra-dition, he suggested in his memoirs, understood history only in terms of the state. He wrote: "That there existed a society outside the state, that this society changed and that its changes owed nothing to the state's actions, good or bad—this idea was entirely new and scandalous to right-wing his-toriography." A few historians had begun to reveal "the existence of an autonomous social space, in which nonpolitical forces—religious, eco-nomic, cultural—had free play," but this space was "scarcely imagined by the pre-Annales historians."[48] Ariès thus enthusiastically endorsed the Annalistes' view that they had enlarged the "historian's territory" by cre-ating an alternative to narrowly political history. Dissatisfied with the

46. Ariès et al., Écrits pour une Renaissance, 212, 220, v–vi.
47. Ariès et al., Écrits pour une Renaissance, 204.
48. Ariès, Un historien du dimanche, 56.

intellectual possibilities offered elsewhere, he eventually found his way to the intellectual space that Febvre and Bloch had cleared.

But Ariès's description of his intellectual development is not fully adequate. He had in fact read Taine with care and appreciation, and his own right-wing political milieu in fact encouraged its members to engage with other early advocates of social history.[49] Maurras called on his followers to turn to Sainte-Beuve, the literary critic and historian, as an antidote to the inadequacies of Michelet and Chateaubriand. Part of Sainte-Beuve's appeal to Maurras lay precisely in his effort to develop a "natural history of the feelings."[50] Maurras sought similarly to appropriate the medievalist Fustel de Coulanges for the Action Française and in 1905 launched his followers on a dramatic campaign to celebrate the anniversary of Fustel's birth.[51] Thirty years later Fustel remained a patron saint of royalist historiography. A reviewer in the royalist *Revue des questions historiques* praised him for having carried out "a reform in the manner of writing history." The reform, according to the *Revue,* consisted in rejecting the political history of Langlois, Seignobos, and Lavisse, precisely the objects of *Annales* criticism during the same years. Instead, Fustel sought to know "what those people [in the past] ate, how they dressed"; he "loved to enter as much as he could into the detail of lives, and he used to say, 'I am after men, both those of the past and those of today.'"[52] Like Taine and Sainte-Beuve, Fustel could be read as calling for a history that focused on the private.

With this background in mind, it is instructive to consider some of the overtones of Ariès's scholarly work. His work displays remarkable inventiveness and brilliance. At the same time, Ariès's political values are readily visible beneath the scholarly surface. Like his political writings, his historical work stresses the brutality of the transition to modernity. His pioneering *Histoire des populations françaises,* first published in 1948, stated the issue with particular force. At this most fundamental level, the

---

49. Ariès supplied a substantial preface to François Leger's *La jeunesse d'Hippolyte Taine.*

50. Maurras, *Trois idées politiques,* 260.

51. For excellent discussion of these efforts, see Hartog, *Le XIXe siècle et l'histoire,* 168–94; specifically on the Fustel de Coulanges affair, see Weber, *Action Française,* 36–38; Capot de Quissac, "L'Action Française," 139–91.

52. Gérin-Ricard, "L'héritage de Fustel de Coulanges," 3–11. Cf. Bloch, *Historian's Craft,* 24–25. Bloch at once acknowledges Fustel's point, emphasizes its nineteeenth-century air by stressing his concern with "man" in the abstract, and imitates his language: "The good historian . . . knows that wherever he catches the scent of human flesh, there his quarry lies." Hartog, in *Le cas Fustel,* 165, also notes the degree to which Lavisse and Seignobos have been targets for widely divergent schools of historical writing. In Ariès's youth, the right-wing students' association at the Sorbonne remained the Cercle Fustel de Coulanges.

level of birth and death, he argues in the book, humanity must be divided between two modes of existence: "during the greatest part of its existence, humanity has never succeeded in affecting its demographic existence. . . . In modern times, on the contrary, . . . life escapes from the realm of natural, uncontrollable forces, and bends before human science. . . . The principal factor of fecundity is, henceforth, the conscious, voluntary thought of man, of the individual or of the state. One cannot imagine, in fact, a more profound revolution in morals and behavior. This is, indeed, the most important fact in our history, though it has escaped the attention of historians and sociologists."[53] Looking back on statements such as these, Ariès in 1971 acknowledged the simplifications they contained and explained that he would now probably rewrite them in more nuanced form. Yet he held to the book's central theme of difference, as helping to explicate "the aggression of modernity" against the traditional world; rewritten in 1971, his book would remain an exploration of a fundamental change in human nature.[54]

Philippe Ariès brought to *A History of Private Life* a sensibility that was critical of the modern world and sharply attuned to its differences from traditional society. His historical writing emerged from an intense engagement with the contemporary world and an interest in acting within it, forming only one element in a larger interest in the nature of modernity itself. This combination of fear and fascination (so runs a central argument of this book) characterized many nineteenth-century students of French history, supplying one of the principal motors propelling the early development of social history. But in the years after 1945 such conservatism was an unusual choice among Parisian intellectuals. The experience of occupation and decolonization had discredited Charles Maurras and his followers, leaving left-wing politics the norm among French intellectuals,[55] in contrast to mood during Ariès's student days, when the Right had typically dominated the Quartier Latin. It is thus striking that Ariès could move so easily into the intellectual world of the *Annales* school, without any apparent strains or transformations on either side. What does his easy integration into the *Annales* historical world tell us about the movement's interactions with the society around it?

There can be no single answer to such questions, for even in its earliest

53. Ariès, *Histoire des populations françaises*, 344.
54. Ariès, *Histoire des populations françaises*, 5, 6.
55. Judt, in *Past Imperfect*, 16–44, acutely analyzes the degree of change that this represented.

days the *Annales* brought together historians of differing temperaments and political views; and few expressed their political positions so clearly as Ariès, or turned to the past with such hopes of finding insight into the contemporary world. In his memoirs, Ariès himself attributed his sudden success partly to the atmosphere that surrounded the events of May 1968. To the 1968 generation, he appealed as an outsider historian, a "marchand de bananes" (as he heard himself described, by those who misunderstood his research position) who stood outside the system of degrees, examinations, and cooptation that dominated French academic life, and who interested himself in elemental experiences such as family life and childhood, rather than more conventional topics. To all this was added Ariès's success with readers outside France: French historians took serious note of his work only after its success in the United States.[56]

But alongside these external conditions, there were also deeper intellectual affinities between Ariès and his new colleagues. Ariès exemplified the ideal of linking historical study to reflection on contemporary life, in just the way that Febvre and Bloch had urged since the 1920s. Nor in the end were *Annales* politics quite so remote from Ariès's as might be imagined. Febvre and Bloch were of the freethinking political Left, but their correspondence during the 1930s shows them as infuriated by the Soviet historians they encountered.[57] They enjoyed warm relations with some French Marxists, and the Marxist specialist on the French Revolution Georges Lefebvre collaborated with them during the journal's early days. But they viewed the theory itself with good-natured condescension. Febvre admired the intelligence and hard work of the young Marxist sociologist Georges Friedmann, but he also wrote mockingly to Bloch about the young man's enthusiasm; Friedmann's eyes filled with tears at every mention of Marx's name, Febvre remarked.[58] Characteristic of their situation at the center of the French political spectrum, during the 1950s members of the *Annales* movement were denounced by both members of the Communist Party, for their supposed pro-American tendencies, and by conservatives, as communists.[59]

Bloch translated this political centrism into a briskly practical vision of French modernization, spurred by his reflections on the French defeat of 1940 and his disdain for the policies that had produced it. He dismissed

56. Ariès, *Un historien du dimanche*.
57. Müller, *Marc Bloch, Lucien Febvre*, 1:419, 420–21, 424.
58. Müller, *Marc Bloch, Lucien Febvre*, 1:391.
59. Le Roy Ladurie, *Paris-Montpellier*, 224.

antimodernist criticisms as barely more than propaganda. "Every day I hear 'back to the land' sermons on the radio. The French people . . . are told: '. . . You had become the chaff of the great city, of the factory, perhaps, even, of the school, whereas what your nature craves is the village or the market-town familiar to your ancestors, . . . the small compact society governed by its local notables.' . . . These bucolic recommendations are, however, nothing new. They were made familiar to us, in the years before the war, through a whole literature of renunciation. It was forever, this literature, lashing what it called 'Americanization.' It denounced the dangers of the machine and of material progress." In fact, he argued, some degree of American-style modernization would be necessary for France's resurrection. "If only to preserve what can, and ought to, be of value in our great heritage, we must adapt ourselves to the claims of a new age."[60] Adaptation might involve genuine losses, but Bloch expressed little sense that the modernization process involved a tragic clash of civilizations.

But Febvre used more dramatic language, and his view of modernization as a clash of civilizations closely resembled Ariès's. In 1946 his "Manifesto of the new *Annales*" (discussed in Chapter 4) sought to situate the journal within a postwar world marked by the "prodigious acceleration" of contacts among once-isolated societies. "That is how our world has been destroyed," he told the journal's readers, in a striking reinterpretation of what World War II had meant. "All the drama is there, in the drama of civilizations. It was visible in 1932. It is playing itself out in 1946."[61] Globalization had helped produce the war itself, and it made the postwar world a dangerous place, one that made ever-new demands on its intellectuals.

This contemporary experience of modernization, Febvre argued, would necessarily shape the historian's agenda, and the younger generation of *Annales* historians agreed. In a 1959 article François Furet, who would eventually serve as editor of the journal, summarized the importance that many younger French intellectuals attached to these questions: "The future will doubtless show that the history of these past ten years in France has been dominated by two great problems: the economic modernization of the country, and decolonization."[62] On the one hand, France itself was undergoing rapid economic development; on the other, like other Europeans the French were defining their relations with their onetime colonies.

60. Bloch, *Strange Defeat*, 147–48, 149.
61. Febvre, "À nos lecteurs," 2.
62. Furet, *Itinéraire intellectuel*, 55.

For France, of course, both processes were especially violent, with war in Indochina and Algeria, and a variety of political struggles at home. Furet noted the parallel between these two movements. In France itself, new forms of industrial organization confronted traditional small enterprises, while elements of this confrontation were replayed in the relations between the advanced metropole and its more backward colonies. Furet's contemporary Emmanuel Le Roy Ladurie, who would eventually join him on the editorial board of the *Annales,* likewise exemplified the centrality of these questions for intellectuals in the 1950s and 1960s. Until 1956 a member of the Communist Party, Le Roy Ladurie participated in an intense round of student militancy supporting anticolonial movements in North Africa and Asia, and his first work of historical scholarship concerned French colonialism during the late nineteenth century.[63] Postwar French historians could scarcely avoid the issues that Febvre's manifesto raised.

And, just as Febvre had urged, these themes appeared in their historical work on the early modern period, as well as in their immediate political engagements. Fernand Braudel's *The Mediterranean and the Mediterranean World* (published in 1949) showed how the early modern world could be understood in terms of precisely those circulations, interchanges, and conflicts that worried Febvre about the twentieth century, for much of the book dealt with encounters between more and less developed culture zones: in it, shepherds from the mountains encounter urbanites from the plains; north Italian bankers encounter aristocratic Spain, a country lacking the cultural resources to exploit its own wealth; and Islam encounters Christianity. In each case, cultural encounters produce misunderstandings and anger, and occasionally they produce violence. In Braudel's sixteenth century as in Febvre's twentieth, new contacts between peoples produce dramatic, unpredictable consequences. Braudel only hinted at the contemporary relevance of these encounters, but the issue clearly concerned him: "I would go so far as to say," he wrote in the work's preface, that the problems he had studied "serve to illumine our own century, that they are not lacking in that 'utility' in the strict sense which Nietzsche demanded of all history."[64]

A similar imagery of civilizations in conflict runs through the greatest work of the following generation of *Annales* historical writing, Le Roy

63. Le Roy Ladurie, *Paris-Montpellier*, 88–90, 117–18.
64. Braudel, *Mediterranean and the Mediterranean World*, 1:19.

Ladurie's *Les paysans de Languedoc*, published in 1966. Despite its title, the book has much to say about the region's merchants and officials, and one of its principal concerns is to understand how these groups managed to enforce their will on the much more numerous peasantry. For explanations, Le Roy Ladurie looked closely at the influence of geography, agricultural technology, and institutions. But his analysis suggests that bourgeois power rested ultimately on psychological mechanisms: fear dominated the peasants' outlook, shaping their economic and political choices, constricting their personal lives, and reducing their capacity for political action, even when rebellion might have been effective. Le Roy Ladurie spoke of "that traditional, ethnological, neurosis of traditional societies, which today is disappearing from the more advanced societies." Sexual repression was central to this traditional outlook. It at once expressed the society's material impoverishment—which allowed no margin for excessive pleasures— and weakened the will of oppressed groups to resist their oppressors. "Materially impoverished, sexually very repressed, traditional society . . . thus seems characterized, among its popular classes, by a double series of frustrations and scarcities, which reciprocally reinforce and shape one another."[65] Hence Le Roy Ladurie explored with particular attention peasants' use of sexual imagery at moments of political and social conflict. His analysis of the 1579 Carnival of Romans (an analysis that he later expanded into a full book) stressed the hesitancy with which peasants confronted their social superiors, a hesitancy expressed in symbols of masculinity: whereas bourgeois adopted various phallic symbols as their emblems, peasants and workers used images of neutered animals. Sorcery testified to the same fears; Le Roy Ladurie focused on a particular kind of sorcery, by which bridegrooms were rendered impotent.

Thus for Le Roy Ladurie material and psychological poverty went together. Early modern society "did not possess, at least not yet and not sufficiently—widely disseminated among elites [*les groupes dirigeants*] and among the people—the outlook, the culture, the ethic, the political values, the education, the reformist spirit, the drive for happiness, which would have permitted the economy's 'takeoff.'"[66] Hence the critical importance of literacy, as an engine of cultural change during the early modern period. "The advance of education is inseparable, even among the lower classes, from a certain transfiguration of psychologies, and from a general softening of behavior [*moeurs*]," leading to a decline of violence and of religious

65. Le Roy Ladurie, *Paysans de Languedoc*, 359, 360.
66. Le Roy Ladurie, *Paysans de Languedoc*, 360.

fanaticism. These processes led to a division between two almost completely distinct societies: in the backcountry, illiteracy, violence, and "religious fanaticism, complete with neurotic symptoms"; in the towns,
literacy, peace, and religious good sense. "Produced in greater numbers,
these men—educated, sharp-witted, practical and calculating—in the long
run would produce solid economic growth [*les bonnes croissances*]."[67] Elsewhere in *Les paysans* he speaks of how "anguish returned in full force,
with its ancient hallucinations, and one sees reappear, in the behavior of
the masses, recurrences of a 'pensée sauvage'"—an allusion, of course, to
the term that anthropologist Claude Lévi-Strauss had applied to contemporary non-European peoples.[68]

In his casual allusions to "la société traditionelle," "'le décollage,'" "les
bonnes croissances," and "la pensée sauvage," Le Roy Ladurie in his historical writing thus insisted on analogies between underdeveloped Europe
and the contemporary world—a world that, like sixteenth-century Languedoc, included its own struggles between underdeveloped peasants and
the bourgeois who held power over them. He viewed that encounter with
a complete lack of sentimentality about traditional life. *Les paysans* repeatedly stresses the material and psychological miseries that the lower classes
suffered in traditional French society, and Le Roy Ladurie underlined this
point a decade later, in his 1975 book *Montaillou*: "[T]hanks to him," he
wrote of one of the book's characters, the shepherd Pierre Maury, "I have
encountered in a lower-class milieu the fragile image of a certain happiness in the Old Regime."[69] Happiness was rare and fleeting for ordinary
people in traditional society, his remark indicated, and the happy man on
whom he had stumbled was in fact exceptional in a variety of other ways,
a wandering shepherd, unencumbered by wife, family, or communal ties;
and in any case his happy wanderings were cut short by the Inquisition,
which imprisoned him for heresy. A powerful streak of anger runs through
Les paysans's explication of how the Old Regime functioned. In these circumstances, the book makes clear, peasant rebellion was a normal, altogether justified fact of early modern life.

But if the book's sympathies are with the lower classes, its historical
analysis repeatedly points to their need for outside political leadership.
On their own, they could produce only an ineffectual, distorted imitation
of true rebellion. In the later sixteenth century, he wrote, a peasantry

67. Le Roy Ladurie, *Paysans de Languedoc*, 365–66, 367.
68. Le Roy Ladurie, *Paysans de Languedoc*, 247.
69. Le Roy Ladurie, *Montaillou village occitan*, 196.

assaulted on all sides "turned to escapism, a prey to old hallucinations, giving itself up to all its demons; in place of a real liberation, it attempted the adventure of a satanic revolt. Between these imaginary revolts and true popular revolts, . . . there were geographical, chronological, in some instances familial overlaps. But above all, between sorcerers' sabbaths and popular revolts there were deeper linkages, at the level of mental structures and the unconscious mind." Class hatred was justifiable, but its effectiveness was limited by peasant psychology. Only cultural change could make possible an authentic resistance to injustice—and such change could come only from those who held power in society. If the rebellions of the sixteenth century failed, he wrote, this was because "reasonable struggles . . . were not yet guided by an enlightened elite, bearers of the Enlightenment and of a modern conception of man."[70] Literacy would be the avenue from collective neurosis to reason, and the primary agents of literacy would be the Old Regime's social elites, its clergy and administrators.

With this vision of class conflict, Le Roy Ladurie's account of the confrontation between bourgeois and peasants takes an unexpected turn. Only when the bourgeoisie's victims have taken on its culture can they resist it effectively; and they can acquire these cultural tools only through the actions of the bourgeoisie itself, either in the form of an "élite éclairée," perhaps recruited from the peasantry itself or through the actions of established institutions. Despite its genuinely radical sensibility, then, *Les paysans* ultimately adopts an interpretive scheme that focuses on the role of enlightened leadership. Like Jean Jaurès (as seen in Chapter 2, above), Le Roy Ladurie's radicalism did not cut him off from the broad consensus in French historical culture about the value of enlightened thought. On the contrary: like scholars ranging from Jaurès on the Left, through Lucien Febvre in the Center-Left, to Charles Maurras on the far Right, Le Roy Ladurie presented enlightened rationality as a precondition for effective action in the world, political resistance included. Given this agreement on the central issues of historical change, Ariès's right-wing views proved no barrier to effective collaboration with *Annales* scholars. As argued throughout this study, French historical culture transcended party politics.

In *A History of Private Life,* Philippe Ariès and his team revisited historical questions that Alfred Franklin had explored late in the nineteenth century. Documents and techniques had of course accumulated in the century

---

70. Le Roy Ladurie, *Paysans de Languedoc,* 244, 246–47.

since Franklin wrote, but to a surprising degree twentieth-century scholars used sources that he used—and in such fields as the histories of eating and cleanliness they largely repeated his findings. In other respects,
however, Franklin's history of private life differed profoundly from that
of his successors. Three interrelated differences seem especially important. First, Franklin's private life was above all a life of the body and its
care. Histories of clothing, cleanliness and dirt, medical care, and the like
received the bulk of his attention, and he stressed the importance of extending historical research into these domains. From these researches he drew
the message that Mikhail Bakhtin and others have read in Rabelais himself. For Franklin understanding physical life in the past undermined
respect for social distinctions and hierarchies. Hence a second important
difference from his successors: in his work, study of the private reveals
society's divisions, rather than its coherence. Dissent, far from being
impossible or unthinkable, in fact inheres in the private, for the body naturally resists social orderings. In its lack of dignity, the body served Franklin as a figure of democracy. Third, Franklin's history tended to stress
commonalities between past and present—again partly because of his
emphasis on the body's role in private life. His late medieval men and
women shared the economic urges of their modern descendants, just
as they shared physical traits. They too sought this-worldly comforts and
pleasures. As a result, they turned to the marketplaces where such comforts were on offer.

In contrast, differences between past and present constitute a central
theme in *A History of Private Life*. Modernity, so these volumes argue,
brought with it new sensibilities, new psychologies, new relationships
among people and between people and the material world; it constituted
a break with a millennial past. In this emphasis, as Ariès understood, *A
History of Private Life* fits well within the traditions of *Annales* historiography. Febvre, Braudel, and Le Roy Ladurie all stressed the fundamental
barriers between different cultures, and all three explored the political
implications of this vision of culture. Cultural differences, they suggested,
produced political power, allowing some groups to dominate others and
causing real social damage. Yet the radicalism in this position, with its
stress on inequality and privation, allied with a stress on the creative role
of elites within French history. On their own, the Rabelaisian traditions
of French popular culture could neither disrupt existing societal structures
nor even produce personal happiness. Prosperity and psychological stability awaited the adoption of literacy, manners, and forms of introspection

first developed at court and among the upper bourgeoisie. Whereas Franklin saw public and private as fundamentally opposed histories, then, the *Annales* group presented them as mutually reinforcing. Private lives do not disrupt or challenge political structures, but rather display the extent of their power to shape particular situations; this is in some measure a history of how political and cultural norms function within the personal microcosm. As a result, the political messages of this history are ambiguous. It highlights the injustices of the Old Regime, but it also stresses the role of the regime's elites in bringing about a better society. In this sense the intellectual journey taken by Ariès, from the world of French conservatism to the social history of the *Annales* group, was an easier one than might be imagined. Beneath real differences they shared central assumptions about how societies functioned and changed.

6

NOBLES AS SIGNIFIERS:
MAKING SENSE OF A CLASS STRUCTURE

As Europe's traditional ruling class, the nobility holds a central yet ambiguous place in an examination of modern historical thought. Aristocratic persons and deeds had constituted the core of traditional historical narrative, which described great men and their doings. But already by the late eighteenth century, writers had also begun to describe nobles as ill adapted to the conditions of modern life, which had little place for their commitments to the values of honor and autonomy, and which required instead the harsh pursuit of economic advantage. In his play *Goetz von Berlichingen* Goethe described its sixteenth-century noble hero as bewildered by the changes around him, and especially bewildered by his own son's preference for learning over violence. Two generations later, Charles Dickens presented his Sir Leicester Dedlock as a contemporary nobleman confused about the Industrial Revolution: "'He is called, I believe—an—Ironmaster,'" Sir Leicester says of a local capitalist, "with gravity and doubt, as not being sure but that he is called a Lead-mistress; or that the right word may be some other word expressive of some other relationship to some other metal."[1]

This contradiction—between nobles' centrality in long-standing ideas about historical action and their irrelevance to what contemporaries saw as the main stories of modern life—applied especially to France, whose great Revolution had been specifically directed against the nobles, killing and exiling thousands of individuals and destroying the system of laws from which they had benefited under the Old Regime. Hence the importance of understanding how historians have depicted nobles and what assumptions they have made about them. Throughout this book, I have argued that French historians in the nineteenth and twentieth centuries turned to history as a way of understanding the modern condition, and thus as a way of understanding their own lives. As a subject so closely bound up with questions about modernity itself, I want to suggest in this chapter, nobility constitutes a test case for the view of historical writing that I have sought to develop.

In France, I will argue, intellectuals' fixation on the problem of modernity produced a paradoxical mixture, rendering historical nobles at once central and invisible. On the one hand, nobles and the concepts surrounding them were deeply embedded in nineteenth- and early twentieth-century thought. In addition, many of the classics of French literary culture depicted aristocratic doings, so that the period's most important literary debates also raised issues about nobles and their place in French life; as seen in Chapter 2, this was precisely Stendhal's complaint about seventeenth-century French culture. On the other hand, the meanings that historians and other writers assigned the group were contradictory and shifting. Elsewhere in Europe, nobles might stand as symbols of conservative values and of national traditions. These ideas appealed to some French writers, but more typically writers attached the traditions of national identity to the monarchy and presented its relationship to the nobles as mainly hostile, dominated by a long struggle to eliminate the nobles' powers and lawless excesses. Celebrating the kings' role in French society necessarily raised questions about the nobility's opposition to the work of centralization, and nobles tended to become troubling symbols of a wider rebelliousness. They symbolized other failures to adapt to the conditions of

---

1. Dickens, *Bleak House,* 449.

modern life as well. For intellectuals seeking to understand the emergence of modern France, the nobility ultimately had only negative meaning, as an embodiment of the social qualities that had to be overcome in the process of political and economic modernization.

The extent of the nobles' disappearance from professional historical writing about France deserves emphasis: despite some exceptions, until the 1980s they played a strikingly small role in academic writing about the early modern period.[2] This fact is especially striking given the French historical profession's abundant research, conceptual daring, and wide influence from the 1920s onward. In this domain, in fact, intellectual influences tended to move eastward across the Atlantic, with French scholars eventually taking up themes first developed by American and British colleagues. Many of the elements that dominate contemporary visions of the nobility can be traced to the American Robert Forster's *Nobility of Toulouse in the Eighteenth Century*, which appeared in 1960.[3] Forster argued for the nobility's essential modernity. Feudalism (he found) meant little to most nobles. They had few seigneurial powers, and only about 8 percent of their income came from feudal rents; like the contemporary English gentry, their money came from the grain and other products that their farms produced. They thought as capitalists, managing their farms for maximum profit and knowing that profit would come from the marketplace, not from the exercise of medieval powers. As such, over the eighteenth century they were a rising, not a falling, class. They rose the more easily in that they enjoyed close relations with the royal administration, which assisted aristocratic families often and generously.

It is a suggestive footnote in publishing history that Forster's book appeared next to Robert Fogel's disruptive study of American railways, another Johns Hopkins dissertation, in the series Johns Hopkins University Studies in Historical and Political Science.[4] Like Fogel's study, *Nobility of Toulouse* offered an early example of the quantitative approaches

2. In this respect, histories of the Old Regime contrast dramatically with those of the Middle Ages; French medievalists have given particular attention to the aristocracy.

3. Other influences should also be noted: J. H. Hexter, whose collected essays appeared a year later and had less to say about the French case, argued forcefully for the continuing wealth, political influence, and sound educations of nobles throughout Europe (Hexter, *Reappraisals in History*); and R. R. Palmer, in *The Age of the Democratic Revolution*, also drew attention to signs of political and economic health in the eighteenth-century nobility, and above all stressed similarities between French and British nobles, in contrast to a long historiographical tradition stressing their differences.

4. Fogel, *Union Pacific Railroad*.

that would dominate American historical writing in the 1960s and 1970s. This new quantitative history, both works suggested, would have a skeptical, nominalist thrust, undermining certainties about how social categories corresponded to the realities they meant to describe, jumbling distinctions that had previously organized much historical writing, and pushing historical writing toward conclusions that had unsettling political overtones as well. Unlike Fogel's work, whose paradoxical arguments provoked immediate protests, Forster's book did not attract much notice on its appearance; there was no review, for instance, in the *Journal of Modern History* and no debate in the middlebrow press, though there was a long and thoughtful review in the *Annales*. But Forster's book soon received attention from other historians, and in retrospect it can be seen to have inaugurated a rapid and surprisingly complete historiographical revolution. In 1964, Alfred Cobban referred warmly to it as one basis for his own revisionist views on the French Revolution. In the mid-1970s, François Furet and Guy Chaussinand-Nogaret presented similar ideas in France, and by the 1980s these views had become established orthodoxy. Other orthodoxies have clustered around them. In the 1980s, William Beik, James Collins, Roger Mettam, and others suggested that absolutist governments of the seventeenth century worked in close partnership with the nobility, rather than seeking to push it from power or domesticate it. Similarly, Norbert Elias's work on court society—written in the late 1930s but coming to historians' notice only after its republication in 1969—has drawn attention to the aristocracy's role in shaping modern values and modes of behavior.[5] Conversely, among the wave of great French regional studies from the 1960s, only Jean Meyer's addressed the nobility directly; it is scarcely visible in the great studies by Pierre Goubert, Emmanuel Le Roy Ladurie, Pierre Deyon, and others.[6]

To some extent, this neglect can be attributed to the political culture of French academia, and notably to French academic Marxism during the post–World War II era. During these years French intellectuals were especially unsympathetic to the idea of a leisured and privileged class, which believed itself entitled to rule. Jean-Paul Sartre, the iconic intellectual of the era, expressed this view with particular force in 1960: social differentiation "occurs in a society whose members produce always *a little less* than is necessary for the whole, so that the constitution of an

5. A history discussed in Chartier, *On the Edge of the Cliff,* 107–23.

6. Goubert, *Beauvais et le Beauvaisis;* Le Roy Ladurie, *Paysans de Languedoc;* Deyon, *Amiens, capitale provinciale;* Meyer, *La noblesse de Bretagne au XVIIIe siècle.*

unproductive group has for its condition the undernourishment of all, and that one of its functions is to select those who are to be eliminated. . . . [T]he unproductive groups, always in danger of being liquidated because they are the absolutely Other . . . internalize this ambivalent otherness and comport themselves vis-à-vis the individuals either as though they were Other than man (but positively, like Gods), or as though they were the only men in the midst of another species."[7] Sartre's language echoes that of the abbé Sieyès, but it also parallels the neo-Malthusian interpretations that dominated postwar social history in France. Pierre Goubert, among others, sought to show that early modern France was indeed a society that produced less than it needed, and he sought to document the consequences: abundance for some meant starvation for others.[8] From such a perspective, it would seem, few historians could think seriously about nobles, and especially few could attempt a sympathetic reconstruction of their motives and potential contribution to society; Richard Cobb described Georges Lefebvre's "lack of understanding of the nobility" as bound up with a larger inability to understand the Old Regime's culture.[9] Conversely, the more sympathetic treatments of nobility that have come out since 1970 seem to show the influence of French historians' retreat from Marxism as a guide to either contemporary politics or historical research.[10]

But Marxism's declining intellectual appeal over the past generation does not suffice to explain the contemporaneous rise of nobiliary studies or the character that those studies have taken. For one thing, strong and explicit Marxist commitments have proved no barrier to studying the nobility, and seem even to have encouraged some historians in sympathetic interest in the subject. Jean Nicolas's *La Savoie au dix-huitième siècle* focused on the nobility from an explicitly Marxist perspective; and its author moved directly from that work to study working-class protest movements.[11] Lawrence Stone's *Crisis of the Aristocracy* likewise came out of the Marxist historical tradition, indeed was undertaken in defense of that tradition. Nor, conversely, were American historians of France especially hostile to Marxist analyses during the 1950s and 1960s. Postwar Anglo-American historians accorded immense respect to the work of

7. From *Critique de la raison dialectique,* cited in Lichtheim, "Sartre, Marxism, and History," 222–46, 235.

8. See Goubert, *Beauvais et le Beauvaisis.*

9. Cobb, *Second Identity,* 99.

10. For a compelling instance of this retreat, see Le Roy Ladurie, *Paris-Montpellier.*

11. Nicolas, *Mouvements populaires et conscience sociale.* It is relevant to the argument that follows that eighteenth-century Savoy was not part of the French monarchy.

Lefebvre, Albert Soboul, and other Marxist scholars. Lefebvre himself was invited to supply both an opening benediction to the newly founded *French Historical Studies,* in 1958, and the journal's first substantive article as well; in the same year, Richard Cobb (whose views were about to change dramatically) wrote in the *Journal of Modern History* that "any French specialist of the Revolution would accept the general premises laid down by MM. Lefebvre and Labrousse" about the nature of social structure.[12] Admiration of this sort ebbed after 1964, but interest in the alternative Marxism represented by E. P. Thompson rose to fill some of the gap thus created. Marxism's changing fortunes, it appears, offer only a partial explanation for changing approaches to the nobility, either in France or in the United States.

Having pushed Marxism somewhat to the margins of this intellectual history, we might turn to a second line of explanation, resting on the nobility's real place in modern French society. Despite signs of the "persistence of the Old Regime,"[13] nobles held a weak position in nineteenth- and twentieth-century France in comparison with their prominence elsewhere in Europe. One element of weakness was the legal anarchy that surrounded their status. The Constituent Assembly abolished all titles in 1790, but after 1800 governmental policies oscillated. Napoleon reintroduced some of the terminology of nobility with his establishment of the Legion of Honor in 1802. There followed the creation of princes of the empire, in 1806, and finally in 1808 the establishment of an imperial aristocracy—while at the same time all other claims to nobility, including the claim to have held noble status under the Old Regime, were declared illegal. The Bourbons' return in 1814 brought an ambiguous restoration of nobility: the Charter declared that "the former *noblesse* takes up again its titles; the new keeps its own." These privileges were also declared to confer no concrete advantages whatsoever, but the Restoration did establish a Chamber of Peers, numbering 184 nobles in 1814, expanding to 365 by the end of the regime, and it gave titled nobles real legislative power. The institution survived the Revolution of 1830, but its existence was debated from the outset: in 1831 the creation of hereditary peerages was abolished, and there was debate about the propriety of the government controlling false claims to nobility. Nobility itself was again outlawed in 1848, but Napoleon III restored it in 1852.

12. Cobb, "Era of the French Revolution," 118–30, 119.
13. Mayer, *Persistence of the Old Regime.*

All this legislation remained intact through the Third Republic—leaving in practice a confusion of usurped and authentic titles, uncontrolled by state authority and (with the disappearance of the Chamber of Peers, in 1848) disconnected from any privileges or powers. Contemporaries believed that false claims to nobility were rising, particularly through the assumption of the *particule* "de" as part of a name—a practice that continued throughout the Third Republic. Napoleon III sought to control the process, by fining unauthorized claims to nobility, but this had little effect, especially given the nineteenth-century's profusion of periodical literature; "the great plague of the nineteenth century has been the proliferation of armorials," wrote an angry nobleman in 1939, adding that "this orgy of fantastical genealogies" continued in his own time.[14] But such self-ennoblements apparently did not produce numerical growth in the order, partly because the nineteenth century's practices radically changed the nobility's structure. Formal titles became far more frequent during the nineteenth century than they had been during the Old Regime, aided by the altogether new practice of "decrescendo," by which the sons of a count, for instance, assumed the title of viscount. Conversely, mere country gentlemen found themselves in a much more difficult situation, lacking titles to special status and unable to claim higher rank without appearing ridiculous.

As the century progressed, then, nobility increasingly meant titled nobility, often with plutocratic connections; grandeur at the top of the order tended to go with decay at the bottom. In these circumstances, all numerical estimates were approximate, indeed acknowledged to be fictitious, but the numbers proposed were very low. On the eve of World War I, one authority claimed that there were only five thousand noble families in France.[15] But in contrast to the Old Regime, when the vast majority of nobles had been undistinguished country gentlemen and -women, these predominantly titled families were an ostentatious presence in French society, and new institutions added to their prominence: from 1815 through 1848, the Chamber of Peers, which gave them a political voice that they had not had during the Old Regime; the Jockey Club, founded in 1833, which explicitly sought nobles as members; even the Automobile Club,

---

14. Pradal de Lamase, "L'idée de noblesse en France," 322. My overview here of nineteenth-century practices regarding nobility is taken partly from this article; see also the excellent work of David Higgs, *Nobles in Nineteenth-Century France*.

15. Saint Martin, *L'espace de la noblesse*, 13.

in which nobles figured prominently, founded in 1895.[16] All this might have very little meaning to outsiders. Proust's Baron de Charlus uses his title to denote his family's very ancient origins; but at a luncheon party his wealthy bourgeois hosts understand nothing of this status and assume that a local marquis (his family ennobled only under Louis XIV) ranks more highly than a baron. The aristocratic world and its forms of distinction, so the novel suggests, were now little known to outsiders, indeed were incomprehensible except to those directly concerned with living them out. Nobles themselves survived, but plenty of evidence suggests their loss of vitality as a group.

But—as both literary critics and historians have observed—the socially marginal may be symbolically central, and their small numbers did not prevent the nobility from playing a large role in nineteenth-century imaginations.[17] As an illustration of both this centrality and the complexities that attended it, we may turn to one of the nineteenth-century's best-known aristocrats, the count of Monte Cristo. Set in the France of 1838, Alexandre Dumas's novel abounds in aristocratic titles and doings. Alongside the count himself, its cast of principal characters consists of the count, countess, and viscount de Morcerf, the baron de Danglars, and Monsieur de Villefort; many of the secondary figures carry titles as well. The characters refer often to military action: two have fought in Algeria, and the impact of the Napoleonic wars continues to resonate. Questions of honor arise often and often lead to dueling; the count himself proclaims that he will die if he fails to avenge a public insult, by killing the man who insulted him.

Yet despite these surface trappings, the novel consistently undercuts the idea of aristocracy itself. "'He is undoubtedly some noble lord,'" a character says of the count, to the general agreement of others who have witnessed his manners and personal qualities. But of course the count is nothing of the kind. He is an altogether self-made man who happens to have a great deal of money, and he presents himself as such to his friends; "'I should never have passed myself off as a great nobleman,'" he tells one of them, "'were it not that I was repeatedly told this was absolutely necessary for anyone who travels a lot.'" The count de Morcerf, a successful military man, claims to be from "'one of the oldest families in the south

16. Saint Martin, *L'espace de la noblesse*, 147.
17. Walkowitz, *City of Dreadful Delight*; Stallybrass and White, *Politics and Poetics of Transgression*.

of France'" and has the genealogies to prove it, but he is in fact another self-invented figure, a onetime fisherman who has made his way in the world through scheming and betrayal. Yet in a final twist, Morcerf's son—like Monte Cristo himself—displays a stereotypical aristocratic bravado and an intense commitment to maintaining his own honor; at the end of the novel he too embarks on a military career, to atone for his father's disgrace. Conversely, Maximilien Morel, the son of a Marseillais business-man who makes no claim to aristocratic title, embodies military valor and indifference to monetary gain.[18] *The Count of Monte Cristo* thus presents an aristocratic society from which authentic nobles are mostly absent. Aristocratic values and practices remain vigorous, but they have only weak connections to aristocratic persons—whose claims to ancient lineage in any case are usually fictional.

The historian Ernest Renan supplies a comparable example of the nine-teenth century's fascination with the concept of aristocracy and its appar-ently paradoxical readiness to disconnect aristocratic values from persons of noble blood. Renan offers an especially compelling example because (as seen in previous chapters) he was among the dominant figures in the historical culture of the later nineteenth century, one of the three on Gabriel Monod's list of the nation's "maîtres de l'histoire." Renan came from a modest social background; his father was a sea captain, born of peasant ancestors, and his mother kept a grocery store. He trained for the priest-hood (first in Brittany, then at the Parisian seminary of Saint-Sulpice), lost his faith, and turned instead to a secular academic career, with daz-zling success: in 1860 he was named a knight of the Legion of Honor, in 1861 professor at the Collège de France. The 1863 publication of his *Life of Jesus* made him one of the nineteenth century's best-selling authors, and its effort to historicize Jesus made him the particular target of con-servatives. The government suspended his classes, and prominent clerics denounced him as an enemy of traditional values. For many of the same reasons, after 1871 he became a central figure in the culture of the newly founded Third Republic. He was gloriously restored to his position, and at his death in 1892 the government organized a state funeral. It also sought (unsuccessfully) to have his body buried in the Panthéon.[19]

Republican hero, provincial outsider made good, and the victim of both imperial and clerical power, Renan nonetheless turned to concepts

18. Dumas, *Count of Monte Cristo*, quotations at 393, 406.
19. For an overview of this career, see E. Renan, *Souvenirs d'enfance et de jeunesse*, 5–16; see also Monod, *Les maîtres de l'histoire*, 1–49.

of aristocracy to make sense of his own life in the modern world and for a political understanding of that world. This language could serve a variety of functions and moods, allowing him to express both embittered anxiety about where the world was heading and ironic detachment. "The idea that the nobleman is one who does not work for a living, and that all commercial or industrial enterprise, however respectable, diminishes the man who undertakes it and excludes him from the first circle of humanity—this idea is disappearing day by day. That is the difference that forty years can produce in human affairs. Everything that I once accomplished would today seem an act of lunacy; and sometimes, looking around me, I believe that I live in a world I no longer recognize."[20]

The crisis that followed the Franco-Prussian War brought more tragic and more practical expressions of these views. "The noble concerns of the old France—patriotism, enthusiasm for beauty, love of glory—have disappeared with the noble classes who represented the soul of France"; and his proposed remedies turned mainly on restoring aristocratic institutions. What he called "the basis of provincial life" in each corner of a restored France would be "an honest country gentleman"; in Paris, there would need to be "a permanent aristocratic center," combining functions of the House of Lords and the Académie française, that would allow the survival of French superiority in the arts and sciences. The military would require even more direct infusions of aristocratic values, for "what is the nobility, in fact, if not the military function considered as hereditary and placed at the first rank of societal functions? When war disappears from the world, nobility will disappear as well, but not before." The restoration of France following its terrible defeats—"18 March 1871," he wrote, "is the day the French *conscience* has been the lowest in the past thousand years"—could come only with the restoration of aristocratic values and institutions.[21] Such comments defined the nobility as more than just a group of people or even a set of social roles; rather, nobles represented a full array of attitudes toward life, centering on neglect of economic calculation, refusal to subordinate honor to the market economy, commitment to family loyalty and to military pursuits. Yet in Renan's account (as in Dumas's) these attitudes and values had no necessary connection to any particular

20. E. Renan, *Souvenirs d'enfance et de jeunesse*, 203.
21. Renan, *Histoire et paroles*, 601, 623, 624, 615. In his views of military valor, of course, Renan directly repeated eighteenth-century ideas to which David Bien and Rafe Blaufarb have drawn attention.

group of people; at no point did Renan suggest for himself any form of aristocratic lineage.

Renan stressed the incompatibility between aristocratic values and those needed for success in a modern commercial society, and this view was widely shared. Its prevalence had important implications for how the history of actual nobles was written in the nineteenth century. Defined as misfits within the market economy, they could scarcely be anything but a social class in decline, incapable of adaptation to a world that increasingly required individuals to evaluate their economic interests with care. As they looked at the documents dating back to the Middle Ages, leading nineteenth-century historians claimed to discover that this in fact had been the case throughout French history. Alexis de Tocqueville described the French nobility as visibly declining from the eleventh century to his own times, under the combined pressures of the monarchy and the bourgeoisie; and he viewed the absolutist governments of the seventeenth century as completing this work of destruction, eliminating nobles from any real role in the nation's life.[22]

François Guizot's lectures on the course of "French civilization" offered the same idea. For Guizot, "the most active and important [*décisif*] element" of that civilization, the one that determined its character, consisted of the communes, the bourgeoisie, the third estate, terms that Guizot treated as synonymous. Thus for Guizot, in contrast to the tradition of Burkeian conservatism, the nation's essence lay not in its traditional great families, rising above and protecting the rest of the population, but rather in its active, changing, economically adventurous bourgeoisie. The development of this class constituted the central theme of French history, and that development was a story of ongoing struggle. "For more than six centuries, allied with the monarchy," it worked "without interruption to ruin the feudal aristocracy"; and once the aristocracy had been defeated, it moved on to attack its onetime ally, the monarchy. "It's the most powerful of the forces that have dominated our civilization," and its existence was a unique fact in world history. "Nowhere else will you encounter a social class that, starting from nothing, weak, despised, almost invisible at the start, rises by a continuous movement and unceasing labor; strengthening itself from one period to the next, to invade and absorb everything around it, power, riches, culture, influence; changing the nature of society

22. His views are discussed in Dewald, *European Nobility*, 7–12.

and government; and finally becoming so dominant that one can say that it is now the country itself."[23]

Guizot's commitment to this view of his nation's history is especially striking in view of his contemporaries' keen awareness of French economic backwardness in comparison to conditions in England, with its cotton mill owners and ironmasters. At a time when French landed wealth still mattered more than industrial or commercial, when even voting rights favored landowners, Guizot could nonetheless view the bourgeoisie as "le pays même." As striking is his stress on the place of conflict in French social development. The third estate struggled "sans relâche" (a phrase he found apt enough to repeat), leaving no margin for even momentary alliances. This was a history in which real blood was shed, producing absolute gains and losses, and ultimately "the ruin" of the aristocracy.

Guizot's vision thus detached the nobility from the nation's most important traditions, those that had come to fruition in his own times. Similar critiques emerged from nineteenth-century aristocrats themselves. The baron de Barante (a peer under the Restoration) argued in 1821 that aristocratic domination of society might have made sense in a purely rural society, "but commerce, industry, learning require another form of protection, and moreover have the force to insist on it."[24] For Barante as for Guizot, the story of the middle class was one of continuous advancement. "An intermediate class had been created, first weak and few, then endowed with power, wealth, and culture. It was thus necessary to give steadily more attention to its needs." As it rose, "the aristocratic edifice of feudalism, long besieged, weakened by so many attacks, everywhere undermined, collapsed completely beneath the blows of royal power."[25] For Barante, these processes had already begun during the seventeenth century, but the eighteenth brought them to full flower. As "the nobility without any political function, without a real occupation, lost its energy from one generation to the next," "wealth, culture, and manners spread throughout the nation. Each day the inferior approached more closely the superior."[26] Tocqueville's best-selling *Democracy in America* would repeat these formulations a few years later.

Like Tocqueville, Barante assigned much of the blame for the nobility's loss of energy to the monarchy, which had limited its functions without

23. Guizot, *Histoire de la civilisation en France*, 4:211, 212.
24. Barante, *Des communes et de l'aristocratie*, 26.
25. Barante, *Des communes et de l'aristocratie*, 31.
26. Barante, *Des communes et de l'aristocratie*, 43, 45.

restraining its privileges. But Barante was more impressed by the nobility's contemporary failings than by its sufferings under the Old Regime. The Restoration, he wrote, had converted honest landlords and small-town mayors, nobles who had adjusted in a constructive manner to the demands of the Napoleonic era, into pathetic office-seekers and connivers—in effect repeating the experience of the Old Regime itself, in which society's natural leaders had turned themselves into servile courtiers.[27] Barante's call for a liberal aristocratic regime, in which society's natural leaders would play preeminent roles, only highlighted the moral and economic failings of the actual French nobility.

Later in the nineteenth century, the duc d'Aumale's *Histoire des princes de Condé* used comparable language for somewhat different purposes. Aumale identified closely with the Condé family, and especially with Louis II de Bourbon, the Grand Condé. He owned Condé's estate at Chantilly, including the family archives on which his history was based; like several of the Condé princes he had been a successful general, and he peppered his text with remarks about the enduring problems of generalship, suggesting that no absolute barrier separated the nineteenth century from the Old Regime; above all, he too was a Bourbon prince (a son of the deposed Louis-Philippe) who had been excluded by political circumstances from participating in the nation's public life.[28] Aumale was thus well situated to detect the continuities in aristocratic power that scholarship since 1960 has emphasized, but the brief and infrequent interpretive comments in his text stress instead decline. Of a moment in the Fronde, for instance, he wrote, "[W]as this not a sign of the approaching [democratic] era? Do we not see here clearly the contrast between an impotent feudalism in decay and the imposing appearance of democracy in its cradle?"[29]

But like many of his contemporaries, Aumale had little enthusiasm for the aristocratic politics of the Old Regime. Early in the reign of Louis XIII, he wrote, "the party of the 'Grands'. . . , united only to destroy the remnant of authority that kept their petty ambitions in check, prepared itself for a new effort to reestablish in France a bastard form of feudalism."[30] Conversely, Richelieu's pacification of the aristocratic Huguenots ensured that "henceforth there were only Frenchmen in France" and that Protestants

27. Barante, *Des communes et de l'aristocratie*, 77.
28. Aumale, *Histoire des princes de Condé*, 2:218; on similarities of seventeenth-century politics with those of Napoleon, see 5:378.
29. Aumale, *Histoire des princes de Condé*, 6:16–17.
30. Aumale, *Histoire des princes de Condé*, 3:114.

would contribute to "the great edifice of national unity."[31] Such comments show the extent to which Aumale shared the nineteenth century's view of French state-building as a process that had continued through the early modern period, and that had set absolutist kings against aristocratic rebels. Whatever his admiration for the Grand Condé, his hero's turn to rebellion violated fundamental duties to the nation. "Shall we follow some," he asked, "in saying that the idea of the Patrie . . . has only just now been revealed to modern societies? . . . No, whatever the claims, France was not born yesterday, and it is not just from yesterday that our ancestors began to love and serve her."[32] Aumale admired the Condés, but his historical perspective—like Guizot's—categorized their aristocratic politics as mere distractions in the history of French state-building.

These cases suggest how nobles might fade out of the nation's history, leaving them ghostly outsiders to the processes that mattered for French identity. A similar shifting can be detected in nineteenth-century discussions of race, a growing preoccupation among French intellectuals. The two topics inevitably intertwined, for "race" had been essential to the Old Regime's definition of nobility itself: although nobility could be acquired in other ways, its essence lay in purity of lineage, which allowed the development of such aristocratic qualities as courage and generosity.[33] These ideas survived among nineteenth-century writers: in Benjamin Disraeli's novel *Sybil,* the heroine is a descendant of medieval Saxon nobles, and she and her father display the characteristic bravery and honor of their lineage. But increasingly intellectuals attached such imagery to whole peoples, rather than just the stratum of the nobility, further reducing the nobility's importance as a repository of specific personal qualities. Comte Arthur de Gobineau's *Essai sur l'inégalité des races humaines,* whose first volumes appeared in 1853, represented the strongest expression of these views, in an emphatically emotional register, emphasizing pessimism about the future of France and of Europe more generally. Gobineau cared deeply about nobility, and some of his views indicated the survival into the nineteenth century of Old Regime ideas about its meaning. He had some claim to the status himself, since in the eighteenth century his family had held offices in the sovereign courts of Bordeaux, but his claim to be a count was murkier; to support it, he spent several years assembling

31. Aumale, *Histoire des princes de Condé,* 3:224.
32. Aumale, *Histoire des princes de Condé,* 5:383, 384.
33. Jouanna, *L'idée de race en France.*

a half-fictional, half-historical version of his family's history, extending back to the Viking invasions of Normandy.[34] Ernest Renan's wife, possibly Gobineau's former mistress and in any case his passionate admirer, summarized the dynastic vision that dominated that work: "[O]ne sees a family developing, transforming itself, moving from place to place over the centuries, [yet] keeping its fundamental nature, remaining itself in all circumstances, reproducing long-dead ancestors, imprinted with pride and all the melancholy of ancient memories."[35] Here was the Old Regime's ideology of *race* updated to new social circumstances: in his qualities and attitudes, the noble embodied historical survival, allowing medieval values to contribute to the modern world.

As with Alexandre Dumas and Ernest Renan, however, Gobineau's language of nobility concealed instabilities that ultimately left his readers uncertain of both what nobility was and how it interacted with the surrounding society. Gobineau believed the races of humanity to be altogether dissimilar, so much so as to raise the possibility of separate creations for each of them, but he also believed that they tended inevitably to intermarry. The result was a steady decline of human energy and achievement. When this process of racial mixing was completed (in the near future, he predicted), "men will all resemble each other," and this common humanity "will be of the most revolting baseness." Humankind would lose its capacity to dominate nature, and instead would come to resemble the other animals. So reduced in energy and capacities, it would not last long, and indeed signs of depopulation were already everywhere visible. China "has never had fewer inhabitants than today"; Germany, England, and France were no more populous now than in the late Roman Empire, while Italy and Spain had lost three-fourths of their populations.[36] Race dynamics thus explained "the fall of civilizations," which he described as "the most striking and at the same time the most obscure of all historical phenomena" (1:141; see also 1:170).

Throughout Europe, this fatal tendency to racial mixture had begun early, as Germanic tribes intermarried with the conquered peoples of Roman Europe, and the tendency was especially marked in France, both because of its strong monarchy and because French territory grouped together a Germanic north and a Mediterranean south, giving special encouragement to racial mixing. "The ethnic decomposition of the French

34. Gobineau, *Oeuvres,* introduction.
35. C. Renan, *Les lettres de Cornélie Renan à Gobineau,* 30.
36. Gobineau, *Oeuvres,* 1:1164–65. Further page references appear parenthetically in the text.

nobility began when Germanic tribes mingled their blood with that of the Gallo-Romans; but decline moved quickly, partly because the Germanic warriors died in great numbers in the incessant wars of the time, and partly because frequent revolutions replaced them with men risen from lower in society" (1:1091n). Thus Gobineau like Tocqueville and Guizot made decline the central narrative in the nobility's history, and like them he believed that the French monarchy contributed to the process. Already by the fourteenth century the monarchy had succeeded in coaxing the nobility "into habits akin to servility," which left the noble merely a "decoration" of the monarchy. "It hardly needs to be added that the nobles allowed themselves thus to be degraded because their blood was no longer sufficiently pure to allow them to feel the wrong, and to give them sufficient strength for resistance. Less romanized than the bourgeoisie, which in turn was less romanized than the common people, they were nonetheless very romanized" (1:1091). Urbanization only completed this work of racial decline, for in the great cities the observer encountered "a frightening spectacle of ethnic anarchy," with inhabitants showing traces of ancestry from throughout the world (1:284). In the end, despite his aristocratic self-image, Gobineau's thinking led him to downplay aristocratic lineage and to stress instead the racial makeup of specific regions. Racial purity survived in the regions of the north (to which only France north of the Seine belonged), rather than among the nobilities. "Here subsist the last remnants of the Aryan element, disfigured, impoverished, but not altogether vanquished. Here too beats the heart of modern society, and consequently of modern culture [*civilisation*]" (1:1098, 1099).

Gobineau wrote in a tense relationship with the intellectual establishment of his day. Unlike Renan's, his works enjoyed neither popular success nor the endorsement of established figures, and he suffered repeatedly for his readiness to make extravagant claims in fields that he did not know well.[37] Religious conservatives disliked the materialistic assumptions in his arguments, and Tocqueville considered their political implications pernicious.[38] French historians tended to view him as an overly enthusiastic autodidact; and in 1856 he continued to complain about the

37. Characteristically, in 1858, three years after the appearance of the *Essai*, he announced in a letter to Alexis de Tocqueville that he had discovered the proper reading of cuneiform texts, in the course of completing a six-volume history of Iran. "Jamais alchimiste n'a été plus heureux," he wrote to another friend, but the episode ended badly, with the Parisian specialist community rejecting his findings. Tocqueville, *Correspondance*, 291, 291 n. 1.
38. Tocqueville, *Correspondance*, 199, 200, 203.

silence surrounding his book.[39] But if Gobineau was not entirely representative of his contemporaries' thinking, neither was he an outsider to Parisian cultural circles. Tocqueville noticed him early on, employed him as a secretary, secured him a place in the French diplomatic corps, and pushed him (unsuccessfully) for a place in the Academy of Moral and Political Sciences. They sustained a warm correspondence until Tocqueville's death in 1859. Cornélie Renan likewise mobilized her husband on Gobineau's behalf, to secure reviews in prominent journals, and herself spoke warmly of his books in salon situations.[40] Years earlier, Gobineau and Cornélie had met at the salon of Cornélie's artist father, where Gobineau had also met the historian Augustin Thierry. To roughly the same degree, Gobineau's ideas also were in contact with those of his contemporaries. More respectable writers such as Renan and Taine (as seen above) also made race central to their understanding of world history. Renan, whose good-humored self-identification with aristocratic values has already been noted, enthusiastically advocated French imperial adventures; France's working classes, like its nobility (he wrote), descended from the warlike Franks, and the grand adventures of foreign conquest and rule alone could provide suitable outlets for these warrior instincts.[41] Elsewhere, he spoke in comparable terms of the Celtic culture that survived in western Brittany. "If racial excellence were to be measured by purity of blood and inviolability of character, no race . . . could compete in excellence with the surviving remnants of the Celtic race." The Celts' qualities paralleled those conventionally attributed to the nobility: a fierce opposition to modernity, a sense that the individual life constitutes "a link in a long tradition," a readiness to undertake arduous quests for idealistic purposes.[42] Despite his divergences from his contemporaries, Gobineau illustrates the variety of ideological schemes into which the vision of nobiliary decline might be fitted.

With varying emphases and assessments, the authors of the accounts traced here agreed in limiting the nobles' place in French national development, defining them as irrelevant to the emergence of both the state and the capitalist market. Other writers took these suggestions of nobles' inability to conform to the forms of modern life much further. For them,

39. Tocqueville, *Correspondance*, 266.
40. C. Renan, *Les lettres de Cornélie Renan à Gobineau*, 38–40.
41. Discussed in Chapter 1, above.
42. Renan, *Histoire et paroles*, 308–9, 311.

the noble was not merely unable to function successfully within bourgeois society, but was also unwilling to accept its constraints: the noble
shaded into the bohemian rebel. The Goncourt brothers, whose family
had been ennobled in the eighteenth century, spoke repeatedly of their
inability to adapt to the rules of the nineteenth century. "We feel ourselves . . . to be émigrés from the eighteenth century. We are déclassé
contemporaries of that refined, exquisite, supremely delicate, rebellious
[d'esprit enragé] society." On this view, nobles constituted a society of the
disobedient, frondeurs unwilling to live conventional lives. For the Goncourts, this view allied with an assertiveness about aristocracy as fundamental to artistic excellence: "[N]othing beautiful in the arts has been
achieved except by aristocracies. Works by the people and for the people
. . . are only pyramids, roads, viaducts."[43]

Dumas's fictions suggested another form that aristocratic rebellion
might take, a questioning of sexual and gender conventions. In his La reine
Margot (first published 1844–45) the heroine's very aristocratic friend
Henriette de Nevers proclaims herself "free, my queen, do you understand? Do you know how much happiness there is in this word free?"
Henriette emphasizes that she is free from her husband's control, as well
as from the rest of the world's, and that she is free in her sexual choices
as in other matters. As a princess, Marguerite cannot enjoy the same
degree of liberty, but she responds in similar terms: she and her friend,
she acknowledges, are united in the untrammeled pursuit of pleasure.[44]

During these years, the Old Regime's aristocratic women and their sexual outlawry fascinated professional historians as much as popular novelists. In the 1840s, both Charles-Augustin Sainte-Beuve and Victor Cousin
wrote significant studies of seventeenth- and eighteenth-century women;
twenty years later the Goncourts themselves wrote a study of women in the
eighteenth century.[45] All these authors portrayed women as mixing illicit
sexuality with politicking and learning. Sainte-Beuve showed Madame de
Pompadour patiently tutoring an ignorant and boorish Louis XV in appreciation of the arts. "Arriving at that position, eminent but little honorable,"
of royal mistress, wrote Sainte-Beuve, she "considered herself as destined
to aid, summon around her, and encourage, suffering merit and men of
talent of all kinds. . . . It was not her fault that no one can speak of the

43. Goncourt and Goncourt, Journal 1:905, 1020.
44. Dumas, La reine Margot, 147.
45. Discussed in Chapter 1, above.

'age of Louis XV' as they do of that of Louis XIV."[46] Cousin came close
to obsession with the beautiful, sexually adventurous *frondeuses* of the seventeenth century, whom he found all the more attractive for their eventual
middle-aged penitence. These themes continued into the twentieth century. In about 1902, Charles Maurras reviewed the career of the aristocrat Mademoiselle Coigny as an example of patriotic heroism: yet another
in the series of atheistic libertines, entertaining multiple lovers, she nonetheless played an important role in bringing legitimate monarchy back
to France in 1814. Maurras of course celebrated her political role, but also
the absolute indifference she displayed to religious ideas. After death, she
believed, there would be "nothing. No future. . . . This is what gives the
brief elegy of her life and loves an intensity of interest and emotion."[47]
Again, the aristocratic woman embodied freedom from pious convention—and in this case personal non-conformity made possible political
heroism.

   These formulations came from intellectuals who exercised enormous
influence on nineteenth- and early-twentieth-century culture, and their
vision of the noble as rebel was hugely popular. Dumas's books were especially popular, of course. Twenty years after *La reine Margot* appeared, the
Goncourts overheard some men in a bar discussing the novel, and concluded that Dumas "has truly been the history teacher of the masses."[48]
A host of imitators produced other efforts drawn from the dramatic events
and characters of the sixteenth and seventeenth centuries.[49] Even the sober
duc d'Aumale drew attention to the overlap between his carefully documented exploration of the Gascon nobles who participated in the Fronde
and that of Dumas; this "most seductive of narrators has engraved their
image in everyone's memory."[50]

   At loftier levels, as seen above, Sainte-Beuve and Cousin heavily influenced the institutional structure of nineteenth-century intellectual life;
Cousin had a say in most French academic careers through midcentury,
while Sainte-Beuve's weekly newspaper columns helped determine literary careers. With this stimulus, their scholarly contemporaries pursued
and edited documents that displayed the early modern aristocracy's ungoverned lives. Marguerite de Valois's own memoirs were published, and

46. Sainte-Beuve, *Portraits of the Eighteenth Century*, 449.
47. Maurras, *Romantisme et révolution*, "Mademoiselle Monk," 206–26, quotation at 216.
48. Goncourt and Goncourt, *Journal*, 1:995.
49. Summary in Dumas, *La reine Margot*, postface, by Eliane Viennot, 625–38.
50. Aumale, *Histoire des princes de Condé*, 6:13.

from that publication there followed late in the nineteenth century a careful biography, by one of Ernest Lavisse's collaborators. Gédéon Talle-mant des Réaux's immense collection of wild stories about seventeenth-century high society had remained almost unknown until the manuscript appeared on the market in 1803; a first edition (in six volumes) appeared in 1833–35, a second (ten volumes) in 1840, a third (nine volumes) in 1854–60. This last was a complete edition, save for (a contemporary noted) "the suppression of some passages whose cynicism passes all bounds."[51]

Tallemant's case typified how prurient fascination with aristocratic amorality intersected with careful scholarship, and with a nervous effort to contain the seditious effects of these examples. Reviewing in 1857 the third edition of Tallemant, Sainte-Beuve noted that "the seventeenth century is more in fashion than ever" and that contemporary historians had absorbed Tallemant's Rabelaisian stories "without citing him . . . and pretending to despise him" for his vulgarity.[52] The sieur de Brantôme's works had been republished in the eighteenth century, but the nineteenth century saw two major new editions (the second in eleven volumes); an 1876 overview of "Brantôme the historian" praised the author's insights, but added "we do not wish even to glance at" his *Dames galantes*, "the fruit of a perverted imagination, instruction in debauchery worthy of Aretino."[53]

A more sober example of this interplay between literary imagery and historical documentation was the mid-nineteenth-century publication of a seventeenth-century account of the Grands Jours d'Auvergne by Esprit Fléchier. The events themselves took place in 1665 and represented an especially dramatic confrontation between the monarchical state and an unruly local aristocracy; in response to complaints about feudal lawlessness, Louis XIV sent a deputation of magistrates to the province (among the most backward in France) to execute summary justice on nobles who abused their local influence. The result was a wave of executions and lawsuits, and an affirmation of royal control over even remote regions. This was a confrontation very much in keeping with nineteenth-century ideas about the progress and achievements of absolutist monarchy. After a first edition in 1844, in 1856 the scholar Adolphe Chéruel (responsible for a number of other archival publications) superintended an annotated version of Fléchier's account of these events.[54]

51. Michaud and Michaud, *Biographie universelle*, s.v. "Tallemant."
52. Sainte-Beuve, *Causeries du lundi*, "Tallemant et Bussy" (19 January 1857), 13: 172, 188.
53. Pingard, "Brantôme historien," 218.
54. Chéruel, *Mémoires de Fléchier*. The edition has served as a standard account since; see,

The edition provoked widespread interest, hence the readiness of the already-famous Sainte-Beuve to supply an introduction. Sainte-Beuve noted that the 1844 publication "obtained the greatest success in both in the wide public and among cultivated readers [*esprits*]."[55] Taine also supplied a review in the middlebrow *Journal des Débats,* presenting the document as a narrative of cultural and social confrontation. Fléchier's "portrayal of provincial mores and Parisian elegance," he wrote, in its "authentic, instinctive contrasts indicates a revolution that is drawing to a conclusion: an aristocracy of petty tyrants, men of action, is becoming a salon of cultivated, well-behaved courtiers." Taine's language suggested his dislike of the new dispensation, with its absolutist politics and neoclassical culture, but in keeping with the other historians considered here he mainly stressed the backwardness of the seventeenth-century aristocratic order, a world of "little private despotisms" and "little private wars" that preceded the monarchy's forcible entry onto the scene. "These robberies and killings of the weak, this regular exchange of ambushes and assassinations among the strong, this custom of affronting and murdering the forces of law and justice, constitute feudal mores through nearly the whole of the Middle Ages."[56] But both Sainte-Beuve and Taine expressed also an ambivalent view of the Parisian side of this encounter. A polished cleric and future bishop, a participant in the salon culture of the Hôtel de Rambouillet, tutor to an important *parlementaire* family, Fléchier himself perfectly embodied the new Parisian culture. But Sainte-Beuve's introduction draws attention to the complexities of this culture, noting the affinities between Fléchier's stories and the bawdy tales of another salon habitué, Tallemant himself. Sainte-Beuve found disconcerting the mix of gallantry and refinement with wild behavior—and the visiting Parisians' ease in moving from festivities, dancing, and flirtation to torture and executions.

Over the nineteenth century, thus, novelists, antiquarians, and scholars combined to produce a collective portrait of the aristocratic character as essentially ungovernable: uncalculating, violent, selfish, amoral. The image had attractive features, which Dumas and the Goncourts emphasized, but it was mainly negative, suggestive of childishness rather than of social leadership. For this reason, conservative thinkers in France approached

---

for instance, Le Bigre, *Les Grands Jours d'Auvergne.* I am grateful to Albert Hamscher for suggesting that I investigate Fléchier and nineteenth-century responses to him.

55. Chéruel, *Mémoires de Fléchier,* iii.

56. Taine, *Essais de critique et d'histoire,* 224, 232, 235.

the nobility with ambivalence. Of course they had available and intermittently used the social vision laid out in the eighteenth century by Edmund Burke, according to which nobles embodied important elements of the national character and served as living examples of the continuity between past and present. "By the sure operation of adequate causes," as Burke proclaimed, the British House of Commons was "filled with everything illustrious in rank, in descent, in hereditary and in acquired opulence, in cultivated talents, in military, civil, naval, and politic distinction that the country can afford"; no wonder that the country advanced so well toward political and social modernity.[57] In describing his hopes for French reconstruction after 1871, as we have seen, Renan echoed some elements of this vision of the relationship between aristocracy and nation: in both country and city, aristocracy was to be the foundation for a new, more solid national identity. But even he also noted examples of aristocratic disruptiveness, and others pushed these ideas much further. Nobles seemed fundamentally at odds with their society's most basic arrangements, and this from the early days of French history.

Hence conservatives proved surprisingly ready to speak disparagingly of their nobles. Taine's critical history of the Revolution offered no defense of the French nobles, nor even of nobles elsewhere. To be sure, like Tocqueville he offered a positive view of their social role in the centuries before Richelieu, when they continued to reside in the countryside and their local influence remained strong. By the later seventeenth century, however, they had become pure influence-peddlers, concerned only to preserve the amenities that they and their relatives enjoyed. "If one looks at the castes and coteries, their isolation made their egoism," he wrote. "From bottom to top, the legal and moral powers that ought to have represented the nation represented only themselves, and everyone sought to advance himself at the expense of the nation." Patriotism was thus another victim of aristocratic self-interest; French nobles had never hesitated to betray the nation and in defense of their interests had regularly conspired with foreign powers, even helping them in their invasions. "The nature of an aristocracy that thinks only of itself is to become a mere coterie. Having forgotten the public, it comes as well to neglect its subordinates; having separated itself from the nation, it separates itself from its followers." Even nobles' much-praised indifference to monetary gain was not a sign of lofty ideals; it showed merely the debilitating influence of court life, in which

---

57. E. Burke, *Reflections on the Revolution in France*, 50.

"there was no time or taste for anything else, even for the things that touch a man most closely, public affairs, estate management, the family."[58]

Like Tocqueville, Taine blamed the monarchy for much of this disorder. In the seventeenth century it had destroyed the authority that nobles had exercised in the countryside, but for Taine the monarchy's cultural impact was still more important. It had insisted on a rigid classical culture, which disparaged discussion of the realities of life, requiring that all topics be reshaped so as to fit within the limits of polite, measured discourse. Because of this classicizing program, in the eighteenth century the French language "was unsuited to depict living things, the individual as he really exists in nature and history"; writers had simplified their subject matter until there remained only "a residue, . . . an empty abstraction."[59] French classical culture had toxic effects on the aristocracy's outlook and behavior; still worse, it accounted for the dangerous abstractions of French enlightened philosophy—abstractions that the Revolution would eventually seek to implement. But unlike Tocqueville, Taine had doubts about the principle of aristocracy itself, which he viewed as a source of social dysfunction. "When the laws establish unequal social conditions," he wrote in another work, "no one is exempt from insults; . . . human nature is humiliated at every level, and society is only an exchange of affronts."[60] The Goncourts disagreed with Taine about the value of the eighteenth-century nobility, whose amorality and indifference to convention they admired, but they shared his dislike of classicism: "Under every empire," they noted privately in 1863, "there is a move toward antiquity, toward classical sources. Tyrannies extend enslavement even to matters of taste."[61] They had in mind both Louis XIV and Napoleon III.

The conservatives who followed Taine tended to reverse these evaluations and to see the state as the maker of France—and the state-sponsored culture of French classicism as one of its principal tools. Writers and ideologues presented far-reaching versions of this idea, as essential to the creation of French identity. Thus Charles Maurras argued that France was not a natural entity, but the product of its kings' efforts, aided by the culture that the monarchy sponsored. When in 1898 Maurras listed the various qualities that marked "old France" before 1789, he left nobles off the list altogether, noting instead the old monarchy's sensible approach

58. Taine, *Les origines de la France contemporaine*, 1:52, 58, 96.
59. Taine, *Les origines de la France contemporaine*, 1:149.
60. Taine, *Les philosophes classiques*, 113.
61. Goncourt and Goncourt, *Journal*, 1:922; see also 1:821.

to religion, municipal government, and culture; and he viewed the aristocratic René de Chateaubriand as precisely the figure in nineteenth-century
culture who had most threatened this inheritance, another instance of
the aristocrat as rebel. "From his ways of fearing demagogy, socialism, a
Europe-wide republic, one comes to realize that he wanted them with all
his heart. . . . This noble spirit . . . imagined the new regime with some
horror. But he loved horror."[62] For Maurras, real conservatism lay not
with these romantic "naufrageurs," but with the monarchy that had created the nation. "Our France is a work of art. It is a political work of art
born of the collaboration of an obliging nature and the thought of our
kings."[63] During the Occupation of the 1940s, the right-wing philosopher
Thierry Maulnier offered another version of this position: "Other nations
can have, as the principle of their unity, their territory, the form of their
work, and, at the very least, the relative homogeneity of their blood. Open
to numerous invasions, dedicated to very diverse activities, born of ethnically disparate elements, France molded itself into a unique substance
only by the slow work of history. It is a nation forged by the hand of man.
French civilization has been one of the principal means by which the
French nation has been made."[64] To Maurras as to his follower Maulnier,
the essence of French national identity lay not in the disruptive nobles,
but in the disciplined forces of the state and its culture.

I have argued that, despite the important differences among them,
nineteenth-century currents of thought problematized many approaches
to the history of the nobility. The writers considered here detached nobles
from the main lines of French national development, whether political
or social, and they suggested that the nobles had no necessary relationship
to the positive values commonly associated with them: valor, indifference
to money, independence. Nobles seemed too rebellious to symbolize conservative values, yet they were clearly too privileged to stand for the political Left. If medieval nobles could be an important subject for investigation,
their counterparts during the early modern period, a period marked by the
development of state, capitalism, and a distinctive national culture, could
not. They could provide only victims of modernization, not participants.

62. Maurras, *Trois idées politiques,* 245–46, 248.
63. Quoted in Carroll, *French Literary Fascism,* 71. Elements of this idea, with numerous
anthropological and scientific underpinnings, survive in Le Bras and Todd, *L'invention de la
France.*
64. Quoted in Carroll, *French Literary Fascism,* 246.

These ideas remained a vigorous presence in French historical thought into the 1960s. Here I can only briefly suggest this continuity—and the accompanying discomfort with the topic of nobility itself—by considering the work of three major historians. Lucien Febvre's 1912 dissertation *Philippe II et la Franche-Comté* offers an especially significant example, because Febvre played such an important role in French academic life between the foundation of the *Annales d'histoire économique et sociale* in 1929 and his death in 1956. Despite his advocacy of historiographical innovation, Febvre's views of the nobility fitted comfortably within the analytical framework sketched out in the previous century by Guizot and Tocqueville. The work's real subject, he explained in the introduction to his thesis, "is the struggle, the furious combat between two rival classes, nobility and bourgeoisie," a struggle that underlay the more superficial political conflicts of the period.[65] In the sixteenth century, "reduced to the revenues of his lands, the nobleman, amid rising fortunes, remained stationary, and thus declined. He witnessed, powerlessly, the dislocation and destruction of the old system of estate management that once had made the grandeur and wealth of his ancestors."[66] The result was a tendency to violence and a hatred of the group's successful rivals, the bourgeois magistrates of the parlement, who enjoyed judicial powers over the nobles along with their economic successes. "The unruly nobility, . . . the daring esquires, the country gentlemen deep in debt . . . , satisfying on the highways their instincts for brutality and brigandage, found themselves face-to-face with the hated magistrates" of the cities.[67] Falling behind economically, unable to use violence as a means to economic recovery, wrote Febvre, "the whole nobility united against the common enemy, the *parlementaire*."[68]

After World War I, Marc Bloch presented a similar view of the nobility's evolution, though he expressed less interest than Febvre in the political ramifications of social changes. Bloch's *French Rural History*, first presented as a series of lectures in 1930, stressed the inappropriateness of feudal habits for the conditions of the late Middle Ages and the sixteenth century. Thus for Bloch as for Febvre, the essential social fact of this period was the nobility's decline, as the group's outmoded economic reasoning encountered new circumstances. Bloch stressed the importance of the correlative process, by which bourgeois landowners brought new values to

65. Febvre, *Philippe II et la Franche-Comté*, 9.
66. Febvre, *Philippe II et la Franche-Comté*, 145.
67. Febvre. *Philippe II et la Franche-Comté*, 254.
68. Febvre, *Philippe II et la Franche-Comté*, 431.

the French countryside. Armed with the distinctive outlook required for success in the modern world, magistrates bought up properties from peasants and nobles alike, and in doing so they reconstituted the seigneurial system. "This advance by the bourgeoisie, followed by such rapid entrenchment," Bloch concluded, "was the most decisive event in French social history, especially in its rural aspect." Although ennobled, Bloch emphasized, these men and women "were accustomed to handling considerable liquid assets with caution, skill and even boldness. . . . In short, they had acquired the capitalist mentality. Such was the leaven which would transform seigneurial methods of exploitation."[69] Bloch saw this renewed seigneurial system surviving to 1789, and a reinvigorated system of large properties surviving into his own times. But these successes did not profit the nobles. Rather, they represented precisely the triumph of the French bourgeoisie, in much the same terms that Guizot had used.

As a final example, we may turn to the historian Roland Mousnier, whose dissertation *La vénalité des offices* appeared in 1945, and who continued to exercise an important influence on historical practice at the Sorbonne into the mid-1970s.[70] In contrast to Bloch and Febvre, Mousnier held conservative political views, consonant with his early training at the French military academy of Saint-Cyr; and much of his work—in the tradition of French conservatism—explored the process by which the French state brought its civilizing influence to an unruly society. His differences of background and orientation from Febvre and Bloch make all the more striking his essential agreement with them on the history of the nobility. Indeed, Mousnier was still more emphatic in presenting conflict between nobility and bourgeoisie as central to French historical development; in his view, French modernization represented the bourgeoisie's triumph in this struggle.

Mousnier explored these questions with particular clarity in a 1958 article.[71] Against those who might argue for a convergence of interests

69. Bloch, *French Rural History*, 125–26.

70. In some ways Mousnier's influence on the French historical profession probably equalled that of Lucien Febvre himself, for Mousnier directed a wide array of dissertations during the 1960s and 1970s.

71. The article was his entry into the prolonged debate with the Russian historian Boris Porchnev, a debate whose implications dominated the last two decades of Mousnier's academic career. Porchnev had argued that early modern France was dominated by an aristocratic state, which channeled tax revenues to an alliance of nobles and magistrates, in effect replacing the revenues that nobles lost as the seigneurial system fell apart. In important respects, this idea is basic to contemporary understanding of absolutism.

between nobles and monarchy, he argued that in the seventeenth century the high nobility wanted to "ruin the entire work of the monarchy [*l'oeuvre monarchique*], and truly return to the feudal order which, in fact, no longer existed."[72] The fact that many of the crown's own servants held aristocratic titles did not change the character of this struggle, he argued, because their formal status fell well short of real nobility; the administrator was "a noble, but not a gentleman or a member of the feudal hierarchy. . . . An official, ennobled by his position, was a bourgeois. . . . In fact the officials of the seventeenth century had habits and customs that sharply distinguished them from the gentlemen, even when they acted as seigneurs."[73] Real assimilation of bourgeois into nobility thus remained an illusion, whatever the new nobleman's properties or even his behavior. In Mousnier's view (as in Guizot's) the French state relied on this group in its work of constructing the French nation. He wrote: "I see nothing to change in the theory according to which the progress of the absolute monarchy was advanced by the possibility of opposing bourgeois against nobles [*gentilshommes*] . . . in reconstructing the state, the monarchy relied on the bourgeoisie, and I maintain that it left to the bourgeoisie a significant share in political and administrative power."[74] For Mousnier as for other French conservatives, thus, the genuine nobility remained essentially irrelevant to understanding the real nature of French society. He too saw France as the creation of its kings, and the nobility mattered in this story mainly for its efforts to block the monarchy's work. To be sure, the French bourgeoisie also required disciplining by the monarchy, but for Mousnier its place in the nation's history was altogether different from that of the old nobility. For if the bourgeois had to submit to the state's disciplining, they also participated in its powers; they were the king's agents, and this position made them in the end the real makers of the nation.

That historians of such varied professional and ideological commitments as Febvre, Bloch, and Mousnier shared essentially the same view of the French nobility suggests the importance and durability of the literary traditions that this chapter has examined. These traditions influenced popular novelists, editors of historical texts, professional historians, and public intellectuals alike. They disagreed on specific points and might attach

72. Mousnier, "Recherches sur les soulèvements populaires," 335–68, 364.
73. Mousnier, "Recherches sur les soulèvements populaires," 365.
74. Mousnier, "Recherches sur les soulèvements populaires," 365.

entirely different evaluations to the facts they described: Taine disliked the French state of the Old Regime, for instance, whereas Maurras and Mousnier admired it. But despite their differences, the writers considered here nonetheless shared a coherent view of what had happened to the nobles and what nobility meant within French history. At its core was the idea that, by the seventeenth century at the latest, nobles had essentially been removed from the important stories of French national development. France itself was the creation of its kings, working together with its bourgeoisie. The nobles embodied the forces resisting this process of creation. Their anarchic impulses had to be controlled, to make way for the modern, conscientious self.

This historical consensus stressed the inevitability of class conflict between nobles and bourgeois, and it presented the nobles as the inevitable losers in a fight whose origins could be traced to the high Middle Ages. It is easy to see Marxism in such conceptual schemes, and certainly they fitted easily into Marxist interpretive frameworks. But in fact the full range of French historians shared these ideas, including conservatives such as Maurras and Mousnier. Their consensus illustrates a pair of arguments that I have sought to make throughout these studies. First, conventional political labels do little to clarify the development of French historical thought, which arose from widely shared intellectual concerns, rather than from those of any single political group. Second, twentieth-century scholars continued to wrestle with problems of national identity that their nineteenth-century predecessors had laid out. They brought new scholarly tools to the task, but they continued to work within an inherited intellectual framework. Given the strength of this consensus, it is not surprising that challenges to it arose first among American historians. Only outsiders to French culture, it seems, could set aside ideas that had been part of French historical culture over the 150 years between Guizot and Mousnier.

7

AN ALTERNATIVE PATH TO RURAL HISTORY

 Interest in peasants and rural life has counted among the distinctive features of historical thought since World War I, and it has stimulated some of the twentieth century's great works of historical writing. Nowhere, it would seem, are the democratic tendencies of modern historical thought more visible, especially as concerns the medieval and early modern periods. Before the Industrial Revolution, peasants constituted the vast majority of Europe's population, but they had almost no impact on high politics or culture. A history centering on them can only be a history of ordinary experiences, with only indirect references to the narratives of state-building and intellectual change that dominated so many nineteenth-century conceptions of progress. Centering historical inquiry on peasants, moreover, inevitably confronts the historian with questions of otherness, as the university-trained scholar seeks to understand groups who made little use of the written word and (so much research has emphasized) held alien beliefs.

In previous chapters I have touched on some aspects and implications of French writing on rural history, by considering classic works by Marc Bloch, Emmanuel Le Roy Ladurie, and others. In this chapter I attempt to clarify these French approaches to the topic by exploring a comparative example, the alternative interpretations of rural history offered by mid-twentieth-century German scholars. The effort is especially worth undertaking because of the closeness of the two societies and the frequency of scholarly exchange between them. From Victor Cousin on, French intellectuals viewed Germany as a source of inspiration and challenge. In the mid-nineteenth century, both Ernest Renan and Hippolyte Taine studied German thought closely. Early in the twentieth century, Bloch spent a year in Germany before World War I, and Lucien Febvre taught brief courses there every year during the 1920s. After the war, they devised their plan for the journal *Annales d'histoire économique et sociale* on the model of a German journal; their intent, as Bloch wrote to the Belgian medievalist Henri Pirenne, was "to create, in an allied country, an international review of economic and social history, with the potential of replacing the *Vierteljahrschrift für Sozial und Wirtschaftsgeschichte.*"[1] Yet despite this intellectual parentage and some striking similarities of method, French and German historians of rural society in fact proceeded to very different results. Comparing their approaches confronts us again with the fact that social history's development cannot be seen as a matter of empirical science only. In both countries, peasant studies developed within established intellectual frameworks, and these determined what questions historians asked, what answers they expected to find, and what interpretations they found plausible.

In the case of peasant history, I will argue, the principal contrast between these two intellectual traditions concerned ideas about agency and social differentiation. Mid-twentieth-century German scholars were eager to see the preindustrial peasantry as full historical actors, altogether able to make intelligent political choices. In contrast, French scholars consistently stressed peasants' misery and the limits that it posed on their dealings with the world. Only dimly able to understand their own situation,

1. Lyon and Lyon, *Birth of Annales History*, 6, 12. ("A serious question arises," added Febvre a few months later, "that of German and, by extension, Austrian participation" in the new journal. Although it was "obvious" that German scholarship could not be ignored, "it is also obvious that this [new] review cannot accept the collaboration of German authors.")

on this account, peasants had to find enlightened leadership from other social groups, who possessed the mental tools needed to define reasonable political goals. This interpretive difference leads to a further point, about the political and ideological implications of historical writing. In contrast to their French colleagues, most of the German historians whom I consider here were political conservatives; at least one was an active member of the National Socialist movement, and others cooperated fully with it. Yet these authoritarian commitments did not prevent them from taking up the history of ordinary people, or from attributing a high degree of political rationality to those they studied. In this case as in others that this book has presented, political ideologies worked in complex ways, producing a mixture of implicit messages, some of them democratic, others authoritarian. Neither the topic of peasant history nor the idea of peasant agency implied a univocal stance toward contemporary politics.

However complex their responses to it, though, French and German historians of the peasantry shared an intense engagement with the world in which they wrote. Both groups were especially concerned with the processes of modernization that they saw going on around them and with understanding the divisions that these processes produced between premodern and modern societies. Historical examples (I argue) served them as a means of coming to terms with these differences, sometimes implicitly, often explicitly. Twentieth-century French writers (as has been seen above) were especially alert to changes taking place in colonial and postcolonial contexts. Germany had never matched France's imperial ambitions, and after 1918 it lost the few colonies it had held. Rather than through comparisons of Europe to Africa and Asia, German intellectuals tended to think about issues of modernity within a European context, in terms of contrasts between west and east. Images drawn from Poland and Russia served some of the functions that colonial imagery served for French scholars, and these images posed closely related questions, about defining modernity and determining its sources. Partly for that reason, the National Socialist era represented a period of striking creativity in German thinking about rural history. After 1939, when the German state took over eastern Europe and western Russia, it called on a wide range of scholars to supply the expertise needed for managing these territories; even earlier, German governments had encouraged historians to think about how eastern European society functioned. To examine German approaches to rural society is thus to examine an especially important instance of the relationship between historical practice and its political environment.

In 1946, as has been seen above, Lucien Febvre presented a "Manifesto of the New *Annales*," reorienting his journal to meet the new conditions of the postwar world. In order to remain useful, he claimed, scholarship had to move in new directions as the external world changed—and the war had changed the world profoundly. As a point of comparison, we may turn to the first postwar edition of the *Vierteljahrschrift für Sozial- und Wirtschaftsgeschichte (VSWG)*, founded in 1903 and probably the world's first scholarly journal devoted to social history.[2] The *VSWG* resumed publication in 1949, after a brief certification process from the Allied occupying forces. Its editor remained Hermann Aubin, a specialist on eastern Europe, who had begun serving in 1925 and would continue in office until 1967, two years before his death; during the National Socialist years he had been an energetic though not especially successful academic politician, close enough to the regime to hope that he might take over the great cultural history institute at the University of Leipzig, but not close enough to succeed.[3] The *VSWG*'s manner of resuming publication was almost perfectly antithetical to Febvre's approach in the *Annales*. Its editors acknowledged the war only in patriotic form, with a page commemorating five of its regular contributors killed since 1939. It offered no discussion of the issues that a post-war social history might need to confront and nothing comparable to Febvre's reflections on how the war had changed the world. The editors' choice implicitly claimed scientific status for their enterprise. Historical knowledge could develop without reference to outside events, because academic research functioned according to its own imperatives.

Instead of with editorial comment, the journal opened directly with its first substantive article, on the effects of agrarian reform in nineteenth-century eastern Europe. As its author noted, this was the reworked version of an *Habilitationschrift*, the second dissertation that formed a normal step in German university careers. He had carried out research in 1939, funded by the National Socialist regime's Institute for Eastern Research, and defended the work before an academic jury in 1943; part of it had

---

2. For an insightful overview, see Oexle, "Was deutsche Mediävisten," 89–127.

3. On Aubin, see Burleigh, *Germany Turns Eastward*, 300–321; Schulze, *Deutsche Geschichtswissenschaft*, 314; Raeff, "Some Observations on the Work of Hermann Aubin," 239–49.

been lost during the chaos of the war's end. Like the journal's silence about contemporary conditions, its first article thus also symbolized continuities with the intellectual life of the 1930s and early 1940s. Even the article's substantive concerns bespoke continuities. It explored relations among culture, ethnicity, and social change in eastern Europe and suggested that social transitions were best managed where German traditions and institutions were strongest; where such traditions were weaker, the transition to modern society was a far more unstable, even dangerous process.[4]

The article was the work of Werner Conze, a historian who in the 1950s and 1960s came to play a dominant role in the development of German social history. During these years he guided numerous dissertations in the field, and he also enjoyed a position of considerable institutional dominance, controlling an institute for the funding and publication of social-historical research. Conze, in other words, was not merely a representative figure within the German historical profession, but rather played a crucial role in defining its methods and objectives in the postwar era. His own reflections on his career and intellectual development thus hold particular interest. He provided some of these in an autobiographical fragment published in 1983, three years before his death, and in it, in keeping with the publication history of his *Habilitationschrift*, he stressed continuities between the intellectual worlds of the 1930s and those of the 1950s and 1960s. In the first place, little needed to change within the historical profession itself, "since the few historians who had been Nazis left the public arena either through death or through loss of office." (In fact of the 110 German history professors in 1945, 20 were condemned after the war for National Socialist activities and theoretically disqualified from teaching; all were reintegrated in 1951.)[5] For the rest, most of the professoriate worked within traditions of research and interpretation set in the nineteenth century, privileging political history; for them, "neither the year 1933 nor 1945 influenced the course of their individual studies"—except for those who took up issues of the German "'destiny'" or "'going astray,'" both of which Conze placed in quotation marks, to indicate a certain ironical distance. (Elsewhere he wrote that "the 'revision of the German idea of history' was, under the psychological

4. Conze, "Die Wirkungen der liberalen Agrarreformen," 2–43. For Conze's position within postwar German historiography, see Schulze, *Deutsche Geschichtswissenschaft*, 254–65, 281–301, appendix.
5. Schulze, *Deutsche Geschichtswissenschaft*, 124–27.

pressure of the victors' preachings and our own scruples, sometimes excessive, sometimes masochistic.")[6] Conze did not count himself a political historian, yet he too saw his work as continuing prewar themes.
"Already before the war . . . I took a position against the 'traditional'
event-oriented history [histoire historisante], and sought a way to join more
analytical methods to the traditional hermaneutic forms of interpretation."
And so to conclude: "The decisive experiences and turning points in my
scientific development took place in the years before and after the war.
The personal and political shocks of the year 1945 constituted no new
beginning or break in continuity; they simply confirmed and strengthened my course."[7]

   I will return shortly to consider what exact intellectual currents Conze
had in mind as he formulated this view of his career. First, however, it
is necessary to consider the place of statements such as Conze's within
recent historical thinking. A handful of German historians have begun to
explore them and to underline the vitality of German historical research
in the 1933–45 period. An excellent recent conference volume follows a
series of historians through these years, including Conze himself, and
seeks to evaluate the degree of continuity in their thought.[8] Michael Burleigh has demonstrated the enormous vitality of historical studies of eastern Europe during these years; even after the outbreak of war, researchers
(Conze himself was one) continued to receive significant stipends for
studies of the region's society and culture.[9] Götz Aly has mainly pursued
the search for smoking guns, hard evidence of close collaboration between
historians and Nazi extermination efforts.[10] Winfried Schulze, by contrast,
has viewed the question mainly in terms of modernization. The National
Socialist period involved a dramatic acceleration of German social and
technological change, Schulze has written, and the development of historical thought was one such domain. Technologies that developed during the 1930s remained important in the postwar world, whatever their
associations with National Socialist crimes; in just the same way, historical
techniques retained their full scientific value, whatever the circumstances
in which they originally developed.[11]

---

6. Conze, "Die deutsche Geschichtswissenschaft," 21–43, 31.
7. Conze, "Der Weg zur Sozialgeschichte," 73–81.
8. Lehmann and Melton, Paths of Continuity.
9. Burleigh, Germany Turns Eastward.
10. Aly, Macht-Geist-Wahn, 153–79.
11. Schulze, Deutsche Geschichtswissenschaft, 302–11. In two extended reviews, Georg Iggers

Neither vision seems fully satisfactory. Our task as students of historical writing is not merely to condemn past errors, in the manner of Aly; nor can one be satisfied with a purely technical vision of historical writing, such as Schulze presents—as the examples below are intended to illustrate. Whatever modifications one may wish to bring to these positions, however, it is also important to note the lack of resonance that they have had except among a limited band of specialists. In the United States, it is probably fair to say, commonsense orthodoxy has remained closer to the view enunciated by Fritz Stern, in an essay that he republished in 1987. Stern presents the National Socialist years as essentially a vacuum in German historical thought, a time (he writes) in which "we [Americans] were the custodians of German history; in 1945 we returned to Germany as conquering reeducators. It took some time for German historians to recover from the inner and outer emigration, from the ready submission of many of them to the dictates of National Socialism." Only after 1960 did there emerge a "renewed vitality among German historians and a willingness to challenge the prevailing conservative consensus."[12] Stern's remarks suggest a considerable gap in historical interpretation, the more remarkable in view of his own distinction as an historian and his command of the field. This disjuncture perhaps expresses the moral assumptions of American liberalism, which has readily taken for granted the centrality of the Holocaust in twentieth-century thought. Such assumptions allow little room for a view such as Conze's own, which presents not a vacuum but a plenum of German historical studies in the interwar years, and even during the war itself, and which saw no decisive intellectual break coming from knowledge of the Holocaust.

Werner Conze's first dissertation had appeared in 1934. It was undertaken at the University of Königsberg, on the far eastern edge of Germany as then defined, and it concerned a subject of intense local interest: in *Hirschenhof* (as the dissertation was titled) he studied a German "language island" in Livonia, seeking to follow what happened as German immigrants settled in Slavic territory (in this instance within the Russian

---

summarizes this literature and explores its implications; for Schulze, see Iggers, review of *Deutsche Geschichtswissenschaft*; for Willi Oberkromme, see Iggers, review of *Volksgeschichte*.

12. Stern, "Americans and the German Past," quotation at 267. See also the very similar formulation presented by Arnoldo Momigliano in 1961 in "Historicism in Contemporary Thought."

empire) during the eighteenth and nineteenth centuries. Conze noted in introducing the work that his dissertation formed part of a developing field of "language-island studies," indicating a widespread interest in understanding how German societies functioned within this alien territory. However scholarly, such studies had also obvious practical overtones, at the very least as a basis for nationalistic claims to these territories, and for this reason they continued to receive funding even during the war itself. Conze's introduction paid due homage to this vision of German influence in the Slavic east. In southeastern Europe, he wrote, this amounted to the "fulfillment of a historical mission for the states of the East, which could be carried out only by German peasants, creating there a German cultural territory."[13] In the case of Hirschenhof, the settlers' heroic efforts added to the drama of the tale. Conze described the difficult years after the colonists' arrival in the region, when famine repeatedly threatened in a barely cleared environment, then traces their growing prosperity in the nineteenth century—prosperity that allowed a tenfold population increase between 1766 and 1858.

Studies of the German peasant community (especially when the community found itself among Slavic populations in eastern Europe) held obvious ideological resonance in the 1930s, as they had already in the nineteenth century, in the work of Wilhelm Heinrich von Riehl.[14] At the same time, *Hirschenhof* shows no signs of Hitlerian racism. The work includes only two references to Jews, neither of them hostile, plus a third reference that was positive though implicit—to the Jewish Hans Rothfels, Conze's dissertation director, who had been forced to leave his professorship at Königsberg in 1933 and flee to safety in the United States.[15] A year after Rothfels's emigration, Conze warmly acknowledged his teacher's influence, which included Rothfels's suggesting the dissertation topic itself. Nor did Conze suggest deep cultural (let alone racial) divides between the German settlers of Hirschenhof and their Slavic neighbors. The Germans proved more advanced in artisanal trades than did the groups they settled among, but their agriculture was relatively backward, and even in the late nineteenth century they showed less interest in education than other groups (11–12, 124 ff.). Even their sense of German identity developed haltingly. Early on they divided along regional lines, according to the

13. Conze, *Hirschenhof,* 8.
14. The author of *Land und Leute* (1853). For an interesting case of Riehl's wider influence, see Eliot, "Natural History of German Life."
15. Conze, *Hirschenhof,* 94, 106, 3. Further page references appear parenthetically in the text.

parts of Germany from which they came. Belief in a larger German identity emerged only in response to the rising national claims of their Slavic
neighbors. The Hirschenhof colonists remained blithely convinced of their
own superiority and never dreamed of intermarriage with other local
groups, but the boundaries of their community were local, not national.

Given all this, it is not surprising that Conze's text could be reprinted
entirely unchanged in 1963, without embarrassing expurgation. In this
sense it abundantly verifies his claim to intellectual continuity. The republication testified to another continuity, that of German historians'
interest in German communities outside the German state. After World
War II, the subject became a major preoccupation for Conze and his colleagues; in keeping with these interests, the republication was financed
by the "Deutsche-Baltischen Landmannschaft" and by the Ministry for
Refugees and Greater German [gesamtdeutschen] Questions (132–33).

The book's methods point in a similar direction. Conze displayed some
anxiety about maintaining the boundaries of historical research, emphasizing that he was not attempting a study of folklore; and much of the
work concerns itself with the colony's politics and institutions. Yet he
could not avoid addressing modes of life within the village, and for these,
unconventional historical sources were needed. In his phrase, to understand these aspects of village life "the narrower historical methods must
in many places be left behind"; in any event, as he noted, "this mode of
research is no longer something new or unusual, especially for language-
island studies" (10). Interdisciplinary social history was thus an established professional fact, perhaps needing defense but not lengthy apology.
The interlocking questions of family structure, land use, and population
provided the main focus for this approach. The Hirschenhof colonists
practiced a rigorous form of primogeniture, pushing younger sons into
artisanal work and ensuring that farming families had large amounts of
land. The system required constant migration to Riga, the only city nearby,
but at that price the agrarian settlement retained its vitality. Here Conze
drew a fundamental distinction between German and Slavic culture areas,
a distinction that continued to preoccupy him in later research. In most
regions of the east, he argued, German settlements were alone in exercis-
ing this kind of Malthusian control, and the result was a growing contrast between German settlements and those of surrounding peoples: the
latter were quickly condemned to rural overpopulation and immiseration, ensuring that "the superiority of German colonists over their alien
[fremdvölkischen] neighbors was not lost." The distinction mattered less

around Hirschenhof, where Germans held most lordships and enforced on all tenants German patterns of inheritance. The tense relationship between land and population would be a central theme in Conze's later work; he presented Hirschenhof as a counterexample, showing how traditional German institutions could cope with the threat (79).

Such comments suggest Conze's desire to blur the distinction between political and social histories, his alertness to the presence of political forces in the social realm. Certainly his treatment of peasant politics is itself striking, for he repeatedly stressed its seriousness, sophistication, and effectiveness. The German peasants viewed themselves as enjoying special rights within the Russian empire, and they used every available means to defend themselves. They used the law effectively, sent representatives to St. Petersburg, and on a few occasions resorted to violence, as in 1827, when they rebelled against efforts to dismantle their self-run law court. Such movements rarely concerned only money, Conze argued. Instead, they turned on village pride, independence, and collective identity. Conze claimed to detect such values even in his own time: "[I]n the consciousness of the colonists there remains even today a lively sense that they had formed a distinctive order against the formerly unfree peasants. With this pride they had also a sense of being bound in an immediate relationship to the Russian czar" (50–77; quotation at 73). Mentalities endured, and the historian needed the methods of folklore in order to understand them.

At this point we encounter an apparent tension in Conze's position—and in that of other historians writing in the 1930s about the German peasantry. Conze wrote under an authoritarian regime and endorsed many of its principles. Yet he, like his fellows, tended to dwell positively on instances of peasant rebelliousness and to stress its rational, considered qualities. A much more dramatic example of the same phenomenon was supplied by Günther Franz, the leading student of the German Peasants' War of 1525. Far more than Conze, Franz was an enthusiastic participant in the National Socialist regime, in fact an SS officer. In 1935 he publicly denounced the historian Hans Rosenberg as Jewish and claimed to find in Rosenberg's work typically Jewish qualities; the identification rested entirely on race, since Rosenberg's mother was Christian, and Rosenberg himself had been baptized a Christian.[16] Franz also included celebratory

16. Winkler, "Pioneer in the Historical Sciences"; more generally on Franz, see Theibault, "Demography of the Thirty Years War Re-visited."

comments about the National Socialist regime in his published scholarly work. Yet he published his history of the Peasants' War in 1933, and the work received new editions in 1939 and 1943. Like Werner Conze, Franz stressed continuities in his thought between the 1930s and the 1950s, though with somewhat less self-assurance. When yet another edition appeared in 1956, he introduced it as follows: "Perhaps I might present many issues differently today than twenty-five years ago, yet one can only write such a book once. Thus I have limited myself to removing a few untimely [*zeitbedingte*] sentences from the conclusion" and to updating a few references.[17] Comparison with the book's 1939 edition confirms the accuracy of this claim. Even the book's passages on the anti-Semitic movements of the late Middle Ages remained unchanged from the prewar edition. Franz's vision of the peasantry was in fact no different in the 1950s and 1960s from what it had been in the 1930s.

That vision remains important within the profession. Peter Blickle, today the leading authority on peasant movements in sixteenth-century Germany, was Franz's assistant in the 1960s, collaborated with him on sizeable projects, and edited the *Festschrift* that appeared in his honor in 1982. Blickle himself defined what he took to be Franz's contribution to historical studies: "[T]hat the peasant was introduced as a political entity in German history," he addressed his teacher, "is truly your doing." He also stressed the powerful appeal that this vision had for other young historians beginning their studies in the 1950s and 1960s, who turned to Franz even though his Nazi past still barred him from officially directing their work.[18] In some degree, as Blickle suggested in another work from the early 1980s, this vision could serve to found a larger understanding of the patterns of German history. Passivity and obedience were no deep-seated national character flaws, but rather the product of particular historical circumstances, in some instances even of accidents.[19] In effect Franz's legacy was recycled to sustain the view that German political life was not inevitably or forever tainted.

Franz confronts us in especially troubling form with themes that we have already encountered in reflecting on Werner Conze's early work. Franz's historical interpretations developed during the 1930s, yet reappeared without needing even cosmetic changes in the 1950s and 1960s,

---

17. Franz, *Die deutsche Bauernkrieg,* 1972 ed., 1:vii; comparison with 1939 ed.
18. Blickle, *Bauer, Reich und Reformation,* 5, 6.
19. Blickle, *Obedient Germans?*

and indeed came to play an important role in the socially critical history of those years.[20] For Franz's theme was peasant agency and the peasants' ability to resist hegemonic discourses from both church and state. His views formed a particularly striking contrast to what is conventionally taken to be the dominant thread of German historiography. Much of that historiography celebrated the triumph of the state as a rational and benevolent overseer of society's needs and saw in peasant rebelliousness the threat of chaos. Leopold von Ranke, for instance, described the peasants of 1525 as motivated "by long-cherished hatred and lust of revenge, . . . their fury . . . inflamed by the ravings of fanatical preachers." They had begun with reasonable grievances and might have secured remedies for them with sensible behavior. "But it is not in human nature to rest content with moderate success; it is vain to expect reason or forbearance from a conquering multitude."[21]

In contrast, Franz presented the state's triumph as tragedy. Its indifference to the opinions and actions of ordinary people signified the society's loss of creative vitality. Further, the peasants' resistance centered not on economic grievances but on basic political values. They sought to preserve autonomous customs of justice, their right to set their own laws. "In vain the peasants defended themselves during the Peasants' War against the Etatisation of justice . . . in hardly any other domain did the oppression of the population show itself so clearly."[22] Even the state's eventual benevolence showed the damage it had wrought. That the peasants eventually acquired their freedom at the state's generous hand, rather than through their own political efforts, sadly typified the new situation. "The peasant," he concluded, was "no longer the subject but only the object of politics." German society would have been the healthier had the peasants won their freedoms through their own, revolutionary actions.[23] This essentially political conception of the peasants' outlook and demands ran very deep in Franz's work and was not limited to his study of the 1525 rebellion. His other major work on the peasants, which follows them from the early Middle Ages into the nineteenth century, sought to underline the same qualities, within a larger context. In this work, he explained, he

---

20. For brief discussion of the idea that social history was especially a concern of the Left in 1960s Germany, see Introduction, above.

21. Von Ranke, *History of the Reformation in Germany*, 1:352.

22. Franz, *Die deutsche Bauernkrieg*, 1972 ed., 1:68–69.

23. Franz, *Die deutsche Bauernkrieg*, 1972 ed., 1:299–300.

sought to write about the peasants as "the bearers of historical reality and change."[24]

We are used to viewing stress on the agency of peasants and other subject groups as the particular mark of radical history, in the tradition, for instance, of the British historian E. P. Thompson.[25] What are we to make of an analysis that explicitly attaches this vision to the National Socialist triumph? For this was the thrust of the "untimely" statements that Franz felt necessary to excise from later editions of the book. "For the first time since the Reformation," he wrote in 1939, "National Socialism has based a revolutionary movement directly on the peasants, and in so doing it has brought it back into the political life of our people."[26] One link between these two aspects of his thought lay in Franz's understanding of the sources of peasants' political agency. He viewed political and biological vitality as overlapping phenomena, and in this sense at least there was little contradiction between rebelliousness and National Socialist ideals. The peasants' defeat in 1525, he concluded, killed thousands of the ablest among them, and in this represented a permanent loss to German society. "The most daring, most open-minded, the readiest for action [*einsatzbereitesten*, a word with sinister echoes after World War II] forces of the peasantry and the petty bourgeoisie of the cities were rooted out. The Peasants' War thus constituted even from a biological viewpoint an unusually severe loss for our entire nation." Death of the courageous and open-minded meant a reduction in these qualities in future generations. These sentences remained when the book was republished in 1972.[27]

Günther Franz represents an extreme and troubling instance of the intellectual continuities between the 1930s and the 1970s, because his association with the National Socialist regime was so direct and enthusiastic. Whereas nearly all his colleagues were reintegrated after 1951, Franz was effectively barred from university teaching, and he spent the remainder of his career teaching at an agricultural institute. (Blickle, it should be noted, presented this relegation as in some measure a victimization: genuine students were denied Franz, he delicately wrote, "because

24. Franz, *Geschichte des deutschen Bauernstandes*, 7. The study, which Franz wrote with Blickle's collaboration, forms part of a very important five-volume collection on German rural history—another indication of Franz's centrality within the intellectual world of postwar Germany.

25. See, for instance, Thompson's essays on rural society, collected in his *Customs in Common*.

26. Franz, *Die deutsche Bauernkrieg*, 1939 ed., 1:307; see also vi.

27. Franz, *Die deutsche Bauernkrieg*, 1972 ed., 1:299–300.

of political events and personal fate.")[28] Yet his example helps us to understand other cases of intellectual continuity, closer to the mainstream of German historical thought and more successfully integrated into the postwar world—the numerous figures like Conze, for whom National Socialist ideology mattered less and whose writing avoided vivid political commentary. German scholars produced an abundant array of research in the years after 1933, and they continued to do so after the outbreak of war. More important, some of the values that informed this work remained important during the postwar period; younger scholars like Blickle carried on the work and ideas of the older generation. The influence that these works exercised testified in part to their technical sophistication. At the same time, we cannot endorse the view of Schulze and others that sees in these writings only advances in historical technique, in the manner of the other technical disciplines that the National Socialist regime encouraged. These works were very far from pure ideology, but neither were they divorced from the concerns of contemporary life. It is their complexity that renders these ideological components difficult for the historian to pin down. Certainly notions of "radical" and "conservative" do scant justice to them.[29]

Werner Conze completed his *Habilitationschrift* in about 1940, and a first volume appeared in that year, titled *Agrarian Organization in Lithuania and White Russia*.[30] On active military service, Conze nevertheless managed to continue his research after 1940, and in 1943, amazingly, he defended the work at the University of Giessen and received certification as a potential professor. (The last part of the work, as noted above, only appeared in 1949, and then in abbreviated form.) Even given the extraordinary wartime setting, defending his work had not been an easy process. Initially he had wanted to habilitate in Vienna, but historians there found the work too distant from their concepts of research.[31] The vitality of interwar German social history did not ensure its practitioners universal acceptance.

28. Blickle, *Bauer, Reich und Reformation*, 6.
29. As an example of the political ambiguities in these views, cf. Thomas Brady's suggestion that there is "more than a Marxist whiff of history as the history of class conflict" in Blickle's conception of the German "common man." Blickle, *Obedient Germans*, xii, translator's introduction.
30. Conze, *Agrarverfassung und Bevölkerung*.
31. Among the skeptics was Otto Brunner, who would later collaborate closely with Conze on several projects.

Like Conze's dissertation, the new work fitted clearly into contemporary concerns. It appeared in a series, Germany and the East: Sources and Research on the History of Their Relations, edited by Hermann Aubin himself. The topic had practical implications, for such studies provided empirical bases for Germany's dealings with the eastern regions that it now ruled; for this reason Conze received substantial research support from the German Institute for Eastern Research. At the same time, it is again important to recognize how very scholarly Conze's work remained. This was a major piece of research, which relied on the same kinds of sources as the great French regional studies that followed Bloch's *French Rural History*: field maps, seigneurial accounts, tax rolls, in an impressive array of eastern European languages.

The study focuses on interactions between population and resources on the frontier between German and Russian cultures. It starts from a simple Malthusian model, in which each society has a limited number of places. Every expansion of resources—"whether through new clearings or through better organization of social life—creates along with new social positions also the precondition for rapid population growth."[32] But Conze argued against too simple or too narrow a definition of social resources. *Lebensraum,* as he termed it, was not a merely geographical or even technological conception. It rested instead on "the ability and the will of a people to organize, fill up, claim the naturally given landscape through work and struggle."[33] This language has heavily racial overtones, but Conze's argument mainly concerns the place of culture and institutions in economic life. At its center is the notion of "agrarian order" (*Agrarverfassung*), the social and political arrangement of rural space. Changes in these could count for as much as new inventions or discoveries. In the Russian and Polish regions that he studied, this meant above all the introduction of German systems of village organization and lordship.[34] Political decisions underlay the process. The grand dukes of Lithuania, for instance, faced intensified international competition in the sixteenth century, and in response they called in German legal experts to reconfigure their domains. Lands were surveyed, farms consolidated, three-field rotations introduced; these changes in turn led to surplus agricultural production, which could be marketed to the growing cities of the Baltic. The demographic consequences predicted by Conze's Malthusian model soon

32. Conze, *Agrarverfassung und Bevölkerung,* 1.
33. Conze, *Agrarverfassung und Bevölkerung,* 1.
34. Conze, *Agrarverfassung und Bevölkerung,* 62–63.

followed. With the new arrangements firmly in place, he demonstrated, population doubled after 1700. However, again in keeping with his Malthusian model, the number of social places quickly stabilized at its new, higher level. "The number of peasant families had to remain about the same, once all the farms had been settled."[35]

Conze thus presented a simple Malthusian model, with politics as its governing force. In a much later essay, he suggested the general applicability of this vision: "[T]here is no social structure that has not arisen from political forces or whose changes are not politically conditioned."[36] Yet in keeping with the interests that he developed in *Hirschenhof*, he understood political forces in broad terms, as including ordinary people as well as elites. Alongside the politics of lordship, there was a peasant politics of resistance. He found only one large-scale peasant rebellion in these regions, but an almost endless peasant opposition ("Widerstand der Bauern") evident in daily affairs. Most important for Conze's demographic model, Polish and Lithuanian peasants refused to follow the inheritance patterns that the new system demanded. Into the nineteenth century, they sought to follow long-standing customs of partible inheritance.[37] Even in his study of non-German regions, Conze thus continued to stress the vitality of peasant politics and peasants' independence from the cultural powers set over them. Lordship exercised little moral authority over its subjects; it survived only through a process of constant struggle.

Yet such resistance also proved the weak point in the system of Malthusian controls that he had analyzed. For partible inheritance meant population growth, and the region offered few outlets for surplus population. Conze's fears about this situation led him to some of the most starkly ideological statements in his historical writing, concerning both Slavs and Jews—views that he repeated without significant modification in the 1950s, and some of which reappeared in a 1992 collection of essays. In 1953, thus, he wrote of eastern Europe around 1900: "[S]cientific sociological investigation into its ethnic and social groupings would underline the crisis-ridden character of east European social structure. The peasantry, the overwhelming majority of whom had not yet been incorporated into a rationalized, capitalist estate system, lived locked in a prerational, magical stage of consciousness, without self-control . . . untouched by the

35. Conze, *Agrarverfassung und Bevölkerung*, 120; for population growth, see 208.
36. Conze, "Die Strukturgeschichte," 66–85, 77.
37. Conze, *Agrarverfassung und Bevölkerung*, 122, 170, 172–73.

state or its spirit."[38] A few years later he made the same point in a study of German-Polish relations during World War I. In East Prussia and Upper Silesia, he noted, Polish populations benefited from the long period of German rule, which accustomed them to conditions of modern economic activity, a "civilizing process of the Poles under Prussian overlordship." Austrian and Russian districts enjoyed far more independence, and the consequence was overpopulation and the threat of social chaos by the end of the nineteenth century.[39] As concerned eastern Europe, at least, Conze remained an admirer of the Prussian state, as a source of orderly development in what otherwise would have been a chaotic region.

It was from this perspective that Jews appeared in Conze's work—again, in terms that scarcely changed between the early 1940s and the mid-1950s. Excess rural population could find no places in the eastern European cities, he wrote, because "the bourgeois positions lay overwhelmingly in the hands of a German or ethnically German bourgeoisie, or in the hands of the Jews, who had been forced into the cities and who ruled the marketplaces typical of the region."[40] These lines were published after the war, and are scarcely distinguishable from the three references to Jews that I count in his 1940 volume. At no point did Conze express any particular sympathy for the Jews, and certainly he never presented them as connected to German society. But in some ways his harshest statement came in 1953—and was reprinted in 1992: a local bourgeoisie failed to develop in eastern Europe, he wrote, because of the "blockage of the leading positions and enterprises by the Jews in most states."[41] Both before and after the war, Conze used the language of sociological problem in discussing the Jews' situation. Neither race nor religion entered these statements in his main published works (though it appears from recent researches by Götz Aly that in the late 1930s Conze on occasion also expressed more racist views, in statements that appear to have been motivated by academic opportunism.[42]) His assumptions, rather, were those of his Malthusian model. After the introduction of German institutions in the seventeenth and eighteenth centuries, eastern Europe experienced no substantial changes in its productive capacities; it had no new social slots to offer its expanding population. Only social

---

38. Conze, "Die Strukturkrise," 401–21, 405.
39. Conze, *Polnische Nation und deutsche Politik*, 3–17, quotation at 7.
40. Conze, "Die Wirkungen der liberalen Agrarreformen," 28.
41. Conze, "Die Strukturkrise," 416.
42. Aly, *Macht-Geist-Wahn*, 162, 165–66.

conflict and breakdown could follow, and ethnic conflict would be one likely aspect of the process.

To this point, Conze's scholarship abundantly confirms his 1983 statement, that his intellectual orientations changed little over the National Socialist and postwar years—even, it seems, when those orientations were tinged with anti-Slavic or anti-Semitic views. Clearly he was correct to say that his thinking was not in any simple way merely imprinted with National Socialist ideas. In his case, as in that of Günther Franz, this continuity in historical concepts had complex ideological implications. Conze produced research of a very high order, following in the 1930s research standards that historians employ today. Other versions of these ideas would play a central role in the great French rural histories of the 1960s and 1970s. At the same time, his work was never entirely without its ideological elements. It was in part a story about the encounter between German and Slavic cultures, about the social problems of eastern Europe, and about the dangers of disorder. In that encounter, Germans functioned as teachers, bringing order and civilization to what otherwise would be a "prerational," chaotic society.

These highly contemporary concerns did not disappear at the war's end, but they did take on a new and dramatic form: ethnic Germans (like those of Hirschenhof) now found themselves unwelcome in much of Eastern Europe, and millions of them became voluntary or involuntary refugees, seeking asylum within the reduced German borders of 1945. They and their plight were a major preoccupation of West German politics during the 1950s, and in these years Conze joined a team of leading historians charged with writing their history, eventually producing eight massive volumes of analysis and documentation.[43] Robert Moeller has recently explored the development of this project, and has elegantly shown the mixture of scholarly and political motives underlying it. As he notes, it involved many of the most important figures in the postwar historical community: Conze, his teacher Hans Rothfels, his contemporary (and immediate predecessor as president of the German Historical Association) Theodor Schieder, and several younger scholars who would go on to distinguished careers, including Hans-Ulrich Wehler and Martin Broszat.[44] Here I want only to emphasize both the starkness with which the collection addressed the concerns of its era and the echoes that it contained of

43. Schieder, *Dokumentation der Vertreibung*.
44. Moeller, *War Stories*.

prewar scholarship such as Conze's. The divide between history and politics remained as porous in the 1950s and early 1960s as it had been in the 1930s.

The volumes attempt to combine quantitative analyses with vivid eyewitness accounts, and quantification undergirds a simple, though mainly implicit, argument: German deaths in the immediate postwar years were very numerous, reaching the same order of magnitude as Jewish deaths during the war.[45] The collection argues that 2.1 million Germans died in the Polish districts alone, about 16 percent of the German population living there; it attributes 1.6 million of these deaths directly to the events of the expulsion, the remainder coming from the privations and other ill-treatment of these years. The same concern with comparability marks the collection's analysis of its qualitative data, the survivors' accounts of their experiences during the expulsions. For the most part these were presented directly, without editorial comment. But the editors attempted to summarize these documents, often in very strong language, with explicit comparisons to Jewish sufferings a few years earlier: "[A]s once the SS guards in the concentration camps . . . , so now the Polish security forces had a free hand, and in the prisons of East Prussia, Pomerania, and Upper Silesia, the same persecutions and mistreatment played themselves out." Here German civil populations encountered "a true sadism in the invention of tortures and other forms of degradation."[46] In Czechoslovakia as in Poland, the editors found systematic efforts to apply National Socialist techniques to Germans—and this included reopening the National Socialist camps and continuing the tortures inflicted there.[47] The editors acknowledged the rage that local populations must have felt at their former oppressors, but concluded that this played little role in the specific processes of victimization. The Germans who were "persecuted, mistreated, imprisoned, and killed for the most part were not the guilty, and often had no inkling" of the National Socialist war crimes.[48]

Saul Friedlander suggests that such claims to equivalency of suffering, between Jews through 1945 and Germans in the immediate postwar years, have recently acquired disturbing legitimacy in German scholarly discourse, moving "from the periphery to the center of the public scene."

45. For the frequency of such claims in the German literature, though Friedlander does not refer to the refugees project in this regard, cf. Friedlander, *Memory, History, and the Extermination of the Jews.* 13.
46. Schieder, *Dokumentation der Vertreibung,* 1:112 (Einleitung).
47. Schieder, *Dokumentation der Vertreibung,* 4:63.
48. Schieder, *Dokumentation der Vertreibung,* 1:125E.

He sees these efforts as responses to 1980s debates about the efforts of Ernst Nolte and others to normalize Hitler and even to stress his positive achievements.[49] However disturbing such recent claims may be, though, it is important to note that already in the 1950s they had received endorsement from central figures in the German historical profession. We may note also the presence in these analyses of more explicit forms of racial analysis. Alongside their sufferings at the hands of local populations, German civilians in these districts had also to confront the advancing Red Army. Soviet soldiers, so the reports ran, raped an "enormous number" of German women; and this fact reflected "a mode of behavior and mentality [*Mentalität*] . . . that strike European conceptions as strange and repellent." Strange and repellent, in fact, because they originated outside Europe. The Soviet soldiers held to "traditions and ideas still current in the Asiatic regions of Russia. . . . Had such values not been widely shared among the Soviet troops, the forms and number of assaults would have been unthinkable. The fact that Soviet soldiers of Asiatic origins showed themselves especially ungoverned and wild confirms that certain traits of the Asiatic mentality contributed to these horrors."[50]

The editors had enlisted the concept of mentality to play a crude political role. At the war's end, so they argued, German populations directly confronted extreme otherness, and their ensuing sufferings demonstrated the real cultural divide between Europe and Asia. Fear of communism may be have sharpened these differences, but they were in fact much older: the product of ancient ethnic traditions and of the social tensions that Conze had earlier studied in the region. The accounts validated Germany's place on the European side of this divide, showing that innocent Germans had suffered nearly as much as Jews from the war and its aftermath. Like Conze's *Habilitationschrift*, the project ultimately centered on the problem of disorder at the margins of Europe. In those regions, the breakdown of order had remained a constant possibility since the early nineteenth century. The explosions of the war's ends were only a further development in a long chain of circumstances.

In these preoccupations, the refugees project fitted well with Werner Conze's prewar research interests and themes. But in one important respect it pointed toward a decisive break that his work would undergo in the postwar era, a break that his published memoir does not lead us

49. Friedlander, *Memory, History and the Extermination of the Jews*, 34.
50. Schieder, *Dokumentation der Vertreibung*, 1:61E.

to expect and one that forms a suggestive counterpoint to changes in the *Annales* themselves in the same years. After 1945 the *Annales* changed its chronological orientation, turning toward the early modern and away from the problems of contemporary society that had so greatly interested Bloch and Febvre in the 1930s. Conze in the same years turned decisively toward modernity as a subject of historical study. His choice had far more than personal significance, for he was to prove a gifted academic entrepreneur. In 1958 he secured government funding for a Working Group on Modern Social History, and this allowed the establishment of a major publication series on the "Industrial World." Thus fortified, over the following twenty years his seminar in Cologne would be the preeminent center of social history research in Germany, and many of the leading figures of the following generation would pass through it. Conze's turn to the modern brought a large group of other scholars with him.

Conze apparently did not speak directly to this changed emphasis in his work, and to some degree its meaning must remain a matter of speculation.[51] Institutional changes perhaps artificially magnify its significance, for German history departments at that time did not treat the early modern and modern periods as distinct fields of specialization. It nonetheless remains striking that Conze entirely relinquished the rural studies on which he had focused in the 1930s and that the early modern period ceased to hold much importance for him. He used dramatic language when speaking of the need to orient historical studies toward the period from the late eighteenth century on. The Industrial and French Revolutions made this a time of change whose only equivalent had come with the invention of agriculture, around 4000 b.c., a "change in human organization [*Daseinordnung*]" that made insignificant traditional chronological divisions like that marking the end of the Middle Ages.[52] The new world thus created called for new historical methods. "For researching history since the eighteenth century, we can no longer make do with the traditional questions and methods of [early] modern history, for over the past century or two our historical life has undergone such a far-reaching structural change; we need to work with altogether new questions and methods, if we are to understand properly our time of great revolutions, both industrial-technical and political."[53] It is consistent with these positions

51. Irmline Veit-Brause, in "Werner Conze," 302–3, notes Conze's extreme reticence in discussing his intellectual development and choices.
52. Conze, *Gesellschaft-Staat-Nation*, 72–73.
53. Conze, *Gesellschaft-Staat-Nation*, 96.

that Conze also turned his attention away from Russia and eastern Europe, despite his impressive command of the languages needed for their study. After the mid-1950s, he became a historian of the modern West, above all the West of the nineteenth century.[54]

This preoccupation led to a variety of research agendas. Conze spoke of the need for close study of workers' experiences during industrialization, and he suggested that careful attention to the biographies of ordinary men and women might be a way to get at these, as well as other characteristic experiences of the modern era.[55] He stressed the widening of history's subject matter—"which seems almost limitless"—in these circumstances.[56] Most important, these interests led Conze to participate in and strongly support another of the great collective projects of German postwar historical writing, a massive dictionary of fundamental historical concepts.[57] He served as one of the project's two senior editors (the third editor, Reinhard Koselleck, had been his assistant), and wrote numerous articles for it. In some respects a history of ideas, the dictionary sought to trace deep levels of historical change. The very conceptions with which people organize their worlds have histories, so runs the project's fundamental argument; uncovering these is essential to understanding the depth of the changes that have occurred in the modern era. This concern directly translated Conze's sense that the revolutionary changes of modernity far outweighed all others of written history. Fundamental structures of perception have changed, so that the same words now have different meanings. The project located these changes in the years around 1800 and argued that together the French and Industrial Revolutions transformed our understanding as well as our ways of living.

Conze's shift to modernity, coinciding so exactly with the *Annales* historians' move toward the preindustrial, raises questions about the sources of intellectual choice in both France and Germany and may suggest some splintering of European thought in the postwar years. Bloch and Febvre certainly had more contact with German scholarship than their postwar successors. We can offer other hypotheses on why Conze and his associates turned so decisively toward study of the industrial world. Obviously,

---

54. Even his 1958 study of German-Polish relations centers on the German administration of Poland during World War I. Conze, *Polnische Nation und deutsche Politik.*

55. Conze, *Gesellschaft-Staat-Nation,* "Sozialgeschichte," 86–94.

56. Conze, "Die deutsche Geschichtswissenschaft," 21–43, 39–40.

57. Brunner, Conze, and Koselleck, eds., *Geschichtliche Grundbegriffe.* For an excellent overview, see Tribe, "The *Geschichtliche Grundbegriffe* Project," 180–84.

complicated guilts and memories attached to Germany's position in eastern Europe before 1945, and to the entire tradition of inquiry centering on the region. German ambitions in the region had ended, and to that extent the study of economic underdevelopment too had lost its practical relevance for German scholars. There was less reason to examine rural communities like *Hirschenhof*, whereas French scholars remained engaged by the colonial and postcolonial world and believed their studies of preindustrial Europe relevant to understanding that world. Possibly German concern with the modern world also reflected the rising influence of Anglo-American social science in the 1950s, with its rigorous distinctions between industrial and preindustrial societies and its concern with modernization theory. And, as several scholars have suggested, emphasizing the cataclysmic changes brought by Europe's modernization allowed German scholars to view their own recent disasters as part of a larger set of problems, an extreme manifestation of the tensions that the industrial and political revolutions unleashed in all societies.[58]

However relevant, though, these suggestions do not add up to complete explanation, and all admit of counterarguments. One might have expected the Cold War, for instance, to stimulate interest in eastern European studies, including the study of Russian and Baltic agriculture. Conze himself claimed that postwar circumstances particularly favored study of the region. "It is certainly the moment today," he wrote in 1958, "with the detachment of a sadly experienced, sobered generation, to take up in an objective way German-Polish relations";[59] but in fact the subject had ceased to be of central importance in his thought. Ultimately, it is perhaps the underlying similarities between French and German interpretation in these years that deserve emphasis. Both represented efforts to establish a frontier between premodern and modern worlds and to establish the difference between them as structural. Systemic difference became a central theme in both traditions, a difference so vast as to have created an epistemological chasm between modern historians and the premodern subjects of their studies.

What relevance do these German comparisons have for understanding the history and functions of French social history? First, the examples of Günther Franz and Werner Conze demonstrate, yet again, that social

---

58. On the importance of this theme, see Schulze, *Deutsche Geschichtschreibung*, 226–27.
59. Conze, *Polnische Nation und deutsche Politik*, v.

history can as easily derive from authoritarian as from radical or critical political impulses.[60] Like most of his colleagues in the German profession, Conze held conservative political beliefs and cooperated enthusiastically with the National Socialist regime. He offered no apologies after 1945, and he treated with some irony those who sought to reflect on "the German catastrophe." There is no sign that he viewed the Holocaust as an especially important fact about the German or Western experience, or that other experiences from the 1930s and 1940s significantly redirected his thinking. Franz was a still more extreme example, a committed National Socialist. In twentieth-century Germany as in nineteenth-century France, the study of how societies functioned in the past was often a response to discomfort with the societies of the present.

But these examples also demonstrate (again, paralleling many of the other examples discussed in this study) the complex ways in which ideologies and social-historical thought might interact, for Franz and Conze regularly used concepts that are normally seen today as characterizing leftist historical thought. Questions of village community and popular agency interested them enormously, and they sought to interpret peasant politics in terms that transcended mere economic interests. Conze also sought to develop a sophisticated neo-Malthusian view of how population and resources interacted, using the sources and many of the analytical tools that would be taken up anew by historical demographers in the 1950s and 1960s. He used the concept of mentality, and in the 1950s his associates on the refugees project used the term itself.[61] His readiness to use these ideas does not mean that they lacked ideological force, or were independent of the circumstances from which they emerged. Rather, Conze's work shows the multi-valence of such concepts and approaches, their capacity to serve a variety of ideological needs—and the multiplicity of implications that they contain. Stress on peasants' capacity for political action, for instance, proved attractive both to National Socialists like Franz and to New Left historians of the 1960s.

Throughout Conze's career, his scholarship in fact responded visibly

60. In this respect, the historical profession fits with recent interest in exploring the roots of modernist thought in the fascist era; as one example, see Carroll, *French Literary Fascism*.

61. Keith Tribe's comments suggest the complex relations between political ideologies and social historical research: "To many readers, this [the *Geschichtliche Grundbegriffe* project] might seem to represent a kind of Marxist historiography. In the German intellectual context, however, it would be more accurately described as 'social liberal.'" Tribe, "*Geschichtliche Grundbegriffe* Project," 183. In fact, both Conze and Otto Brunner were very conservative in their politics.

and directly to needs and pressures in the society around him, and much of it had direct policy implications. This was as true of his studies of the early modern period as of his studies of the recent past. In the narrow sense, his researches served German plans to colonize eastern Europe, and after the war he contributed through the refugees project to reconstituting Germany's national identity, as a nation that also had been victimized by the war. But at a deeper level, his history addressed ideological needs that we have seen preoccupying French historians as well: like them, he was intent on establishing lines of difference between European and non-European, modern and underdeveloped worlds. French historians wrote with intense awareness of their nation's overseas domains and ambitions. For their German colleagues, this border ran instead through eastern Europe; there they found their images of underdevelopment and cultural difference. The images were not quite the same, but they testified to a common interest in applying historical study to the problems of modernity itself.

But if this comparison demonstrates important commonalities, it also displays a fundamental difference between French and German scholarship: whereas German historians stressed peasants' agency, their French colleagues stressed peasants' passivity and their need for guidance from other classes in society. Günther Franz and Werner Conze viewed peasant politics—rational action, directed to attainable goals—as the determining fact about the course of early modern rural development. In contrast, their contemporaries among French historians repeatedly emphasized disjunctures between peasants' collective actions and their real interests, and some suggested the impossibility of a peasant politics. To be sure, in his 1930 lectures on French rural history, Marc Bloch described peasant rebellions as a normal element of the seigneurial regime, akin to workers' strikes in the industrial world. "It was above all in dealing with its enemies," he wrote, "that the small rural collective not only became more conscious of its own identity but also gradually forced society as a whole to accept it as a viable and living institution."[62] Yet even Bloch saw peasants as needing outside leadership for any real resistance to seigneurial power. Incapable of effective political action on their own, he wrote, villagers turned for leadership to their parish priests, "whose minds could better encompass the idea that their miseries were part of a general ill; in a word, men well fitted to play the time-honored role of the intellectual

62. Bloch, *French Rural History*, 170, 169.

by acting as leaven in the long-suffering masses."[63] Only intellectual leadership could translate suffering into effective action.

Soon after, Lucien Febvre offered a still darker reading of the possibilities for peasant politics in Old Regime France. In 1933 he wrote a lengthy review of Georges Lefebvre's book on the Great Fear, a peasant movement during the late summer of 1789. Absolute misery provided the starting point for peasants' actions in these movements, but their psychology led them to fantastical responses to the circumstances they faced. Peasant outlooks, wrote Febvre, were shaped by "a very great receptiveness [to rumor], a credulity powerfully developed by a state of anxious impoverishment, of prolonged malnutrition, of confused but deep emotions that destroyed, among men who lacked intellectual training [*sans culture intellectuelle*], any rudiments of critical sense; finally, [by] a latent fermentation of minds, a subterranean, imaginative reworking of a certain number of simple themes common to rural society." Ultimately, peasant society was characterized by its isolation, "material isolation, moral isolation," and this allowed bizarre rumors "to propagate themselves in the troubled hearts of the French peasants."[64] Such a peasantry could not hope to act effectively on its own. Only with instruction and leadership from others could peasants understand their situation and act to improve it.

French historians in the 1950s and 1960s continued to analyze peasant politics in the terms that Febvre laid out, as reflecting the combined effects of material and cultural poverty. For postwar historians as for Febvre, these circumstances allowed peasants only a limited capacity for political action, and the development of historical demography after 1945 strengthened this line of thought. In his 1960 study of the region around Beauvais, the first major French historical work to use demographic techniques, Pierre Goubert came to conclusions much like Febvre's. "Overburdened with children who died too young," he wrote of seventeenth-century villagers in the region near Paris, "helpless in the face of plague and food shortages, deprived of livestock, land, clothing, food, and above all money, they led lives that were constricted, courageous, pious, and short."[65] Goubert's demographic statistics demonstrated how

63. Bloch, *French Rural History*, 170.
64. Febvre, "Une gigantesque fausse nouvelle," quotations at 827, 828. It is worth noting that Febvre here accepted an estimate of peasants' immiseration that makes their biological survival something of a mystery and that more recent scholarship has tended to revise. For an overview, see Dewald and Vardi, "Peasantries of France."
65. Goubert, *Cent mille provinciaux au XVIIe siècle*, 173.

fully peasants subordinated both their sexual pleasures and their economic interests to the teachings of the Catholic Church. They abstained
from sex before marriage and birth control during it, producing a state
of chronic overpopulation. As a result, "the majority of the peasants of
the Beauvaisis suffered from almost continuous undernourishment. . . .
[D]uring lean years, which were not exceptional, they had to resign themselves to dying in their thousands from lack of food."[66] But Goubert's
peasants offered no resistance to the crushing circumstances of their lives.
Their courage was employed only in the struggle for daily existence.

A few years later, Emmanuel Le Roy Ladurie drew a similar picture of
southern French peasants. In his thesis on the peasants of Languedoc,
he too stressed the reciprocal effects of material and psychological privation, which left peasants incapable of accurately assessing the world they
lived in; as a result most peasant movements amounted to little more than
escapism.[67] In 1974, he extended this analysis to a broad overview of France
during the period 1550–1720. "In the end," he wrote, "I see the French
peasants of the sixteenth century as the objects of history, far more than
as its subjects. The end product of their activity as producers and repro-
ducers was the restoration [following its late-medieval crises] of a system
that oppressed and occasionally crushed them. . . . The great majority,
moreover, was fundamentally silent, walled off by its dialects and folkloric
beliefs, incapable of participating save in brief outbursts in the great
movements of the 1560s."[68] Le Roy Ladurie's language almost exactly inverted the claims of Günther Franz and Werner Conze about the German
peasantry. Franz claimed that the peasantry had been forcibly pushed out
of an active role in German politics following their defeat in 1525; Conze,
that peasants continued throughout the early modern period to maneu-
ver effectively in defense of their own interests. In contrast, Le Roy Ladurie
saw French peasants' political emasculation as self-inflicted, the natural
by-product of a constricted way of life that they themselves defended,
effectively doing their oppressors' work for them. As he had written in
his thesis: "Materially impoverished, sexually very repressed, traditional
society . . . thus seems characterized, among its popular classes, by a double series of frustrations and scarcities, which reciprocally reinforce and
shape one another."[69]

66. Goubert, "French Peasantry of the Seventeenth Century."
67. See Chapter 5, above.
68. Le Roy Ladurie, *Le territoire de l'historien*, 178.
69. Le Roy Ladurie, *Paysans de Languedoc*, 359–60.

It is unnecessary to evaluate here the fundamental accuracy of either line of interpretation, for this chapter is concerned with historiographical traditions, not the realities of peasant history. I do not claim that either German emphasis on peasant activism or French emphasis on passivity was incorrect, or that empirical findings played no role in shaping each tradition. But in both Germany and France, I argue, historians depicted peasant politics in clearer, more absolute terms than the evidence alone could justify. It is consistent with this view that in both countries interpretive orientations remained essentially unchanged over about fifty years, despite the accumulation of new documents and analytical techniques.[70] Peter Blickle and Emmanuel Le Roy Ladurie in the 1970s used much the same language as Günther Franz and Lucien Febvre in the 1930s—much the same, save that positions tended to become more clear-cut over these years, with greater emphasis on German peasants' political action and on French peasants' passive misery, and with a tendency to extend some of these views from specific cases to "traditional society" as a whole. The continuity in each line of thought is the more impressive for the availability of the other. Neither French nor German social historians seem to have taken up the interpretive challenges that their colleagues' work might have posed, or even acknowledged them. In their basic characteristics, it seems necessary to conclude, these approaches should be understood as chosen by the historians who developed them, rather than imposed by the data that they studied.

To some extent, these interpretive choices reflected a difference in political cultures. In stressing peasants' misery, French historians showed the influence of France's revolutionary tradition on their thinking. For Febvre, Goubert, and Le Roy Ladurie, the peasantry's disabling poverty demonstrated the injustice of the Old Regime, its crushing human costs, and its imperviousness to reform. Conversely, national pride encouraged German historians to see their nation's peasants as sturdy defenders of their own liberties; the nation's traditional arrangements, their findings suggested, had produced self-confidence and dignity among its laboring classes. But the political overtones of these views were more complicated than such contrasts suggest. French historians who stressed the peasantry's incapacity for political action at the same time suggested that an autonomous politics among the impoverished and uneducated might be

70. Statistics already available when Febvre wrote, for instance, show that well more than half the peasants of northern Europe were literate in the eighteenth century, and a flourishing trade in popular books addressed their desire to read.

impossible in the present, as it had been in the past. German historians who explored the autonomy of early modern peasant resistance implicitly pointed to the reasonableness of contemporary working-class politics. In both cases, research generated ideas that extended beyond the historians' apparent ideological intentions.

In both cases, finally, historians' scholarly analyses intersected with their contemporary concerns. These were the more straightforward in Germany. Scholars like Werner Conze wrote about peasant political culture as Germany sought to expand its hold on eastern Europe, and as its administrators planned to transplant German settlers to the region. Scholarship was a tool in that process, and an ideological resource as well, demonstrating German farmers' ability to cope with new conditions and exploring weaknesses in Polish social arrangements.[71] French scholars confronted the problem of their nation's overseas empire, already contested in the 1930s but still a political reality through the 1950s. Direct comparisons and oblique references to that reality dotted their writings on the French peasantry, suggesting the injustice of imperial rule and the enduring disabilities that it inflicted—but also suggesting the vast gap that separated colonial subjects from metropolitan readers. In such circumstances the peasantry could never be a topic for purely disinterested scholarship. For French and German scholars alike, to write about the peasantry required addressing questions about how backward social groups functioned and interacted with others, in the present as in the past.

71. For the importance of this planning and for historians' involvement in it, see Aly, *"Final Solution."*

CONCLUSION:

ON THE POLITICS OF SOCIAL HISTORY

"What was history then?" asked Lucien Febvre in 1925. His question referred to the year 1869, when one of Jules Michelet's most important books appeared, and Febvre's answer was blunt: "In spite of the efforts of Michelet to enlarge it, enrich it, and change the traditional idea of it," history in that era "always meant setting out . . . the long struggle of the Kings, to establish in domestic politics a rule of monarchical centralization and absolutism, and their long effort in matters of foreign policy . . . to fill the predestined frame [of French territory] with a land entirely French. . . . The lengthy effort and struggle were all political in character, and history remained before all things a study of politics." Michelet alone, "with his universal divination and foresight," envisioned a broader kind of history, but even he "was able only to foresee, to divine, and to wish: for economic and social history cannot be improvised."[1]

---

1. Febvre, *Geographical Introduction to History*, 54. For clarity, I have changed this translation slightly.

In this study I argue that Febvre was wrong about the history of his discipline and that his opinions have misled historians in the years since he wrote. In fact, the history of society preoccupied French intellectuals from early in the nineteenth century. History itself was crucial to the nineteenth century's understanding of the world, and the subject's centrality ensured that historical analysis would be defined broadly, as extending far beyond politics. In nineteenth-century Paris, histories of private life, women, peasants, religious mentalities, and a variety of related topics all attracted writers and readers. The authors of these studies described themselves as writing a new kind of history, and just like Febvre they deplored their predecessors' narrow interest in kings, wars, and state-building. Their commitment to a broader conception of history in turn forced them to think about fundamental problems of method. They used novel documents and reflected on explanatory schemes that would help them make sense of the strangeness of the past, schemes borrowed from psychology, linguistics, and sociology.

Few of these writers were professional historians, and none devoted himself exclusively to history. Most supported themselves partly as freelance intellectuals, writing in a variety of genres and trying to reach a broad middle-class audience. In that sense their social history was indeed improvised, a history assembled from heterogeneous source materials and resting on shaky theoretical foundations, a history that sacrificed scholarly depth for accessibility to nonspecialist readers. I argue here, however, that a real history of historical thought cannot focus only on professionals, those practicing within university faculties. For one thing, whatever their technical limitations, the writers considered here produced some of the nineteenth century's greatest historical works. They also exercised a powerful influence on their contemporaries and successors, including the professional historians among them. Charles-Augustin Sainte-Beuve, Ernest Renan, and Hippolyte Taine were the most listened-to intellectuals of the later nineteenth century; the Goncourts and Alfred Franklin were less influential, but their works were nonetheless widely read and appreciated. Their importance exemplified a basic fact about French intellectual life. In France (far more than in Germany or the United States) reciprocal influences have always flowed between university professors and public intellectuals, and the latter have often had more influence than the former in defining fields of knowledge. Such interactions dominated nineteenth-century intellectual life, since the French university was then especially weak, and they remained important through the twentieth century. If only because of the attention accorded them, such intellectuals have to be included in the genealogy of modern historical thought.

Above all, they require inclusion because of their understanding of what history and the historian ought to be. "Through psychological analysis," wrote the Goncourts, "through observing individual and collective life, and assessing habits, passions, ideas, moral as well as material fashions, we intend to reconstitute a whole vanished world, from the base to the summit, from the body to the soul."[2] I have quoted variations on that intention from the other nineteenth-century intellectuals examined here, and I have suggested that this program allied with their demand that historians write as detached observers of their society, indifferent to its religious and political beliefs. Only historians who felt themselves to be outsiders in their own times could enter fully into the psychology of others, they suggested, for only they could avoid judging the past by the criteria of the present. Not all could sustain such detachment for the full length of their careers. The successes of their later years made some of them more accepting of a society that treated them so well, and military disaster in 1870–71 encouraged expressions of patriotism. But their writings nonetheless exemplified an ideal of historical analysis that had no reference to their contemporaries' most cherished commitments, progressive and conservative alike: they criticized Catholicism, the Revolution of 1789, and contemporary humanitarianism, all the while showing appreciation for the inventiveness of their own century. As a result they were ready to take on novel historical topics, including the history of Christianity itself, and propose unorthodox interpretations, as in Taine's understanding of French revolutionary violence. Friederich Nietzsche was correct in his belief that "exasperated pessimism" characterized these intellectuals and that he himself would have felt at home among them.

I have sought to demonstrate here that this outlook differed fundamentally from that of many intellectuals around them—and of many since. François Guizot, Jules Michelet, Alexis de Tocqueville, and the great German historians of the nineteenth century all believed that history moved in a clear direction, and they believed that one form or another of providence underlay its movement. Twentieth-century historians were less confident, but their belief in progress retained surprising vigor through most of the twentieth century. Lucien Febvre and Marc Bloch witnessed some of the most terrible events of the modern era, yet both expressed

2. As quoted in Chapter 1, above.

confidence in the superiority of modern ways of life as a source of psychological stability and intellectual creativity. Nor did they doubt France's special mission as a nation. "I was born in France," wrote Bloch. "I have drunk of the waters of her culture. I have made her past my own. I breathe freely only in her climate, and I have done my best, with others, to defend her interests."[3] Not having faced the challenges of twentieth-century European existence, the nineteenth-century intellectuals considered here felt no need to affirm their national identity in this way. They looked skeptically on their nation and times, and their doubts ran deep, manifesting themselves in bohemian lives as well as in published thoughts.

Detachment of this kind helped shape these writers' ideas about historical time. Skeptical about the virtues of the present and about French national greatness, they questioned the central narratives of French history, and especially those that focused on the achievements of the seventeenth century, the era of centralizing government and classicizing culture. Instead, they celebrated popular culture, precisely those modes of thought that Descartes, Racine, and the other seventeenth-century greats had sought to root out. For Sainte-Beuve and Taine, François Rabelais exemplified the real France; the great seventeenth-century texts represented only an artificial outgrowth. Alfred Franklin went farther still, exploring the realities of early modern bodily life in order to demonstrate the fragility of Louis XIV's hold on his society. In making such claims, these writers took sides in an ongoing debate about the roles of ordinary people and elites in French national life. To set Rabelais and La Fontaine against Descartes, as Taine did, implied questioning the role of educated elites in making French civilization. The debate produced surprising configurations. Although men of the Left, Jean Jaurès and Lucien Febvre both dismissed the Rabelaisian tradition in France, and both celebrated the rationalizing achievements of seventeenth-century philosophy. Later *Annales* historians shared this view, tracing a broad "civilizing process" that brought modern emotions and behaviors from elites to lower classes. Although their sources were literary and they were frightened of democracy, Sainte-Beuve, Taine, and the other nineteenth-century intellectuals considered here nonetheless accorded more legitimacy to French popular culture than did their twentieth-century successors.

Giving these writers significant roles in the development of modern historical thinking thus implies reassessing the work of some of the

3. Bloch, *Strange Defeat*, 3.

twentieth century's most important historians. Repeatedly, I have sought to show, twentieth-century historical interpretations echo nineteenth-century debates. I have focused especially on the figure of Febvre, who can reasonably be accounted the most influential historian of the twentieth century. Febvre returned repeatedly to themes that had been developed by earlier writers, and, with the enthusiasm of an intellectual crusader and institution builder, did not worry overmuch about acknowledging antecedents to his ideas or explaining the processes by which he arrived at them. Other scholars have documented his borrowings from his contemporaries, notably from the Romanian émigré scholar Lucie Varga.[4] In these studies I indicate the exaggerated quality of some of his other claims, for instance, that of having introduced questions of psychology and mental structures to historians' notice. But noting such exaggerations is a secondary concern here. The broader point is that historians, like other writers, need somehow to deal with the themes, images, and topics that they inherit from their predecessors. They cope with this requirement (again like other writers) through a complicated process of borrowing, forgetting, and remaking, creating something new from inherited materials.

Reconstructing this process as it occurred in the work of Febvre and other *Annales* historians, as I have tried to do here, draws attention to important themes running through their work, themes linking together historians who disagreed on many specific issues. One such common theme was the value of specialized research, of the sort best carried out by university history departments, as against the claims of the amateur historians who figure so largely in this study. Despite his reputation for interdisciplinary enthusiasm, Febvre was in fact especially concerned to stress the specificity of historical research and the boundaries that separate it from literature, philosophy, and psychoanalysis. More important, the first generations of *Annales* historians made the cultural privations of the early modern past a central theme of their work. Early modern men and women, according to these interpretations, had only a minimum of tools for dealing with the world around them, or indeed for understanding themselves. Their limited vision and hopes to some extent resulted from the harshness of the physical world that they inhabited, but cultural limits also helped create real-world harshness; early modern men and women doubted that they could improve the world, and therefore failed to do so. Such stress on the grimness of the early modern past implied

---

4. Schöttler, *Lucie Varga.*

belief in progress, a confidence in the achievements of modern times, and especially those of French modernity. Great works such as Febvre's *Le problème de l'incroyance,* Bloch's *La société féodale,* Pierre Goubert's *Beauvais et le Beauvaisis,* and Emmanuel Le Roy Ladurie's *Les paysans de Languedoc* made these beliefs explicit.

A paradox thus runs through *Annales* historical writing of the mid-twentieth century. This was a history committed to re-creating the lives of ordinary French men and women and to understanding the full magnitude of the injustices that Old Regime society visited on them. Yet this history ultimately stressed the guiding role of elites in French history. Early modern French men and women could neither control nature nor construct a political order that would meet their most elementary needs; and they derived little satisfaction from their personal lives, which were "constricted, courageous, pious, and short," in the words of Goubert. Change began in the seventeenth century, as intellectuals and courtiers began devising new ways of living. During the Enlightenment these innovations began to reach the countryside, through the work of preachers, schoolteachers, publishers, and other cultural mediators. Neither economic nor political revolution was possible until this work of education had been completed. In this narrative of progress, peasants were the objects and victims of larger forces, not subjects.

Poetry, W. H. Auden claimed, "makes nothing happen." It is otherwise with history. Because of its commitment to deal only with documented truths, history helps constitute our understanding of the real, our beliefs about what is possible and how we can attain it. If (as I argue) we need to think of a wide range of intellectuals as contributing to the development of modern historical practice, we also need to think of professional historians as intellectuals, who contribute to structuring the cultural life of their society, whatever their apparent isolation within the confines of academic life. This is especially the case in France, with its long and powerful tradition of interaction between university and the educated public. It seems appropriate to reflect briefly on what social history as a mode of thought has meant for the values governing daily life in the present.

Normally this question elicits a simple answer, which stresses the essentially democratic impact of twentieth-century historical studies. The practice of social history, it is argued, has allowed once-excluded groups to view themselves as historical actors, full participants in humanity's development, worthy of memory and reflection. Hence new historical topics have tended to emerge as new groups have come to participate in historical studies. Georges Lefebvre, the great historian of the French Revolution, viewed his own intellectual life in exactly these terms. Born to a provincial working-class family in 1874, he reached the university only because of the revolutionary changes that the Third Republic brought to education, and in turn he took up the history of the peasantry as a subject for his doctoral dissertation.[5] In Lefebvre's intellectual life, social experience and the writing of social history intersected. Comparable interactions have recurred throughout the last century. As women and ethnic minorities have entered the historical profession, for instance, they too have brought new attention to new areas of research, and their research has been directly connected to their understanding of contemporary society. On this view, the changing subject matter of history reflects a larger democratization of society as a whole.[6]

But for many of the historians considered here, the lines connecting historical practice, political conviction, and personal experience were more tangled. Some of these figures were outright conservatives, such as Philippe Ariès and Werner Conze, who nonetheless devoted much of their careers to the study of ordinary lives. More characteristic were such figures as Sainte-Beuve, Taine, and Renan, conservatives on some issues and at some times, but in other ways radicals. For the most part they disliked the Old Regime, and they admired much that had been achieved since 1789. At the same time, they all expressed unease about the modern world and fears about where it was heading; they disparaged democracy, and most (Sainte-Beuve appears to be the exception in this regard) relied on racial theories to explain social circumstances. Holding such complicated, even contradictory, views, they offered their readers no Archimedean point of certainty from which to evaluate historical developments; and in their conversation they made a point of undercutting all contemporary pieties. Conservative writers might thus produce radical history—a point recognized by the Catholic Church when it placed Sainte-Beuve's *Port-Royal* on the Index of Prohibited Books. In any case, their divided feelings about modernity encouraged them to look respectfully at other societies and explore the systems that allowed those societies to function coherently. In the mid-twentieth century, the former SS officer Günther Franz offered the most extreme instance of this ideological complexity, stressing the

5. Cobb, *Second Identity*, 84–100.
6. This vision of democratization also characterizes the analyses of Appleby, Hunt, and Jacob in *Telling the Truth About History*.

political agency of oppressed groups like the peasantry while also celebrating an authoritarian and racist regime.

Social histories written by members of the political Left might likewise
have ambiguous implications for contemporary life. This was particularly
the case in histories that explored the distinction between modern and
premodern societies, a distinction that (I have suggested here) has been
fundamental to the development of social history itself. This distinction
mattered enormously in mid-twentieth-century France, a society preoccupied both with its own modernization and with its tense relations to formerly colonial territories. During these years the analogy between Europe's
premodernity and that of twentieth-century underdeveloped societies became a commonplace in historical writing, and inevitably the analogy carried political overtones. To view early modern ways of thought and feeling
as a collection of "vieux délires," in Emmanuel Le Roy Ladurie's phrase,
to be overcome only with the aid of schoolmaster and new technologies,
had implications for understanding the present as well the past. When
Febvre and Bloch drew connections between the comforts of modern life
and the psychological assurance that allows moderns the full development of their abilities, they too affirmed hierarchies between developed
and underdeveloped worlds. Such analogies suggested that underdevelopment was a unitary concept, as applicable to the twentieth century as
to the seventeenth; common civilizing processes were needed in each.

Thus one of this study's claims is that a history of social history can be
written with almost no reference to its authors' stated political ideologies,
despite the importance of ideological struggle during the years discussed
here. Marxism plays an especially limited role in this account. It mattered
a great deal to some scholars, such as Lefebvre and (early in his career)
Le Roy Ladurie. But to most of the figures considered here it had little
significance: Febvre and Bloch treated their Marxist colleagues with good-
humored, mocking tolerance,[7] while Taine and his fellows took a critical
view of all overarching social theories. The ideological sources of social
historical thought lay elsewhere, in ideas and imagery that political opponents might well share. The socialist Jaurès and the conservative Charles
Maurras had the same view of French classicism, and they offered the
same criticisms of Taine's treatment of the subject. These specific shared
opinions emerged from deeper agreements: about modernity itself and

7. See, for instance, Müller, *Marc Bloch, Lucien Febvre,* 1:391.

the progress that led to it, about French national identity, about the nature of culture.

That the past is alien territory, it seems necessary to conclude, is an idea to be applied as fully to the history of history as to its subject matter. For it is not only peasants and artisans who inhabited mental worlds distant from the present, but historians as well. Previous generations of historians had experiences, ideas, and preoccupations that we in the twenty-first century can scarcely understand, let alone share. We have only a remote understanding of the Goncourts' anti-Semitism, Renan's colonial hopes, Taine's racism. Yet despite all these barriers, our lives in some respects resemble theirs more than those of the great twentieth-century historians. From their service in the world wars, Febvre, Bloch, Franz, and Conze all had a direct knowledge of violence that only a small number of contemporary historians share.[8] Having served heroically in both wars, Bloch could describe himself as "'a born fighter,'" in the words of a fellow officer; he knew firsthand what an aerial bombardment felt like and the emotional impact of having sent soldiers on a useless, fatal mission.[9] Their generation also faced an array of political choices specific to their times and places: Franz became a National Socialist activist, Conze a willing participant in planning the ethnic cleansing of eastern Europe, Bloch a resistance fighter, Febvre an uneasy survivor in occupied Paris. Given such gaps between their experiences and ours, it should not surprise us that they viewed the past in ways that we in the twenty-first century cannot share. Nor should we be surprised that ideas that we find congenial, such as the political agency of the peasantry, prove to have troubling origins, bound up as they might be (in the work of Franz and Conze) with ideas about ethnic differences.

To observe these facts is in no sense to undercut the intellectual value of the histories written in the past. On the contrary, these facts should serve to remind us that all history is written in its own times and to serve those times, and that we too write history under these constraints. Like our predecessors, we see the past imperfectly because of our connectedness to the world we inhabit. But like them we may hope to use our historical knowledge as a mode of coping with that world and acting on it.

8. A point eloquently made by John Keegan in *Face of Battle.*
9. Bloch, *Strange Defeat,* 4, 45–46, 54–57.

BIBLIOGRAPHY

Allart de Méritens, Hortense. *Lettres inédites à Sainte-Beuve (1841–1848)*. Edited by
   Léon Séché. 2d ed. Paris, 1908.
Aly, Götz. *"Final Solution": Nazi Population Policy and the Murder of the European
   Jews*. Translated by Belinda Cooper and Alison Brown. London, 1999.
———. *Macht-Geist-Wahn: Kontinuitäten deutschen Geschichte*. Berlin, 1997.
Appleby, Joyce, Lynn Hunt, and Margaret Jacob. *Telling the Truth About History*.
   New York, 1994.
Arendt, Hannah. *Between Past and Future*. London, 1961.
Ariès, Philippe. *Histoire des populations françaises et de leurs attitudes devant la vie
   depuis le XVIIIe siècle*. Paris, 1971. (Orig. pub. 1948.)
———. *Un historien du dimanche*. Paris, 1980.
———. *Le temps de l'histoire*. Monaco, 1954.
Ariès, Philippe, and Georges Duby, eds. *A History of Private Life*. Translated by Arthur
   Goldhammer. 5 vols. Cambridge, Mass., 1987.
Ariès, Philippe, et al. *Écrits pour une Renaissance par le groupe de la "Nation Française."*
   Paris, 1958.
Aron, Raymond. *Introduction à la philosophie de l'histoire*. New ed. Paris, 1986. (Orig.
   pub. 1938.)
———. *Mémoires: 50 ans de réflexion politique*. Paris, 1983.
Aulard, Alphonse. *Taine historien de la Révolution française*. 2d ed. Paris, 1908.
Aumale, M. le duc d'. *Histoire des princes de Condé pendant les XVIe et XVIIe siècles*.
   2d ed. 7 vols. Paris, 1889–92.
Azouvi, François. "Descartes." In *Les lieux de mémoire*. Vol 3. Edited by Pierre Nora.
   Quarto ed. Paris, 1997.
Babbitt, Irving. *Masters of Modern French Criticism*. New York, 1963. (Orig. pub. 1912.)
Babeau, Albert. *La vie rurale dans l'ancienne France*. 2d ed. Paris, 1885.
Baker, Keith, and Steven Kaplan. Editors' introduction to *A Rhetoric of Bourgeois
   Revolution: The Abbé Sieyès and What Is the Third Estate?* by William Sewell
   Jr. Durham, N.C., 1994.
Barante, Amable-Prosper Brugière, baron de. *Des communes et de l'aristocratie*. Paris,
   1821.
Baudelaire, Charles. *Écrits esthétiques*. Edited by Jean-Christophe Bailly. Paris, 1986.
Beauvoir, Simone de. *Le deuxième sexe*. 2 vols. Paris, 1976. (Orig. pub. 1949.)
Berlin, Isaiah. "The Bent Twig: On the Rise of Nationalism." In *The Crooked Timber
   of Humanity: Chapters in the History of Ideas*. Edited by Henry Hardy. London,
   1990.
———. *The Power of Ideas*. Edited by Henry Hardy. Princeton, 2000.
Billy, André. *The Goncourt Brothers*. Translated by Margaret Shaw. New York, 1960.
Blickle, Peter, ed. *Bauer, Reich und Reformation: Festschrift für Günther Franz zum
   80. Geburtstag am 23 Mai 1982*. Stuttgart, 1982.

———. *Obedient Germans? A Rebuttal; a New View of German History*. Translated by Thomas A. Brady Jr. Charlottesville, 1997. (Orig. pub. 1981.)

Bloch, Marc. *Feudal Society*. Translated by L. A. Manyon. 2 vols. Chicago, 1961.

———. *French Rural History: An Essay on its Basic Characteristics*. Translated by Janet Sondheimer. Berkeley and Los Angeles, 1966.

———. *The Historian's Craft*. Translated by Peter Putnam. New York, 1953.

———. *Strange Defeat: A Statement of Evidence Written in 1940*. Translated by Gerard Hopkins. New York, 1968.

Bourget, Paul. *Essais de psychologie contemporaine: Études littéraires*. Paris, 1993.

———. *Oeuvres complètes*. 2 vols. Paris, 1899.

Bouwsma, William. *A Usable Past: Essays in European Cultural History*. Berkeley, 1990.

Braudel, Fernand. *Écrits sur l'histoire*. Paris, 1969.

———. *The Mediterranean and the Mediterranean World in the Age of Philip II*. Translated by Siân Reynolds. 2 vols. New York, 1972.

Brunner, Otto, Werner Conze, and Reinhard Koselleck, eds. *Geschichtliche Grundbegriffe*. 8 vols. Stuttgart, 1972–89.

Buckley, Michael J. *At the Origins of Modern Atheism*. New Haven, 1987.

Burguière, André. "Histoire d'une histoire: La naissance des *Annales*." *Annales: ESC* 34 (November–December, 1979): 1360–75.

Burke, Edmund. *Reflections on the Revolution in France*. Edited by Thomas H. D. Mahoney. Indianapolis, 1955.

Burke, Peter. *The French Historical Revolution: The* Annales *School, 1929–89*. Stanford, 1990.

Burleigh, Michael. *Germany Turns Eastward: A Study of* Ostforschung *in the Third Reich*. Cambridge, 1988.

Cantor, Norman. *Inventing the Middle Ages*. New York, 1991.

Capot de Quissac, Jean. "L'Action française à l'assaut de la Sorbonne historienne." In *Au berceau des Annales: Le milieu strasbourgeois, l'histoire en France au début du XXe siècle*, edited by Charles-Olivier Carbonell and Georges Livet. Toulouse, 1983.

Carbonell, Charles-Olivier. *Histoire et historiens: Une mutation idéologique des historiens français, 1865–1885*. Toulouse, 1976.

Carrard, Philippe. *Poetics of the New History: French Historical Discourse from Braudel to Chartier*. Baltimore, 1992.

Carroll, David. *French Literary Fascism: Nationalism, Anti-Semitism, and the Ideology of Culture*. Princeton, 1995.

Casanova, Nicole. *Sainte-Beuve*. Paris, 1995.

Charle, Christophe. "Academics or Intellectuals? The Professors of the University of Paris and Political Debate in France from the Dreyfus Affair to the Algerian War." In *Intellectuals in Twentieth-Century France: Mandarins and Samurais*, edited by Jeremy Jennings. London, 1993.

———. *Les intellectuels en Europe au XIXe siècle: Essai d'histoire comparée*. Paris, 1996.

———. *Paris fin de siècle: Culture et politique*. Paris, 1998.

Chartier, Roger. *Cultural History: Between Practices and Representations*. Translated by Lydia G. Cochrane. Cambridge, 1988.

——. *On the Edge of the Cliff: History, Language, and Practices*, trans. Lydia G. Cochrane. Baltimore, 1997.

Chasles, Philarète. *Études sur les hommes et les moeurs au XIXe siècle*. Paris, n.d.

Chéruel, Adolphe, ed. *Mémoires de Fléchier sur les Grands-Jours d'Auvergne en 1665*. Paris, 1862.

Christofferson, Michael. "François Furet Between History and Journalism, 1958–1965." *French History* 15, no. 4 (2001): 421–47

Cobb, Richard. "The Era of the French Revolution: Some Comments on Opportunities for Research and Writing." *Journal of Modern History* 30, no. 2 (June 1958): 118–30.

——. *A Second Identity: Essays on France and French History*. London, 1969.

Cochin, Augustin. *La crise de l'histoire révolutionnaire: Taine et m. Aulard*. 2d. ed. Paris, 1909.

Comte, Auguste. *Early Political Writings*. Edited by H. S. Jones. Cambridge, 1998. (Orig. pub. 1820.)

Conze, Werner. *Agrarverfassung und Bevölkerung in Litauen und Weissrussland*. 1. Teil. *Die Hufenverfassung in ehemaligen Grossfürstentum Litauen*. Leipzig, 1940.

——. "Die deutsche Geschichtswissenschaft seit 1945: Bedingungen und Ergebnisse." In *Gesellschaft-Staat-Nation: Gesammelte Aufsätze*. Stuttgart, 1992.

——. *Gesellschaft-Staat-Nation: Gesammelte Aufsätze*. Stuttgart, 1992.

——. *Hirschenhof: Die Geschichte einer deutschen Sprachinsel in Livland*. 2d ed. Hannover-Döhren, 1963. (Orig. pub. 1934.)

——. *Polnische Nation und deutsche Politik im ersten Weltkrieg*. Cologne, 1958.

——. "Die Strukturgeschichte des technisch-industriellen Zeitalters als Aufgabe für Forschung und Unterricht." In *Gesellschaft-Staat-Nation: Gesammelte Aufsätze*. Stuttgart, 1992.

——. "Die Strukturkrise des östlichen Mitteleuropas vor und nach 1919." In *Gesellschaft-Staat-Nation: Gesammelte Aufsätze*. Stuttgart, 1992.

——. "Der Weg zur Sozialgeschichte nach 1945." In *Forschung in der Bundesrepublik Deutschland: Beispiele, Kritik, Vorschläge*, edited by Christoph Schneider. Weinheim, 1983.

——. "Die Wirkungen der liberalen Agrarreformen auf die Volksordnung in Mitteleuropa im 19. Jahrhundert." *Vierteljahrschrift für Sozial- und Wirtschaftsgeschichte* 38 (1949): 2–43.

Cousin, Victor. *Cours de philosophie: Introduction à l'histoire de la philosophie*. Paris, 1991.

——. *Jacqueline Pascal: Premières études sur les femmes illustres et la société du XVIIe siècle*. 9th ed. Paris, 1878.

Davis, Natalie Zemon. "Censorship, Silence, and Resistance: The *Annales* During the German Occupation of France." *Rivista di storia della storiografia moderna* 14, no. 1–2 (1993): 161–81.

——. "Rabelais Among the Censors (1940s, 1540s)." *Representations* 32 (Fall 1990): 1–32.

den Boer, Pim. *History as a Profession: The Study of History in France, 1818–1914*. Translated by Arnold J. Pomerans. Princeton, 1998.

Descimon, Robert. "Declareuil (1913) contre Hauser (1912): Les rendez-vous manqués de l'histoire et de l'histoire de droit." *Annales HSS* 57, no. 6 (2002): 1615–36.

Dewald, Jonathan. *The European Nobility, 1400–1800*. Cambridge, 1996.
Dewald, Jonathan, and Liana Vardi. "The Peasantries of France, 1400–1789." In *The Peasantries of Europe, from the Fourteenth to the Eighteenth Centuries*, edited by Tom Scott. London, 1998.
Deyon, Pierre. *Amiens, capitale provinciale: Étude sur la société urbaine au 17e siècle*. Paris and The Hague, 1967.
Dickens, Charles. *Bleak House*. Edited by Norman Page. Harmondsworth, U.K., 1971. (Orig. pub. 1853.)
Dosse, François. *New History in France: The Triumph of the* Annales. Translated by Peter V. Conroy Jr. Urbana, 1994.
Dumas, Alexandre. *The Count of Monte Cristo*. Translated by Robin Buss. London, 1996. (Orig. pub. 1844–45.)
———. *La reine Margot*. Paris: Livre de Poche, 1994.
Dumont, Robert. *Stefan Zweig et la France*. Paris, 1967.
Eksteins, Modris. *Rites of Spring: The Great War and the Birth of the Modern Age*. Boston, 1989.
Elias, Norbert. *The History of Manners*. Translated by Edmund Jephcott. New York, 1978.
Eliot, George. "The Natural History of German Life." In *Selected Essays, Poems, and Other Writings*. Edited by A. S. Byatt and Nicholas Warren London, 1990.
Febvre, Lucien. "À nos lecteurs, à nos amis." *Annales: Economies, sociétés, civilisations* 1, no. 1 (1946): 1–8.
———. *Amour sacré, amour profane*. Paris, 1996. (Orig. pub. 1944.)
———. "De 1892 à 1933: Examen de conscience d'une histoire et d'un historien." *Revue de synthèse* 7 (1934): 93–106.
———, ed. *Encyclopédie française*. Vol. 8, *La vie mentale*. Paris, 1938.
———. *A Geographical Introduction to History*. Translated by E. G. Moutford and J. H. Paxton. New York, 1925.
———. "Une gigantesque fausse nouvelle: La Grande Peur de juillet 89." In *Pour une histoire à part entière*. Paris, 1962. (Orig. pub. 1933.)
———. "Histoire sociale ou histoire littéraire." *Revue de synthèse* 3, no. 1 (1932): 39–50.
———. "L'histoire de la philosophie et l'histoire des historiens." *Revue de synthèse* 3, no. 1 (1932): 97–103.
———. "L'histoire économique et la vie: leçon d'une exposition." *Annales d'histoire économique et sociale*, 13 (January, 1932), 1–10.
———. *Martin Luther: A Destiny*. Translated by Roberts Tapley. New York, 1929.
———. "Une mise en place: Sainte-Beuve" and "Taine et son temps." *Annales: ESC* 5, no. 3 (1949): 356–57
———. *Philippe II et la Franche-Comté: Étude d'histoire politique, religieuse et sociale*. 2d ed. Paris, 1970. (Orig. pub. 1912.)
———. *Le problème de l'incroyance au XVIè siècle: La religion de Rabelais*. 2d ed. Paris, 1968.
———. "Renan retrouvé." *Annales: ESC* 5, no. 2 (1949): 200–203.
Febvre, Lucien, and Albert Demangeon. *Le Rhin: Problèmes d'histoire et d'économie* Paris, 1935.
Fink, Carole. *Marc Bloch: A Life in History*. Cambridge, 1989.

Fogel, Robert. *The Union Pacific Railroad: A Case Study in Premature Enterprise*. Johns Hopkins University Studies in Historical and Political Science, 78th ser., no. 2, 1960.

Forster, Robert. *The Nobility of Toulouse in the Eighteenth Century*. Johns Hopkins University Studies in Historical and Political Science, 78th ser., no 1, 1960.

Franklin, Alfred. *Ameline Dubourg: A Tale of the Huguenots*. Translated by JHD. New York, 1883.

———. *Bulletin de la Société de l'histoire de Paris et de l'Ile-de-France*, 65 (1918): 24–25.

———. *Histoire de la Bibliothèque Mazarine et du palais de l'Institut*. Paris, 1901. Reprint, Amsterdam, 1969.

———. *La vie privée d'autrefois. Arts et métiers, modes, moeurs, usages des parisiens du XIIe au XVIIIe siècles. D'après des documents originaux ou inédits*. 27 vols. Paris, 1887–1902.

Franz, Günther. *Die deutsche Bauernkrieg*. 2 vols. Munich and Berlin, 1939. 9th unrev. ed. 2 vols. Darmstadt, 1972.

———. *Geschichte des deutschen Bauernstandes von frühen Mittelalter bis zum 19. Jahrhundert*. Stuttgart, 1970.

Friedlander, Saul. *Memory, History, and the Extermination of the Jews of Europe*. Bloomington, 1993.

Furet, François. *Interpreting the French Revolution*. Translated by Elborg Forster. Cambridge, 1981.

———. *Un itinéraire intellectuel: L'historien journaliste de* France-Observateur *au* Nouvel Observateur *(1958–1997)*. Edited by Mona Ozouf. Paris, 1999.

Fustel de Coulanges, Numa. *La cité antique*. Edited by François Hartog. Paris, 1984.

Geertz, Clifford. *After the Fact: Two Countries, Four Decades, One Anthropologist*. Cambridge, Mass., 1995.

Gérin-Ricard, Lazare de. "L'héritage de Fustel de Coulanges." *Revue des questions historiques* 62 (November 1934): 3–11.

Gobineau, Arthur comte de. *Oeuvres*. Edited by Jean Gaulmier. 3 vols. Paris, 1983.

Goncourt, Edmond de, and Jules de Goncourt. *La femme au XVIIIe siècle*. 2 vols. Édition définitive. Paris, n.d. (Orig. pub. 1862.)

———. *Histoire de la société française pendant la Révolution*. Édition définitive. Paris, n.d.

———. *Journal: Mémoires de la vie littéraire*. 3 vols. Paris, 1989.

———. *Manette Salomon*. Paris, n.d. (Orig. pub. 1867.)

Gosse, Edmond. *More Books on the Table*. New York, 1923.

Gossman, Lionel. *Basel in the Age of Burckhardt: A Study in Unseasonable Ideas*. Chicago, 2000.

———. *Between History and Literature*. Cambridge, Mass., 1990.

Goubert, Pierre. *Beauvais et le Beauvaisis de 1600 à 1730: Contribution à l'histoire sociale de la France du XVIIe siècle*. Paris, 1960.

———. *Cent mille provinciaux au XVIIe siècle: Beauvais et le Beauvaisis de 1600 à 1730*. Paris, 1968.

———. "The French Peasantry of the Seventeenth Century: A Regional Example." In *Crisis in Europe, 1560–1660*, edited by Trevor Aston. Garden City, N.Y., 1967. (Orig. pub. 1956.)

Greenhalgh, Paul. *Ephemeral Vistas: The Expositions Universelles, Great Exhibitions, and World's Fairs, 1851–1939*. Manchester, 1988.

Grenier, Albert. *Camille Jullian: Un demi-siècle de science historique et de progrès français, 1880–1930*. Paris, 1944.

Gruettner, Michael. *Arbeitswelt an der Wasserkant: Sozialgeschichte der Hamburger Hafenarbeiter, 1886–1914*. Göttingen, 1984.

Guizot, François. *Histoire de la civilisation en France depuis la chute de l'Empire romain*. 3d ed. 4 vols. Paris, 1840.

Hanotaux, Gabriel. *Histoire du Cardinal de Richelieu*. New ed. 6 vols. Paris, n.d.

Hartog, François. *Le XIXe siècle et l'histoire: Le cas Fustel de Coulanges*. Paris, 1988.

Hauser, Henri. *La modernité du XVIe siècle*. Paris, 1930.

Hegel, Georg Wilhelm. *The Philosophy of History*. Edited by C. J. Friedrich. New York, 1956.

Hexter, J. H. *On Historians*. Cambridge, Mass., 1979.

———. *Reappraisals in History*. Evanston, 1961.

Higgs, David. *Nobles in Nineteenth-Century France: The Practice of Inegalitarianism*. Baltimore, 1987.

Himmelfarb, Gertrude. *The New History and the Old*. Cambridge, Mass. 1987.

Hunt, Lynn. "Does History Need Defending?" *History Workshop Journal* 46 (Autumn, 1998): 241–49.

———. "French History in the Last Twenty Years: The Rise and Fall of the *Annales* Paradigm." *Journal of Contemporary History* 21 (1986): 209–24

Iggers, Georg. *Historiography in the Twentieth Century: From Scientific Objectivity to the Postmodern Challenge*. Hanover and London, 1997.

———. Review of *Deutsche Geschichtswissenschaft nach dem Zweiten Weltkrieg (1945–1965)*, edited by Ernest Schulin, and of *Deutsche Geschichtswissenschaft nach 1945*, by Winfried Schulze. *History and Theory* 31, no. 3 (1992): 335–43.

———. Review of *Volksgeschichte: Methodische Innovationen und völkische Ideologisierung in der deutschen Geschichtswissenschaft 1918–1945* by Willi Oberkromme. *History and Theory* 33, no. 3 (1999): 395–400.

Jaurès, Jean. *Histoire socialiste de la Révolution française*. 6 vols. Edited by Albert Soboul. Paris, 1983–.

Jouanna, Arlette. *L'idée de race en France au XVIe siècle et au début du XVIIe*. Rev. ed. 2 vols. Montpellier, 1981.

Jouhaud, Christian. *La main de Richelieu, ou le pouvoir cardinal*. Paris, 1991.

Judt, Tony. "The Believer." *New Republic* 222, no. 7 (2000): 40–47.

———. *Past Imperfect*. Berkeley, 1992.

Kaplan, Steven. *Farewell, Revolution: The Historians' Feud, 1789/1989*. Ithaca, 1995.

Keegan, John. *The Face of Battle*. London, 1976.

Kelley, Donald. *The Descent of Ideas: The History of Intellectual History*. Aldershot, U.K., 2002.

Keylor, William. *Academy and Community: The Foundation of the French Historical Profession*. Cambridge, Mass., 1975.

Laslett, Peter. *The World We Have Lost*. New York, 1965.

Le Bigre, Arlette. *Les grands jours d'Auvergne: Désordres et répression au XVIIe siècle*. Paris, 1976.

Le Bras, Hervé, and Emmanuel Todd. *L'invention de la France: Atlas anthropologique et politique.* Paris, 1981.

Le Roy Ladurie, Emmanuel. *Montaillou village occitan de 1294 à 1324.* Paris, 1975.

———. *Paris-Montpellier: P.C.-P.S.U, 1945–1963.* Paris, 1982.

———. *Paysans de Languedoc.* Abr. ed. Paris, 1969.

———. *Le territoire de l'historien.* 2 vols. Paris, 1974–78.

Leger, François. *La jeunesse d'Hippolyte Taine.* Paris, 1980.

Lehman, A. G. *Sainte-Beuve: A Portrait of the Critic, 1804–1842.* Oxford, 1962.

Lehmann, Hartmut, and James van Horn Melton, eds. *Paths of Continuity: Central European Historiography from the 1930s to the 1950s.* Cambridge, 1994.

Lepenies, Wolf. *Sainte-Beuve: Auf der Schwelle zur Moderne.* Munich and Vienna, 1997.

Lepetit, Mathieu. "Un regard sur l'historiographie allemande: Les mondes de *l'Alltagsgeschichte.*" *Revue d'histoire moderne et contemporaine* 45, no. 2 (1998), 466–86.

Lévi, Bernard-Henri. *Adventures on the Freedom Road: The French Intellectuals in the 20th Century.* Translated by Richard Veasey. London, 1995.

Lévy-Bruhl, Lucien. *L'âme primitive.* New ed. Paris, 1963. (Orig. pub. 1927.)

———. *History of Modern Philosophy in France.* Chicago, 1899.

Lichtheim, G. "Sartre, Marxism, and History." *History and Theory* 3, no. 2 (1963): 222–46.

Lloyd, Geoffrey E. R. *Demystifying Mentalities.* Cambridge, 1990.

Lowenthal, David. *The Past Is a Foreign Country.* Cambridge, 1985.

Lyon, Bryce, and Mary Lyon, eds. *The Birth of Annales History: The Letters of Lucien Febvre and Marc Bloch to Henri Pirenne (1921–1935).* Brussels, 1991.

Marx, Karl. *Selected Writings.* Edited by Lawrence H. Simon. Indianapolis, 1994.

Maurras, Charles. *Romantisme et révolution.* Paris, 1922.

———. *Trois idées politiques: Chateaubriand, Michelet, Sainte-Beuve.* In *Romantisme et révolution.* Paris, 1922. (Orig. pub. 1898.)

Mayer, Arno J. *The Persistence of the Old Regime: Europe to the Great War.* New York, 1981.

Maza, Sarah. *Servants and Masters in Eighteenth-Century France: The Uses of Loyalty.* Princeton, 1983.

Megill, Alan. "'Grand Narrative' and the Discipline of History." In *A New Philosophy of History,* edited by Frank Ankersmit and Hans Kellner. Chicago, 1995.

Meinecke, Friedrich. *Historism: The Rise of a New Historical Outlook.* Translated by J. E. Anderson. London, 1972.

Meyer, Jean. *La noblesse de Bretagne au XVIIIe siècle.* 2 vols. Paris, 1966.

Michaud, J.-F., and L.-G. Michaud, eds. *Biographie universelle ancienne et moderne.* 85 vols. Paris, 1811–62.

Michelet, Jules. *Cours au Collège de France, 1838–1851.* Edited by Paul Viallaneix. 2 vols. Paris, 1995.

Middleton, Christopher, ed. *Selected Letters of Friedrich Nietzsche.* Chicago, 1969.

Miller, Nancy K. *Subject to Change: Reading Feminist Writing.* New York, 1988.

Moeller, Robert G. *War Stories: The Search for a Usable Past in the Federal Republic of Germany.* Berkeley and Los Angeles, 2001.

Molho, Raphaël. *L'ordre et les ténèbres ou la naissance d'un mythe du XVIIe siècle chez Sainte-Beuve.* Paris, 1972.

Mollard, Jean-Pierre. "Alfred Franklin (Versailles 1830–Viroflay 1917)." *Revue de l'histoire de Versailles,* 198.

Momigliano, Arnoldo. "Historicism in Contemporary Thought." In *Studies in Historiography.* New York, 1961.

Monod, Gabriel. "Bulletin historique, France." *Revue Historique* 26 (1884).

———. *Les maîtres de l'histoire: Renan, Taine, Michelet.* 3d ed. Paris, 1895.

———. *La plume, la faucille et le marteau: Institutions et société en France du Moyen Âge à la Révolution.* Paris, 1970.

Mousnier, Roland. "Recherches sur les soulèvements populaires en France avant la Fronde." In *La plume, la faucille et le marteau: Institutions et société en France du Moyen Âge à la Révolution.* Paris, 1970. First published in *Revue d'histoire moderne et contemporaine* 5 (1958).

Müller, Bertrand. *Bibliographie des travaux de Lucien Febvre. Cahiers des Annales.* Paris, 1990.

———, ed. *Marc Bloch, Lucien Febvre et les "Annales d'Histoire Économique et Sociale: Correspondance.* 3 vols. Paris, 1994–2002.

Nadler, Steven. *Arnauld and the Cartesian Philosophy of Ideas.* Manchester, 1989.

La Nation Française, 1955–60.

Nicolas, Jean. *Mouvements populaires et conscience sociale, XVIe–XIXe siècles.* Paris, 1985.

———, ed. *La Savoie au dix-huitième siècle: Noblesse et bourgeoisie.* 2 vols. Paris, 1978.

Nietszche, Friedrich. *On the Advantage and Disadvantage of History for Life.* Translated by Peter Preuss. Indianapolis, 1980.

———. *On the Genealogy of Morality.* Translated by Maudemarie Clark and Alan J. Swensen. Indianapolis, 1998.

Noiriel, Gérard. *Sur la "crise" des histoires.* Paris, 1996.

Novick, Peter. *That Noble Dream: The "Objectivity Question" and the American Historical Profession.* Cambridge, 1988.

Oexle, Gerhard. "Was deutsche Mediävisten an der französichen Mittelalterforschung interessieren muss." In *Mittelalterforschung nach der Wende 1989, Historische Zeitschrift,* Beiheft 20 (n.s.), edited by Michael Borgolte. Munich, 1995.

Olivier, Gouverneur Général. "Philosophie de l'Exposition Coloniale." *Revue des Deux Mondes,* 8th ser., 6 (November–December 1931): 285–86.

Orsenna, Erik. *L'Exposition Coloniale.* Paris, 1988.

Painter, George D. *Marcel Proust: A Biography.* 2 vols. London, 1959.

Palmer, R. R. *The Age of the Democratic Revolution: A Political History of Europe and America, 1760–1800.* Princeton, 1959.

Pingard, L. "Brantôme historien." *Revue des questions historiques* 19 (1876): 186–224.

Pocock, J. G. A. *Barbarism and Religion.* 2 vols. Cambridge, 1999.

Pradal de Lamase, Martial. "L'idée de noblesse en France." *Mercure de France,* 294, no. 989 (1939): 307–32.

Prater, D. A. *European of Yesterday: A Biography of Stefan Zweig.* Oxford, 1972.

Proust, Marcel. *Contre Sainte-Beuve.* Paris, 1954.

———. *Sodome et Gomorrhe.* Paris, 1989.

Raeff, Marc. "Some Observations on the Work of Hermann Aubin (1885–1969)." In *Paths of Continuity: Central European Historiography from the 1930s to the 1950s*, edited by Hartmut Lehmann and James van Horn Melton. Cambridge, 1994.

Ranke, Leopold von. *History of the Reformation in Germany*. Translated by Sarah Austin. Edited by Robert A. Johnson. 2 vols. New York, 1905. Reprint, New York, 1966.

———. *The Theory and Practice of History*. Edited by Georg Iggers and Konrad von Moltke. Indianapolis, 1973.

Renan, Cornélie. *Les lettres de Cornélie Renan à Gobineau*. Edited by Roger Béziau. *Archives des lettres modernes* 75 (1967).

Renan, Ernest. *L'avenir de la science*. In *Histoire et parole: Oeuvres diverses*. Edited by Laudyce Rétat. Paris, 1984.

———. *Histoire et parole: Oeuvres diverses*. Edited by Laudyce Rétat. Paris, 1984.

———. *The Life of Jesus*. Edited by John Haynes Holmes. New York, 1927.

———. *Nouvelles études d'histoire religieuse*. New ed. Paris, 1899.

———. *Souvenirs d'enfance et de jeunesse*. Edited by Henriette Psichari and Laudice [*sic*] Rétat. Paris, 1973.

Rétat, Laudyce. *Religion et imagination religieuse: Leurs formes et leurs rapports dans l'oeuvre d'Ernest Renan*. Paris, 1977.

Revel, Jacques. "Histoire et sciences sociales: Les paradigmes des *Annales*." *Annales: ESC* 34 (November–December 1979): 1347–59.

Revel, Jacques, and Lynn Hunt. *Histories: French Constructions of the Past*. New York, 1995.

Saint-Martin, Monique de. *L'espace de la noblesse*. Paris, 1993.

Sainte-Beuve, Charles-Augustin. *Les cahiers*. Edited by Raphael Molho. Paris, 1973.

———. *Causeries du lundi*. 16 vols. Paris, n.d.

———. *Correspondance générale*. Edited by Jean Bonnerot. Paris, 1947.

———. *Nouveaux lundis*. 13 vols. Paris, 1868–84.

———. *Oeuvres*. Edited by Maxime Le Roy. 2 vols. Paris, 1960.

———. *Portraits de femmes*. In *Oeuvres*. Edited by Maxime Le Roy. 2 vols. Paris, 1960.

———. *Portraits of the Eighteenth Century, Historic and Literary*. Translated by Katharine P. Wormeley. New York, 1905.

———. *Portraits littéraires*. Edited by Gérard Antoine. Paris, 1993.

———. *Port-Royal*. Edited by Maxime Le Roy. 3 vols. Paris, 1953.

———. *Pour la critique*. Edited by Annie Prassoloff and José-Luis Diaz. Paris, 1992.

———. *Tableau historique et critique de la poésie française et du théâtre française au XVIe siècle*. New ed. Paris, n.d. [1842?].

Scherer, Edmond. *Études sur la littérature contemporaine*. 2d ed. 6 vols. Paris, 1882.

———. *Nouvelles études sur la litterature contemporaine*. 2d ed. Paris, 1876.

Schieder, Theodor, ed. *Dokumentation der Vertreibung der Deutschen aus Ost-Mitteleuropa*. 8 vols. Bonn, 1951–61.

Schöttler, Peter. *Lucie Varga: Les autorités invisibles*. Paris, 1991.

Schulze, Winfried. *Deutsche Geschichtswissenschaft nach 1945, Historische Zeitschrift*, Beiheft 10 (n.s.). Munich, 1989.

Sewell, William. *A Rhetoric of Bourgeois Revolution: The Abbé Sieyès and What Is the Third Estate?* Durham, 1994.

Smith, Bonnie G. *The Gender of History: Men, Women, and Historical Practice*. Cambridge, Mass., 1998.

————. "History and Genius: The Narcotic, Erotic, and Baroque Life of Germaine de Staël." *French Historical Studies* 19 (Fall 1996): 1059–81.

Smith, Bonnie G., Jonathan Dewald, William Sewell, and Roger Chartier. "Forum: Critical Pragmatism, Language, and Cultural History; On Roger Chartier's *On the Edge of the Cliff.*" *French Historical Studies* 21, no. 2 (1998): 213–64.

Sorel, Georges. *Le système historique de Renan*. Paris, 1905–6. Reprint, Geneva, 1971.

Sprigge, Cecil, ed. *Philosophy, Poetry, History: An Anthology of Essays by Benedetto Croce*. London, 1966.

Stallybrass, Peter, and Allon White. *The Politics and Poetics of Transgression*. Ithaca, 1986.

Stendhal. *Racine and Shakespeare*. Translated by Guy Daniels. N.p., 1962.

————. *Stendhal: Du romantisme dans les arts*. Edited by Juliusz Starzynski. Paris, 1966.

Stern, Fritz. "Americans and the German Past: A Century of American Scholarship." In *Dreams and Delusions: The Drama of German History*. New York, 1987.

Stone, Lawrence. *The Crisis of the Aristocracy, 1558–1641*. Oxford, 1965.

Taine, Hippolyte. *De l'intelligence*. 2 vols. 5th ed. Paris, 1888.

————. *Derniers essais de critique et d'histoire*. 6th ed. Paris, 1923.

————. *Essai sur Tite Live*. 7th ed. Paris, 1904.

————. *Essais de critique et d'histoire*. 14th ed. Paris, 1923.

————. *La Fontaine et ses fables*. 25th ed. Paris, n.d..

————. *History of English Literature*. Translated by H. van Laun. 2 vols. New York, 1900.

————. *Notes sur Paris: Vie et opinions de M. Frédéric Thomas Graindorge*. 18th ed. Paris: Hachette, 1913.

————. *Les origines de la France contemporaine*. 2 vols. Paris, 1986.

————. *Les philosophes classiques du XIXe siècle en France*. 4th ed. Paris, 1876.

————. *Sa vie et sa correspondance*. 4 vols. Paris, 1907.

Talbot, Emile. *La critique stendhalienne de Balzac à Zola*. York, S.C., 1979.

Theibault, John. "The Demography of the Thirty Years War Re-visited: Günther Franz and His Critics." *German History* 15, no. 1 (1997): 1–21.

Thompson, E. P. *Customs in Common: Studies in Traditional Popular Culture*. New York, 1993.

————. *The Making of the English Working Class*. New York, 1963.

Tocqueville, Alexis de. *Correspondance d'Alexis de Tocqueville et d'Arthur Gobineau*. Edited by Maurice Degros. Vol. 9 of *Oeuvres complètes*. Edited by J.-P. Mayer. 2d ed. Paris, 1959.

————. *The Old Regime and the French Revolution*. Translated by Stuart Gilbert. Garden City, N.Y., 1955. (Orig. pub. 1856.)

Tribe, Keith. "The *Geschichtliche Grundbegriffe* Project: From History of Ideas to Conceptual History." *Comparative Studies in Society and History* 31, no. 1 (January 1989): 180–84.

Trilling, Lionel. *The Moral Obligation to Be Intelligent: Selected Essays*. Edited by Leon Wieseltier. New York, 2000.

Van Kley, Dale. *The Religious Origins of the French Revolution: From Calvin to the Civil Constitution, 1560–1791.* New Haven, 1996.

Veit-Brause, Irmline. "Werner Conze." In *Paths of Continuity: Central European Historiography from the 1930s to the 1950s,* edited by Hartmut Lehmann and James van Horn Melton. Cambridge, 1994.

Verdès-Leroux, Jeannine. *Refus et violences: Politique et littérature à l'extrême droite des années trente aux retombés de la Libération.* Paris, 1996.

Vigarello, Georges. *Le propre et le sale: L'hygiène du corps depuis le Moyen Âge.* Paris, 1985.

Walkowitz, Judith. *City of Dreadful Delight: Narratives of Sexual Danger in Late-Victorian London.* Chicago, 1992.

Weber, Eugen. *Action Française: Royalism and Reaction in Twentieth-Century France.* Stanford, 1962.

Weber, Max. *The Protestant Ethic and the Spirit of Capitalism.* Translated by Talcott Parsons. New York, 1958. (Orig. pub. 1905.)

Wellek, René. *A History of Modern Criticism: 1750–1950, the Age of Transition.* New Haven, 1965.

White, Hayden. *The Content of the Form: Narrative Discourse and Historical Representation.* Baltimore, 1987.

Winkler, Heinrich August. "A Pioneer in the Historical Sciences: Hans Rosenberg 1904–1988." *Central European History* 24, no. 1 (1991): 1–23.

INDEX

CPSIA information can be obtained
at www.ICGtesting.com
Printed in the USA
BVHW032309270120
570664BV00001B/4